MAKING
SUSTAINABILITY
STICK

MAKING SUSTAINABILITY STICK

The Blueprint for Successful Implementation

Kevin Wilhelm

Vice President, Publisher: Tim Moore
Associate Publisher and Director of Marketing: Amy Neidlinger
Development Editor: Russ Hall
Operations Specialist: Jodi Kemper
Marketing Manager: Lisa Loftus
Cover Designer: Chuti Prasertsith
Managing Editor: Kristy Hart
Senior Project Editor: Betsy Gratner
Copy Editor: Cheri Clark
Proofreader: Julie Anderson
Indexer: Erika Millen
Compositor: Nonie Ratcliff
Manufacturing Buyer: Dan Uhrig

Published by Pearson Education, Inc.
Upper Saddle River, New Jersey 07458

Pearson offers excellent discounts on this book when ordered in quantity for bulk purchases or special sales. For more information, please contact U.S. Corporate and Government Sales, 1-800-382-3419, corpsales@pearsontechgroup.com. For sales outside the U.S., please contact International Sales at international@pearsoned.com.

Printed in the United States of America

First Printing October 2013

ISBN-10: 0-13-344557-7
ISBN-13: 978-0-13-344557-2

Pearson Education LTD.
Pearson Education Australia PTY, Limited
Pearson Education Singapore, Pte. Ltd.
Pearson Education Asia, Ltd.
Pearson Education Canada, Ltd.
Pearson Educación de Mexico, S.A. de C.V.
Pearson Education—Japan
Pearson Education Malaysia, Pte. Ltd.
Library of Congress Control Number: 2013943348

This book is dedicated to all of those "in the trenches"
trying to make sustainability a reality.

Contents

Acknowledgments

This book would not be possible without the support of so many people. I would especially like to thank Tauschia Copeland and Ruth Lee, my co-workers who were most instrumental in the writing of this book. Tauschia, thanks for being my right hand, being my researcher, editor, idea person, and someone I could bounce crazy ideas off of from time to time. You did an amazing job of keeping me on track and getting this to the finish line. Nobody is more responsible for this book's success than you! Ruth, what can I say? You've been my rock not only through this process, but for the past six-plus years while working at SBC. Thanks for constantly challenging me and for pushing me to make this better and more personable. This book and SBC would not be where we are without you.

Thank you Mom and Dad, for embedding my love for reading, writing, and learning at such a young age. Thanks for showing me that anything is possible, and for not only providing the safe nest for me to grow up in but also providing me with the wings to fly.

I want to thank Jeff Evans and Bruce Hutton for being my business mentors in both college and graduate school and Bob Williard and Hunter Lovins, who have served that role professionally.

Ben Packard and Kevin Hagen deserve call outs for encouraging me to write this book during eight boring and scoreless innings of a Mariners game; sorry, fellas, your original title was not accepted.

I also want to thank Libba and Gifford Pinchot, Jill Bamburg, John Gardner, and Lorinda Rowledge for accepting me into the BGI community, which has truly become my second family.

Of course I need to thank all the people who agreed to be interviewed for this book, as your wisdom was invaluable, with special thanks to Mary Kay Chess, John Koriath, and Terra Anderson.

And most importantly, I need to thank the love of my life, Jo. Thank you for being so patient throughout this entire process. Your love, understanding, interest, and encouragement kept me going during those long winter weekends and sunny evenings when the last thing in the world I wanted to do was write. Jo, you were the one who introduced me to sustainability, and you are the biggest influence in not only my work, but my life. There will never be another man who loves, adores, and appreciates his wife in this world more than I do. You are my everything.

About the Author

Kevin Wilhelm is the one of the world's preeminent business consultants in the field of sustainability and climate change. He is the CEO of Sustainable Business Consulting, a Seattle-based consulting firm focused on demonstrating the bottom-line business benefits of sustainability and then leading companies through successful implementation. Kevin brings nearly two decades of experience working with businesses ranging from Fortune 500 multinationals to medium-sized businesses. His clients include Nordstrom, REI, The North Face, Alaska Airlines, Redbox, Expeditors, Drugstore.com, Puget Sound Energy, and more than 75 others.

Previously he wrote the acclaimed *Return on Sustainability: How Business Can Increase Profitability and Address Climate Change in an Uncertain Economy*, and he is a professor at the Bainbridge Graduate Institute, where he teaches various courses on sustainable business.

Introduction

When I opened my office back in 2004, sustainable business was a fairly new topic, and it was frustratingly hard to get companies to understand the business case for sustainability. At the time, they really needed to understand "the why." Years later, after having consulted with more than 75 companies across 17 industries and spoken at countless sustainability conferences, I've realized that the challenge now is to help companies figure out how to implement sustainability, how to make it last for the long term, and how to get "unstuck" if their programs have stalled.

That is why I'm writing this book.

I want companies to fully realize the triple-bottom-line (financial, social, environmental) benefits of implementing sustainability by truly integrating it into everything they do. For years, Patagonia and Interface have been held up as examples of companies that have done this, but I've often wondered why is it that still ten years later we have no other recognizable brands held in the same regard. The reality is that while many companies have set out to do this, few have gone all the way and been successful. I want to change that.

This book pulls from my firsthand experience helping companies implement sustainability using steps outlined in this book, as well as from industry best practices, publicly available case studies, and interviews with sustainability leaders. It is full of wisdom from some of the best thought leaders in the business, leadership, change management, and sustainability worlds, including Jim Collins, Peter Drucker, Peter Senge, Daniel Pink, Stephen Covey, Gifford Pinchot, Bob Willard, and many more. The book is equally balanced between success stories and lessons learned so that you can learn from other peoples' stumbles and failures while minimizing your own.

Many of my clients have agreed to be featured and go on record, while others have preferred off-the-record conversations so that they could be as frank and as honest as possible and share their lessons learned with you and with a larger audience for the greater good.

Implementing sustainability is tough work. When someone asks me, "How do I implement sustainability successfully?" my gut reaction is to respond that it is almost like asking someone, "How do I raise a child?" There are many different ways and distinct variables, so there really is no single answer or magic bullet. In each case you will have a unique context of culture and society that is changing all the time. The same is true with implementing sustainability within your company because you will be facing complex challenges that are unique to your business, people, industry, and geographic reach.

Making Sustainability Stick is written to help you face those challenges. It is not only about providing you with the knowledge of what to do, but also about the keys to behavior change that are so crucial for overcoming the numerous frustrations, barriers, and potential setbacks that you will undoubtedly face.

This 11-step guidebook is designed to provide you with the tools for engaging the head, the heart, and the hands of the people within your organization so that you can successfully integrate sustainability into everything you do—into every decision, product design, market, job description, and business unit!

So if the idea of integrating sustainability into everything your company does seems overwhelming, realize you are not alone in this journey. This book is full of helpful tips, worksheets, new strategies, and illustrative examples that are replicable, funny, and easy to emulate.

We need you! We need your passion and knowledge in this fight. We are at a critical point in history: We are potentially in the middle of a decade of economic malaise, the effects from extreme weather are increasing rapidly, we just passed a critical milestone of 400 parts per million in terms of CO_2 levels, while simultaneously experiencing unprecedented levels of income inequality. Never in our history has the planet faced such daunting social and environmental challenges, and we need all of us working diligently to integrate sustainability into our jobs and companies because business may be the only institution that has the resources that can move fast enough to address these issues. It's up to us—not our kids' generation, but ours. So read on for how to do it and good luck!

How to Use This Book

Every company and every reader of this book will be at a different point in their sustainability journey. Therefore, I've written this book to help you, the reader, no matter what phase you are in. The book is chock-full of tools, activities, and real-world successes to provide you with the blueprint for sustainability implementation.

It is organized around three themes:

1. The Business Case: No matter what, you must always tie things back to this issue. This is the reason you are playing the game. (Chapter 1)

2. Fundamentals: These are the building blocks that are essential for your success. This is the blocking and tackling that will enable you to get to the next phase. (Chapters 2–6)

3. Engagement and Value Creation: This is where you look to score and win the game. This involves change management, employee engagement, and the policies and systems around sustainability that you need to institutionalize so that you can throw deep for the end zone. (Chapters 7–11)

The Hagen-Wilhelm Change Matrix, shown in Figure 1, is designed to help you recognize where your company is and what it still needs in order to truly integrate sustainability into everything you do. In each phase, there are different characteristics, drivers, and leaders. It is important to realize that as you progress as a company, you will reduce your negative social and environmental impacts while driving business growth and value through sustainability.

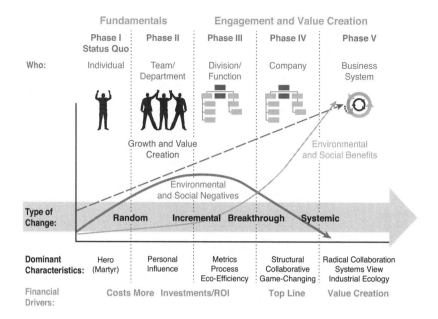

	Fundamentals		Engagement and Value Creation		
	Phase I Status Quo	Phase II	Phase III	Phase IV	Phase V
Who:	Individual	Team/ Department	Division/ Function	Company	Business System

Growth and Value Creation

Environmental and Social Benefits

Environmental and Social Negatives

Type of Change:		Random	Incremental	Breakthrough	Systemic	
Dominant Characteristics:	Hero (Martyr)	Personal Influence	Metrics Process Eco-Efficiency	Structural Collaborative Game-Changing	Radical Collaboration Systems View Industrial Ecology	
Financial Drivers:		Costs More	Investments/ROI		Top Line	Value Creation

Figure 1   Hagen-Wilhelm Change Matrix.

Tips for Reading This Book

Here are a few tips to enable you to get the most out of this book and to personally enhance the relevance of your reading experience:

- If you are *just getting started,* you need to read the book chrono-logically to make sure you first nail down the business case and fundamentals before tackling how to *Make Sustainability Stick.*

- If you are a person or company that has *been at this for a while,* feel free to jump ahead to the Part II, "Engagement and Value Creation," chapters.

- If you are *stuck or feel as though you have lost momentum,* take inventory as to where you are on the Hagen-Wilhelm matrix and go back and brush up on your fundamentals. Then pick the specific chapters where your company needs to focus.

These tips are merely suggestions as this book provides illustrative examples, stories, and key insights throughout each chapter of the book; but the goal is to help you implement sustainability successfully and to make it stick for the long term, so read it however it best meets your needs.

1

The Business Case

T here is a strong business case for sustainability. Done right, it adds value, saves money, drives innovation, reduces risk, enhances your brand, and increases both customer and employee loyalty. It is not a cost to your business; it is a value creator.

Whether you are embarking on sustainability for the first time or trying to reignite momentum for it within your firm, the key to making it stick within an organization is to demonstrate the business value it will bring to your company over both the short and long term. This chapter is broken down into several sections to help you do just that. First we'll focus on the external market and public policy forces that provide both risk and opportunities for your company. Then we'll discuss top-line competitive advantage, highlight Interface as an example of a company to aspire to that is fully realizing the benefits of sustainability, and run you through an exercise on using sustainability to protect your brand.

Market Forces

An A.T. Kearny analysis revealed that during the current economic slowdown, "companies that showed a 'true' commitment to sustainability outperformed their industry peers in the financial markets." This study, which looked at 18 different industries, found those that were recognized as sustainability-focused outperformed their competitors, which translated to a differential of $650 million in market capitalization per company.[1]

When I wrote my first book, *Return on Sustainability,* there were very few case studies, books, or reports that demonstrated the bottom-line business benefits of sustainability. Today that has changed, so I'm not going to exhaustively list all of these case studies and reports because Natural Capitalism Solutions has already done that through the *Sustainability Pays*[2] study. This study pulled together more than 45 separate reports that highlight the numerous ways in which companies are realizing value from their sustainability efforts.

They are experiencing these types of value:

- Cost savings
- Reduced risk
- Enhanced brand value and customer loyalty
- Lower recruiting and retention costs
- High employee satisfaction
- Meeting investor expectations
- More engaged suppliers
- Competitive advantage and differentiation
- New top-line revenues

There is a business case for sustainability and I am going to write in depth over the next few pages about the numerous market forces and regulations that are taking place around sustainability that can lead to all of these benefits. While global agreements and federal legislation on environmental and social issues have been stalled, the market hasn't been waiting. It has been moving on these issues. So read on and think through how each of these market forces might apply to your company, and identify both risks you want to avoid and opportunities you want to capitalize on.

The numerous market forces around sustainability are shown in Figure 1.1.

Investor/Stockholder Pressure

Over the past decade, there has been a major increase in interest by the investor community about environmental, climate, and social issues. From 2007 to 2010 alone, SRI (socially responsible investment) assets increased more than 13%, while professionally managed assets overall increased less than 1%.[3]

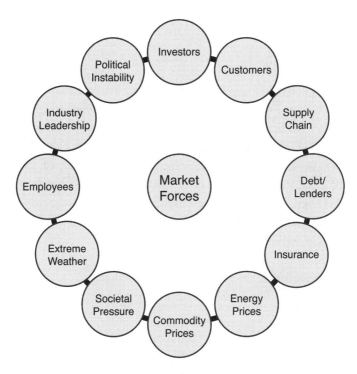

Figure 1.1 Market forces around sustainability.

As of early 2013, SRI investments represented $3.74 trillion or almost 10% of the U.S. investment marketplace.[4] This is being led by investment firms such as these:

- **Pensions:** BlackRock, TIAA-CREF, the California State Teachers' Retirement System (CalSTRS), CALpers, Calvert Mutual Funds.

- **Investment Funds:** Calvert, Trillium, Sentinel Investments, MMA Praxis Mutual Funds, Neuberger Berman Mutual Funds, Parnassus Investments, Pax World, TIAA-CREF.

- **Venture Capital:** Kleiner Perkins and Bright Capital, Acumen Fund, Big Issues Investment, Central Fund, City Light Capital,

Clean Technology Venture Capital, Root Capital, Good Capital, TBL Capital, and many more.

Maximizing Stakeholder Value

Too often there has been the assumption—by investors, CFOs, and skeptics alike—that any investment toward improved social and environmental performance violates fiduciary responsibility. They are following Milton Friedman's frequently quoted belief that "the social responsibility of business is to maximize shareholder value."[5] Well, I want to point out that the two are not mutually exclusive, and I'll tell you why. Over the ten-year period from 2001 to 2011, which featured a recession, 9/11, the financial crisis of 2008, and the recovery, those funds that had a high sustainability or environment, social, and governance (ESG) component of their investment outperformed the S&P 500,[6] as demonstrated in Figure 1.2.

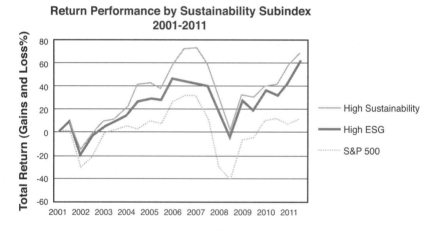

Figure 1.2   Sustainable investing performance.

Based on Sustainability Index Update Q3 2012.[7]

A separate study performed by Ethisphere showed that between 2007 and 2011, these same types of companies "outperformed the S&P 500 by delivering a nearly 27% return to shareholders, compared to the S&P's negative 8.5% shareholder return during the same period."[8]

So, if someone is dismissing your arguments about sustainability, don't try to sell them on the social or environmental issues. If money is all they care about, meet them where they are and say: "Okay, I agree with you. Let's focus only on maximizing shareholder value," and then show them the numbers. This will shut them up pretty quickly and go a long way toward strengthening your business case.

ESG, Its Impact, and Its Long-term Performance

Some key trends in socially responsible investment and ESG include these:

- In 2011, over 50% of pension funds had an SRI portfolio.

- 80% of firms believe there's no performance trade-off between SRI/ESG strategies and traditional investments.[9]

- A study by Notre Dame and Georgetown found that those companies that are large emitters of greenhouse gas (GHG) emissions see their market cap reduced because of these emissions. Specifically, their study found that a company's value declines by $202,000 for every additional 1,000 million tons of carbon they emit.[10]

The Problem with a Quarterly Focus

One problem with traditional investing is today's focus on short-term quarterly earnings. You cannot invest internally for the long term, or effectively implement sustainability, if you are focused only on the next quarter. This is true because many of the decisions you will need to make around sustainability are complicated and involve cultural change, and they don't all pay back in the next 6 to 18 months. Many energy-efficiency projects and low-hanging fruit do, but some of the more innovative and game-changing ideas will not pay back within such a short period.

In fact, there is a movement being led by Paul Polman, the CEO of Unilever, who has stopped reporting quarterly earnings. He stated that he cannot run his company effectively or smartly for the long term if he has to manage this way. He told investors that if they don't like it, that's fine, because Unilever doesn't want them as shareholders with what the company is trying to do. He's lost a few shareholders but also attracted many others who share the company's vision and values, while simultaneously seeing the stock price rise.

The CDP

The other real change is being led by large institutional investors that are backing the Carbon Disclosure Project (CDP), which works with 3,000-plus of the largest corporations in the world to help them ensure that an effective carbon reduction strategy is made integral to their business.[11]

It is taken seriously because, as of mid-2013, 655 institutional investors with more than $87 trillion under management support the CDP's efforts, and Table 1.1 shows CDP's growth over ten years. To give context, this amount is greater than the entire economies of the United States, the EU, Japan, Russia, India, and China combined.

Table 1.1 CDP Reporting

CDP Reporting	2003	2013
Institutional Investors	35	655+
Value of Assets Held	$4.5 trillion	$87 trillion
Companies Surveyed	The Financial Times 500	4,112 globally

The business results from companies reporting to the CDP have been quite positive.

- Companies in the 2011 Carbon Disclosure Leadership Index (CDLI) provided approximately *double the average total return* of the Global 500 between January 2005 and May 2011.

- 61% reported financial savings from addressing climate change.

- Respondents had a payback period of three years or less.[12]

Shareholder Resolutions

The number of shareholder resolutions involving social and environmental issues has also increased dramatically since 2000, as have the number of resolutions that have reached the critical 30% threshold. In

2012, environmental/sustainability proposals were the largest overall percentage of shareholder proposals (34%). This was even greater than political spending (31%), which was at an all-time high due to the 2012 election.[13]

CEOs Agree with the Market

It's not just the market that is speaking on behalf of sustainability; CEOs are increasingly seeing the importance of implementing sustainability into their companies. In fact, a study by the UN Global Compact and Accenture of 766 worldwide CEOs, which included 50 in-depth interviews, found that CEOs believe sustainability to be increasingly important to their companies' operations. The results are listed in Table 1.2.[14]

Table 1.2   Results of CEO Sustainability Survey

Results	2010	2007
Fully embedded into subsidiaries' strategies and operations	96%	72%
Discussed and acted on by boards	93%	69%
Embedded throughout the global supply chain	91%	65%
The basis for industry collaborations and multistakeholder partnerships	88%	59%
Incorporated into discussion with financial analysts	78%	56%

ACTIVITY 1: QUESTIONS TO RELATE SUSTAINABILITY AND THE BUSINESS CASE TO YOUR COMPANY INVESTMENT

- What market forces would interest your shareholders?

- How could you relate any of these issues to current shareholder priorities?

- Has your investor relations department already fielded sustainability-related questions from your investors? If so, around what specific issues?

Consumer Preferences

Consumer preferences are changing toward choosing more environmentally friendly and socially just products. A National Green Marketing Research study conducted by GreenSeal found that four out of five people say they still buy green products and services today even after the U.S. recession.[15]

The strongest force pushing adults toward purchasing green are their kids who "pester" their parents into buying green. The Energy Defense Fund found that 42% of adults admitted to coming under pressure from their children to be more environmentally friendly.[16] Figure 1.3 demonstrates how green consumption preferences around the environment have risen.

Americans Consider Environmental Impact of Their Purchases:

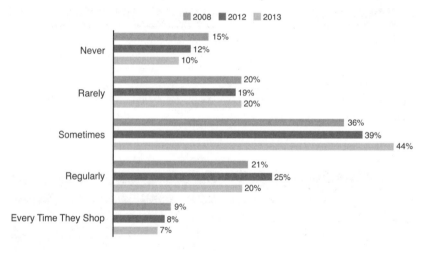

Figure 1.3 Green consumer trends.

Based on Cone Study.[17]

I've found this to be true as I've worked with companies over the past eight years; sustainability is the tiebreaker if price, performance, quality, and convenience are the same. This is more important than any celebrity endorsement.

However, one important point to note is that there is increased skepticism as well. According to this study, more consumers are worried about "greenwashing" and want to verify company claims:

- The Business and Consumer Behaviour 2013 survey showed that in 2012, 23% of consumers switched brands if their regular brand or service provider was having a bad effect on the environment, people, or society, or behaving unethically.[18]

- About one in three consumers say they don't know how to tell whether green product claims are true.

- One in ten consumers blindly trust green product claims.

- 24% of consumers are verifying green claims by reading the packaging. 17% are going online, reading studies.

Companies Are Purchasing Green, Too

In 2013, *Forbes* brought together worldwide green giants to talk about selling sustainable products and the conclusion was that "customers won't pay more for green, but companies will."[19]

Employees

To attract and retain the best employees, companies need to find a way to connect with their employees beyond financial rewards; they need to connect with what they are passionate about. Think about this: How many times have you woken up and gotten out of bed inspired to just make your shareholders more money? You got up for another reason. What was that? Employees want to work for companies that align with their values, and they are more productive when they are connected to a job and work that is meaningful.

Several studies support this idea across all age groups, but especially for Gen Y or millennial (those born after 1982) employees. I've also seen it firsthand with my Gen X (1965–1982) peers and even the baby boom generation; people are craving the opportunity to find more meaning in their day-to-day jobs.

Consider the fact that 86% of baby boomers and 85% of Gen Ys say that it is important that their work make a positive impact on the world. Even in the middle, 75% of those in Gen X see making a contribution to society through their work as important.[20]

Although it might have been okay for our parents' generation to "check their values at the company door" each day and relegate caring about the environment and community to the evenings or by volunteering on weekends, today's workers are not willing to do that. They seek a higher level of engagement and want to make a difference in their day-to-day work.

This is especially important now because employees are feeling more hopeful and mobile than they have at any point in the past few years. They are feeling more confident and will be factoring sustainability into their decisions to work for a company, into whether to leave a job, and even into their pay considerations.

Consider the following four factors in play: recruiting, productivity, compensation, and turnover.

Recruiting

Job seekers care about a company's social and environmental performance:

- According to a 2011 PricewaterhouseCoopers (PwC) study, 88% of graduate students and young professionals factor an employer's corporate social responsibility position into their job decision.[21]

- A Stanford research study found that graduating MBA students rate the Corporate Social Responsibility (CSR) criteria of ethics, treatment of employees, environmental sustainability, and caring for communities and stakeholders high on their list of job criteria.[22]

Productivity

Social and environmental performance of a company increases the productivity of its employees:

- At the highest level, sustainability provides a means of connecting with employees' senses of moral purpose, self-identity, creative energy, and desire to contribute to "making the world a better place."[23]

- One of the strongest endorsements employees give their company is the enthusiastic declaration that the company allows them to put their time and discretionary energy toward their life's work.[24]

Take a look in Table 1.3 at the results from a study by the Hay Group, which found the performance difference from those who found meaning in their work.

Table 1.3   Productivity with Meaningful Work

Type of Job	Performance Difference
Low-complexity jobs	19%
Moderate-complexity jobs	32%
High-complexity jobs	48%
Sales	48%–120%

Compensation

If a company chooses to focus on sustainability, employees are willing to work for less to be part of a company with purpose:

- A Stanford study showed that over 97% of graduating students would make a financial sacrifice to work for a company that exhibited all four characteristics of social responsibility.[25]

- The CSR Branding Survey found that almost 50% of respondents between the ages of 18 and 24 would choose a position with a socially responsible company, even if they had to take a pay cut.

Turnover

Employees are less likely to stay with companies that have a bad reputation or lack a sustainability component:

- The 2010 CSR Branding Survey revealed that 44% of young professionals say they would discount an employer with a bad reputation.[26]

- The aforementioned PricewaterhouseCoopers study showed that 86% would consider leaving a job if their employer's CSR performance no longer held up.[27]

Today's employees want to work for companies that have a reputation as a great place to work. People want to be part of a winning team, one that is not just keeping up with the times but is making a positive difference in the world.

Suppliers and Value Chain

Another market force is the increasing concern that consumers and manufacturers are showing in and around their supply chain. This concern is leading to questions aimed not only at tier 1 suppliers, but also at smaller tier 2, 3, and 4 suppliers, and all the way to the harvesting of the raw materials.

Organizations are being asked about their social, environmental, and climate performance in supplier scorecards, in requests for proposals (RFPs), and in bids for work. This is being led by the largest retailers, such as Walmart, Target, Microsoft, HP, and P&G.

In fact, if you do a quick search, more than 1,000 companies will show up with some type of sustainability requirements in their RFP requirements. Most cities and government agencies (including federal) are also incorporating these into contract bidding requirements. All of this is putting a demand through companies' value chain for not only more sustainable products but also more sustainable practices and services.

Walmart, for example, pushed more than 100,000 suppliers to produce more sustainable products with its "Eco-Index" and released its Environmental Key Performance Indicators in late 2012.

This is an outgrowth of many of the social aspects of sustainability including affirmative action and sweatshop labor issues. While the environment has taken a more primary role as of late, human rights, workers' conditions, and even human trafficking (such as the California

Transparency in Supply Chain Act) are once again playing a major role in supplier questionnaires. Much more media attention is being paid to employees seen jumping to their deaths at the Foxconn factory in China, to the garment factory fires in Bangladesh, and even to employees collapsing from heat inside a major online retailer's Lehigh Valley warehouse here in the United States.

The demand to answer questions around sustainability is such that some manufacturers in Southeast Asia are actually dedicating a person to the job of responding to these social and environmental questionnaires full time because the questions keep changing and the number of requests keeps rising.

Insurance/Risk

The insurance industry has also been getting into the mix of sustainability, primarily because it has the most to lose from a financial perspective as the number and frequency of extreme weather events continues to rise.

According to Evan Mills, a scientist at the Lawrence Berkeley National Laboratory, "Climate change stands as a stress test for the insurance industry in that it now pays an average of $50 billion a year in weather- and climate-related insurance losses, including property damage and business disruptions. Such claims have been doubling every decade since the 1980s."[28]

This is incredibly important to business because the insurance industry is the world's largest industry and represents 7% of global GDP. If they are seeing their costs rise, they are going to pass those fees along to the consumer and businesses. In fact, back in 2007, the National Association of Insurance Commissioners voted to require insurers to submit annual *Climate Risk Reports*.

How Things Are Playing Out

The main drivers of this are the reinsurance companies (such as Swiss Re, Munich Re, Allianz, and Lloyds of London) that provide financial backing to their consumer insurance companies. They are requiring their insurers to think about not only the traditional internal and market risks, but also the aforementioned risks from extreme weather events and natural disasters. In fact, the largest insurers are also asking their client companies questions about climate change during the renewal process of their Errors and Omissions (E&O) policies. So you can just imagine that once CEOs or Boards realize that their E&O insurance might be at risk if their company doesn't have a climate change policy, they'll make sure that the company puts one in place. Smart companies should be proactive and prepare for what nature might throw their way next, to help keep their insurance premiums down.

Extreme Weather Not Global Warming

The hardest market force to predict out of all of them might be extreme weather.

According to NASA, 2012 was the hottest year on record in the United States and the ninth hottest globally ever. In fact, with the exception of 1988, the nine warmest years in the 132-year global weather record have all occurred since the year 2000.[29] While many people talk about global warming and climate change, I prefer to focus on extreme weather events, which are increasingly more common and severe. This is because while there are people still willing to debate whether global warming is occurring, there is less debate about the increase in severity of these extreme weather events.

From a business-case perspective, just think about all the natural and financial disasters that have been in the news over the past seven to eight years, and how each event changed the stakeholder conversation with companies:

- In 2007 the topic of interest was climate change and the collapse of the U.S. housing market.
- In 2008 it was toxins in children's toys from China.
- In 2008–2009 it was the global financial crisis.
- In 2010 it was the BP oil spill.
- In 2011 it was the Fukushima Tsunami.
- In 2012 it was the financial crisis in Greece, the worst drought in the U.S. in 50 years, and Superstorm Sandy.
- In 2013 it was the Cyprus bank default.

As Bob Willard says, sustainability "is a survival strategy to thrive in a new, changing, dynamic world. It's not so much about saving the world, but in preparing the company to prosper in the future."[30]

Banks/Credit Markets

Lenders are also getting into the mix. In addition to adding numerous hoops and other requirements that have made getting loans after the financial crisis more difficult, banks have begun to incorporate social and environmental criteria into their lending practices. They are doing this from a risk-reduction standpoint, in terms of minimizing their loss exposure from fines and extreme weather events, as well as from an opportunity standpoint, in that they are looking to fund more sustainable investments and projects, especially around clean technology and sustainable development.

Two of the primary ways in which this is playing out are through the Equator Principles and through one small but often overlooked section of the Dodd–Frank Wall Street Reform and Consumer Protection Act of 2010.

The Equator Principles

Created by the World Bank in conjunction with the International Financial Corporation (IFC), the Equator Principles have become the respected industry standard for determining, assessing, and managing environmental and social risk in project finance transactions.[31]

The eight Equator Principle Performance Standards include questions about the following:

1. Assessment and management of environmental and social risks and impacts

2. Labor and working conditions

3. Resource efficiency and pollution prevention

4. Community health, safety, and security

5. Land acquisition and involuntary resettlement

6. Biodiversity conservation and sustainable management of living natural resources

7. Indigenous peoples

8. Cultural heritage

Lenders that are following the Equator Principles are beginning to put just as much pressure on companies to change practices as the SRI investment firms, and social and environmental requirements are becoming the norm in major lending agreements.

ACTIVITY 2: QUESTIONS TO RELATE THE MARKET FORCES OF SUSTAINABILITY TO THE CONSUMERS, EMPLOYEES, SUPPLIERS, INSURERS, AND LENDERS OF YOUR COMPANY

Consumers:

- What market forces around sustainability can enhance value to your customers?
- How do your products/services align with sustainability trends?

Employees:

- What are your employees engaged in now? How could sustainability build business value and enhance engagement?

Suppliers:

- Do any of your suppliers have sustainability as a priority?
- Where in your supply chain could you potentially improve sustainability performance and business value at the same time?
- In what ways could environmental factors such as extreme weather impact your value chain?

Insurance:

- In what ways is your company at risk from climate disruption?

Banks/Credit Markets:

- Can you use the Equator Principles to attract new credit or a lower rate from your existing banks?

Nontraditional "Market Forces"

Although they are not "traditional" market forces, I want to talk about two societal factors that are also bringing sustainability to everyday consumers in a way previously not thought of, and that is through the sports and faith communities.

The Sports Community

Sports fans come from every demographic, race, ethnicity, and class. In 2010 the Green Sports Alliance was launched with a mission to help sports teams, venues, and leagues enhance their environmental performance. As of early 2013, the Alliance represented more than 160 teams across 15 leagues. From your greenest, tree-hugging Portland Trailblazers fan to your most skeptical, Budweiser-drinking NASCAR fan, individuals are being asked to find ways to reduce their environmental impact at sporting events, at home, and at work. People are being exposed to these initiatives at sports venues and are starting to bring these questions to their workplaces and wondering why their company isn't following suit.

The Faith Community

The faith community is stepping up to the plate to combat climate change as well; here are a few examples to showcase their efforts:

- The Episcopal Church passed the Genesis Covenant in 2009, which asks all its churches to reduce GHG emissions by 50% within ten years.

- *Ecobuddhism* is a term of its own. The Dalai Lama was the first to sign the declaration, which encourages all people to target 350 parts per million (PPM) on CO2e in the atmosphere as the only way to continue human existence on the earth. It asks people to act now.[32]

- The Muslim Seven Year Action Plan (2010–2017) on Climate Change is an action plan for the global Islamic community. It investigates every level of Muslim activity from daily life to annual pilgrimages, from holy cities to future leader training.

- Former Pope Benedict XVI started a movement within the Catholic faith when he urged international leaders to reach a credible agreement on climate change back in 2011, asking all faiths to "keep in mind the needs of the poor and of future generations."[33]

- The Jewish Environmental and Energy Imperative was signed by 50 Jewish leaders, establishing a goal of reducing Jewish community greenhouse gases by 83% of 2005 levels by 2050.[34]

ACTIVITY 3: QUESTIONS TO RELATE SUSTAINABILITY AND THE BUSINESS CASE OF NONTRADITIONAL MARKET FORCES TO YOUR COMPANY

- What other nontraditional market forces could impact your business? In what way?

- How likely is this and when would you expect this to occur?

- Are any of these influencers or investors?

Public Policy and Regulation

Public policies that you should consider for your sustainability business case are displayed in Figure 1.4 and further discussed in this section.

It seems as though not much has happened globally over the past few years around sustainability. The reality is that there actually has been movement in a number of countries, states, and municipalities that all provide both risks and opportunities to companies. Therefore, when you are making the business case for sustainability within your firm or to your stakeholders, there will be times when the market forces won't be enough and you'll need to demonstrate to key decision makers how current and future regulation might impact their decision making. I've highlighted a few areas in the next few pages to pay attention to.

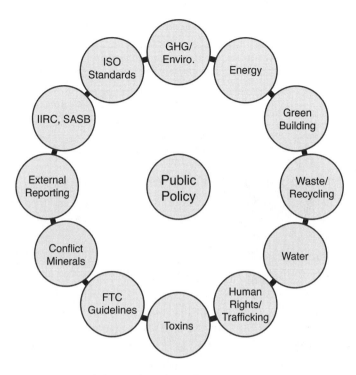

Figure 1.4   Sustainability and public policy.

Energy Prices and Regulations

A major factor in forcing businesses to operate in a more environmentally conscious manner has been the increase in energy prices. For example, oil prices more than doubled in the past decade. As shown in Figure 1.5, in 2003 the average cost per gallon of gasoline in the U.S. was $1.50, and by 2013 it had grown to $3.50.[35] This increase has affected the cost of delivery of any product, good, or service, forcing higher prices on everything from freight to business travel to food. This is expected to only get worse as the Energy Information Administration (EIA) predicts that global demand for fuel will increase by a further 30% by 2030, and a separate study states that if China continues to purchase personal vehicles at its current pace, its demand for fuel could outstrip the global supply by 2030.

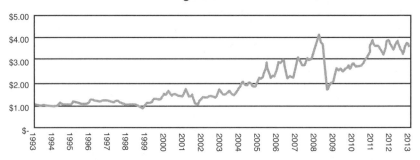

Figure 1.5   U.S. average gasoline price per gallon[36]

While most of the focus has been on oil, the cost of electricity has gone up as well, about 50% in the past decade, from a U.S. average of 8 cents per kWh to 12 cents per kWh. This also affects the bottom line and makes it more difficult to forecast future operating expenses. Controlling transportation and electricity costs will give any company a huge advantage in the marketplace, lower risk, and provide certainty to the CFO and facilities manager who are looking to better manage these variable costs.

Climate Legislation

Although major annual climate conferences have taken place over the past five years at Copenhagen, Mexico City, Durban, and Rio +20 (United Nations Conference on Sustainable Development), all failed to create a global successor to the Kyoto Protocol for a comprehensive climate treaty. However, there have still been a number of individual localized initiatives that have passed and are beginning to make an impact that business needs to pay attention to:

- The European Union's Climate Exchange (ECX), which is a platform for trading carbon credits on the stock market,[37] was launched in 2005 and was aimed at reducing greenhouse gas emissions to 8% below 1990 levels by 2012. Although it struggled early on because it set the cap too high and it put too many permits on the market at too low a price in the coming years, the number of permits was revised in July 2013, which will likely impact business costs in Europe from 2014–2020 as companies look to adapt.

- California just enacted the Global Warming Solution Act (AB32), which creates an in-state carbon cap-and-trade program and requires the state to reduce its GHG emissions to 1990 levels by 2020. Large emitting businesses will have to not only trade and report emissions but also work to reduce emissions, which might impact prices.

- The U.K. requires energy and GHG reporting through its Climate Change Agreements (CCAs) program, and in the U.S. three regional GHG initiatives have been created: the Western Climate Initiative, the Regional Greenhouse Gas Initiative (RGGI), and the Midwest Greenhouse Gas Reduction Accord. Only the RGGI is operational, but when the economy picks up, business should be ready for action across these 22 states and 5 Canadian provinces.

U.S. Mayors' Climate Commitment

Besides California, in the U.S. it has been the nation's mayors leading the charge. As of June 2013, 1,060 mayors of U.S. cities with more than 50,000 people have signed the U.S. Mayors' Climate Protection Agreement, which is a commitment to reduce GHG emissions 7% below 1990 levels by 2012. This means that if your business is located in the U.S., you will be affected because you likely have customers, suppliers, vendors, shareholders, or employees in one of these cities, and because there are signatories in each of the 50 states.

Carbon Taxes

These exist at the federal level in Sweden, Ireland, Finland, Great Britain, and New Zealand. Carbon taxes and costs are found at the provincial level in Quebec and British Columbia, and at the municipal level in Boulder, Colorado. Updates on worldwide carbon taxes can be found at www.carbontax.org.

U.S. Federal Regulation

After the Supreme Court ruled that the EPA did have the ability to regulate GHG emissions, the EPA began requiring the 13,000 largest GHG emitters (those with over 25,000 metric tons of carbon dioxide equivalent, or CO2e, in their Scope 1 and 2 sources) to report their emissions.[38] This has now been expanded to include 41 source categories. Moreover, President Obama signaled in a major policy speech in 2013 that he intends to use the EPA more aggressively to combat climate change through the remainder of his term.

Climate Risk in SEC Filings

As of 2010, publicly traded companies must disclose climate risk in their annual SEC filings, just as they must disclose other types of risk. For most organizations, they might be located in areas that are not impacted by things such as sea-level rise, but they might be exposed to other direct or indirect risks. The specific disclosures require companies to identify risks and potential new business opportunities from legislation and regulation, international agreements and treaties, indirect consequences of regulation or business trends, and physical impacts from climate change including extreme weather events.

ACTIVITY 4: QUESTIONS TO RELATE SUSTAINABILITY AND THE BUSINESS CASE OF ENERGY AND CLIMATE POLICY TO YOUR COMPANY

- In what ways could energy or climate regulation impact your company? Either directly or indirectly?
  - Energy prices
  - Climate legislation
  - U.S. city mayoral commitments
  - Climate risk in SEC filings

Water

In many ways, water has become an issue on par with climate change as an environmental issue. In fact, in 2012 the Carbon Disclosure Project added a water disclosure questionnaire for companies to begin reporting their water use and management of water issues. The fact that 9 out of the last 11 years, at the time of this writing, have been the hottest on record[39] has put new stresses on water availability around the globe.

New regulations surrounding water conservation have been implemented in the U.S. after the record drought that affected the United States in 2012. Both the drought and the new public policies will impact business in the cost, availability, and new regulations related to water use.

Toxins

As consumers are increasingly concerned about toxins and chemicals in products, many countries and states are beginning to outlaw certain types of chemicals. Plastics, plasticizers, and flame retardants have been receiving the most attention; countries are banning and companies are facing pressure about having substances such as bisphenol A (BPA), polybrominated diphenyl ethers (PDBEs), and heavy metals in their products.

The European Union has been leading the charge on various chemical and toxin issues, mostly through its Registration, Evaluation, Authorisation, and Restriction of Chemicals (REACH). It requires "all companies manufacturing or importing chemical substances into the European Union to register these substances with a new European Chemicals Agency (ECHA) in quantities of 100 or more tons per year and will shift to 1 ton per year by 2018."[40] Any company importing goods into Europe could be affected.

This is a major game changer because in the United States the EPA has to prove that a chemical is harmful, whereas REACH requires companies to certify that the chemicals in their products are safe before they are sold to the general public.

FTC Ruling on "Green"

Another recent policy change affecting business was the U.S. Federal Trade Commission's (FTC) ruling on the term "green." As sustainability has become "fashionable" over the past few years, it seemed as though every company was making some type of green claim about their products. Even General Motors typically gets into the mix annually around Earth Day, describing its "green SUVs" that get under 20 miles per gallon. In my firm, we call this "sustainababble," which is displayed in Figure 1.6.

Figure 1.6   Sustainababble.

There was no way for consumers to verify all the claims out there or compare among products, which forced the FTC to come up with new rules to ensure that any claims that companies make about the environmental attributes of their products are truthful and nondeceptive.[41] These updates to the FTC will not only allow consumers to make informed comparisons, but will also force companies to truly know what is in their products and might cost them to do so.

Dodd–Frank, Section 1502

Largely lambasted by most financial institutions for the increase in paperwork that this act has generated, there is a small and important section regarding conflict minerals that has been largely overlooked by the media and most industry executives. Although conflict diamonds have received lots of attention over the years, including through the movie *Blood Diamond,* regulations on diamonds only impact a very small number of companies—primarily, Luxemburg-based De Beers, which owns about 75% of the world's diamond inventory.

This conflict-minerals regulation, however, affects a far greater number of industries and specifically references tin, thallium, tungsten, and gold. Moreover, there is a growing movement to include coltan, which is the key ingredient in most modern communication devices, including the iPhone, iPad, and Galaxy IV, as well as other rare earth elements.

New Accounting Standards

New accounting standards are being created to require the disclosure of social and environmental criteria in traditional financial statements and annual reports. These are being beta tested right now and will be coming to the accounting and auditing world in the next few years, which will affect just about every company.

Numerous countries, primarily in the EU, require state-owned and the largest publicly traded companies to produce sustainability reports, and in a few European countries, pension funds are already required to disclose whether they make socially and environmentally responsible investments and how they do so. Other countries that have adopted a variation of the same type of mandatory corporate social responsibility law include Australia, Austria, Canada, China, Denmark, France, Germany, Greece, Holland, Indonesia, Italy, Malaysia, Norway, Portugal, Spain, Sweden, and the United Kingdom.

This is being led by two organizations, the International Integrated Reporting Council (IIRC) and the Sustainability Accounting Standards Board (SASB). Although there have been other efforts, including the Prince's Accounting for Sustainability Project (A4S), which is working with Global Reporting Initiative (GRI), the IIRC and SASB are the ones leading the charge on developing the protocols for integrated reporting, with SASB looking to combine efforts with GRI for companies to have to create only one report.

A major reason for this new type of integrated reporting, beyond just demonstrating social and environmental impact, is because where companies' true brand value lies has shifted dramatically over the past 35 years. As Bob Willard demonstrates, a company's value has shifted from tangible assets (cash, property, plant equipment, accounts receivable) to intangible assets (goodwill, brand value, etc.) in a major way, going from 95%/5% respectively in 1978 to 35%/65% today. Therefore, a company's value is much more at risk from social and environmental issues because so much of their value is an intangible asset.

ISO Standards

The International Standards Organization (ISO) has also weighed into the frame and begun developing a global process for a monetary evaluation of these intangibles.

ISO has three programs related to sustainability that companies should be aware of, because these might be legal requirements in countries outside of the U.S.

- **ISO 14001:** Specifies the requirements for an environmental management system.

- **ISO 26000:** This standard offers guidance on socially responsible behavior and possible actions.

- **ISO 50001:** This is a management system standard for energy.

External Reporting

All these market forces, regulations, and public policies have led to a tremendous growth in external reporting across the spectrum. Many of the types of reporting around sustainability are contained in Table 1.4.

Table 1.4 Types of Reporting

Reporting Options	
Equity Investing	Calvert, DJSI, SAMs, Domini, Social Funds
EMS	ISO 14001 and ISO 26000
Climate	Climate Registry, Corporate Register, CDP
Governance	AccountAbility 1000, GRI G4 Guidelines
All	GRI, Climate Registry, CR Reporting Awards
Debt/Multinational	IFC Funding, Equator Principles
Workers	SA 8000
Labeling and Third-Party Verification	Green Seal, FSC, Rainforest, B Corp, and 300 more
Integrated Reporting	IIRC, SASB
Sustainability Rankings	Newsweek's Green Rankings, Climate Counts, Corporate Knights

The Top Line and Competitive Advantage

From my experience, although it's interesting and sometimes easier to talk about risk mitigation, compliance, cost savings, and the bottom line, what gets CEOs and upper management truly excited is the possibility of growing revenue with new product(s) or service opportunities to the top line. That is the CFO versus CEO comparison. The former is typically looking for ways to cut costs, and the latter is usually focused on growth and new revenue possibilities.

Why do we always hear about "bottom-line benefits" and "cost-savings"? I think it is because for years business has been looking at social and environmental issues from a defensive posture. They have been more comfortable in thinking about risk reduction.

Take the opposite approach. Play offense. Focus on opportunities and realize that sustainability can be an accelerant for growth and opportunity. Determine what new products or service options your company could create around sustainability that would contribute to the top line of your business. This will get the Board's and CEO's attention.

One example of how much more excited leadership can get about top line than bottom line came from one of our contractor clients. When we first started working with this technology contractor, in our initial meetings we asked them about their business practices. They were pretty humble about everything they did, and we found ourselves just tinkering around the edges in terms of finding ways to potentially save the company money and reduce their environmental footprint at the same time.

However, after about 60 minutes of our initial 90-minute conversation, they began to talk about their "Ship-to-Shore" power program. This is when a light went on for us: There was a huge growth opportunity for them financially. It also just happened to be about the most impactful and sustainable thing the company could do.

We quickly pivoted from focusing on the low-hanging fruit internally and spent the rest of the conversation identifying ways they could build on and grow this business, which would have a greater impact on the planet and also on the company's top line.

Competitive Advantage and Differentiation

One of the least-appreciated business reasons for implementing sustainability is the competitive advantage it can offer your company and the way it can serve as a differentiator between so many of the products and services that are so similar in the marketplace.

As Laszlo and Zhexembayeva write in *Embedded Sustainability*, "Differentiation is all about creating unique (and, to customers, uniquely valued) attributes for your company."[42] Typically, companies try to differentiate themselves using price, performance, aesthetics, or customer service. As mentioned earlier, Generation X and Y consumers tend to choose those companies and products that have environmental or socially just attributes when all other things are equal. So in many ways, sustainability attributes serve as a way to reinforce product quality, process, and brand uniqueness as well as your competitive advantage.

Laszlo and Zhexembayeva also make the case that "in the embedded sustainability model, a product or service that embodies sustainability does not compromise on functionality or price. There are no trade-offs in usability, reliability, or durability. However, the product—whether a light bulb, household cleaner, bank loan, or car—will look and feel very different from its conventional counterparts"[43] in that the consumer will know its sustainability benefits.

One example in the ski industry is that of Stevens Pass, a ski resort in Washington State. While many resorts were struggling to compete against one another, Stevens Pass looked at sustainability as a way to deliver value to its customers (skiers) while finding ways to save money and take action on climate change at the same time.

According to Ross Freeman, former Environment and Sustainability Manager at Stevens Pass, the marketing department was looking for a way to differentiate itself from other local ski areas in the Puget Sound region—Crystal Mountain, The Summit at Snoqualmie, and Mount Baker.

They didn't have access to traditional capital resources, which so many resorts use to build higher speed lifts, gondolas, or new facilities. So the resort decided instead to try to become one of the greenest ski resorts. To do this, they worked with a local waste facility, Cedar Grove Composting, to increase their recycling and compost all of their food waste; the resort also partnered with the utility company to purchase 100% renewable energy, making this one of the greenest ski resorts in North America. They did this because their customers are typically early adopters of sustainability and they've found this to be a true differentiator for their customers.

Differentiation Matters Only If You Use It!

This next example is probably the hardest one I've ever written, but it is also probably the most instructive. Because of the outcome, the former client name has been left out of the story. A few years ago, a company came to us because they had a product that was cheaper, was more efficient, and had a lower environmental footprint than that of their main rival.

One of their largest customers, Walmart, had just released their environmental guidelines and the customer was beginning to ask questions of their suppliers about the environmental attributes of their products. So my firm Sustainable Business Consulting (SBC) and one of our partners began to perform a Life Cycle Assessment (LCA) and carbon footprint for this client's product so that they could share the environmental benefits of their new product with Walmart and hopefully gain market share and increase top-line revenue.

However, our client found themselves bogged down by other priorities and they were not able to provide us with the data we needed to make the calculation. We kept insisting they get us the data immediately because we knew it was necessary to respond to the customer request and that if they dragged their feet any further they would lose their competitive advantage. They just kept saying they were busy and they'd get it to us whenever they could. Eventually, six months passed and one of their competitors stepped in with a product very similar to theirs, was able to respond to the supplier request, and won the business. Our client had the differentiation and competitive advantage, but they never capitalized on it and ended up losing out on millions in the process.

It's not enough to just have the competitive advantage; you need to communicate it and act on it!

The Interface Example

Whenever people talk about transforming their business around sustainability, one gold standard comes to mind: Interface. The carpet manufacturer was the first large company to do this, and the story of Interface and its transformation is inspiring, innovating, and complex all at the same time. For those unfamiliar with what Interface did, I've summarized it in the text that follows, because it is the model for any company trying to fully integrate sustainability into their business operations and make it stick for the long term.

The Story

Interface was just like any other carpet company in the world when it first started. It made petroleum-intensive carpeting that was full of chemicals, was unrecyclable, and was typically thrown away by consumers and companies when the carpet was stained, worn out, or ready to be replaced.

The founder and owner, Ray Anderson, had an epiphany in 1994 and challenged his then 21-year-old company to adopt a bold vision and a new model for business: a sustainable enterprise. He wanted to not only reduce the company's environmental footprint, but transform how business was done—from that of a purchasing model to one of leasing. The idea was that customers could lease individual carpet tiles and replace them as needed versus having to buy an entire new carpet every time. This was a bold and risky idea because it meant potentially sabotaging his own bottom line and how the company had made money for a long time.

He was undeterred, though. He asked his engineers to calculate the company's environmental footprint and set out the most ambitious goal of any CEO of any company at the time: zero impact and zero emissions by 2020. He called this project Mission Zero and it had seven key aspects:[44]

1. **Eliminate Waste:** Remove all forms of waste, in every area of business.

2. **Benign Emissions:** Eliminate toxic substances from products, vehicles, and facilities.

3. **Renewable Energy:** Operate facilities with 100% renewable energy.

4. **Close the Loop:** Redesign processes and products to close the technical loop using recovered and bio-based materials.

5. **Resource Efficient Transportation:** Transport people and products efficiently to eliminate waste and emissions.

6. **Sensitize Stakeholders:** Create a culture that uses sustainability principles to improve the lives and livelihoods of all of stakeholders—employees, partners, suppliers, customers, investors, and communities.

7. **Redesign Commerce:** Create a new business model that demonstrates and supports the value of sustainability-based commerce.

The results have been staggering. As of 2012 the company had seen the following benefits:

- Net GHG emissions were down 82% in absolute tonnage.

- Renewable energy usage was up 30%.

- About 74,000 tons of used carpet had been diverted from landfills.

- Fossil fuel usage was down 60%.

- Water usage was down 75%.

- Renewable and recycled materials usage was up 25%.

From a financial standpoint, these benefits have been realized:

- They've cut costs by $4.5 million.

- Sales have increased by two-thirds.

- Profits have doubled.

The company is halfway to its goal of Mission Zero and it anticipates that it will achieve that goal in 2020. The best part is that all of these efforts have paid for themselves over time. For more information, look up either of these stories:

- Ted Talk by Ray Anderson, at www.youtube.com/watch?v= iP9QF_lBOyA

- Full Interface story, at www.interfaceglobal.com/sustainability/ interface-story.aspx

The circumstances at your company are probably not the same as what Ray had at Interface, but this is the type of thinking and courage that today's CEOs need to embrace because the business case is truly a win-win.

Protecting Your Brand Exercise

A valuable tool I use in my consulting work and in workshops about the business case for sustainability is an exercise called *Protecting Your Brand*. This exercise was designed to help companies think through and hedge against future uncertainty, and address both risks and opportunities in the market and regulatory environments. It is designed to help you forecast into the future and determine what could potentially impact your company from a social, environmental, and financial standpoint across the following three scenarios over time:

1. Business as usual (BAU)

2. Further financial crises

3. Massive market disruption and strict environmental and social regulations

We use this exercise because the market and regulations are constantly shifting around sustainability, and the issues and concerns for most stakeholders right now might change, be passé, or be firmly cemented into society three to five years from now.

We've witnessed this in several ways. Let's use the consumer market for eggs as an example. Five to seven years ago the popular sentiment started shifting toward buying eggs that were organic. Then it slowly evolved as trends changed to local, then cage-free and naturally fed. And soon it became hormone and antibiotic free. Who knows where it will go next, and that is exactly the point. Sustainability is constantly changing and businesses need to plan ahead for ways to protect their brand from both market changes and new public policies.

Going through the Protecting Your Brand exercise will help you articulate potential future policy and market conditions, and determine how those conditions could impact the company. It will help you analyze business trade-offs, risks, and opportunities and uncover ways for your company to prosper by responding to those forces. It enables you to take a proactive stance versus a reactionary one. It will allow you to play both offense and defense.

Each scenario runs across three time periods; the short term (1 to 3 years), medium term (3 to 5 years), and long term (6 to 10 years). Although the latter is truly not "the long term" by traditional standards, because the current average length of a CEO is just over 8 years[45] and the average tenure of an employee is about 4.6[46] years, I decided to use 6 to 10 years as long term.

SBC's Protecting Your Brand Exercise

Think about what might change within the marketplace, your industry, public perception, and what is common consensus among scientists, policy experts, and your industry peers. Read each scenario, run through the risks and opportunities created by each, and then after all ideas have been generated, think about ways to take action.

ACTIVITY 6: PROTECTING YOUR BRAND		
Scenario 1: Business as Usual	Scenario 2: Financial Crises	Scenario 3: Strict Environmental and Social Regulations
The county is very politically divided.	Euro crashes, Japan further devalues. Income equality further expands.	The world wakes up about the environment; political leaders get backbone about what needs to be done! Fracking is outlawed.
Environmental issues and new social regulation are on the back burner, but local actions continue.	Congress fails to deal with budget problems and long-term debt. Inflation returns in a huge way.	New aggressive climate, environment, and social regulations are put into place immediately.
The economy grows at a sluggish rate.	Economy goes back into recession, unemployment rises, S&P is downgraded (again), stock market suffers flash crash.	Fuel costs rise; oil is closer to $200 per barrel.

Scenario 1: Business as Usual	Scenario 2: Financial Crises	Scenario 3: Strict Environmental and Social Regulations
Market pressures happen organically.	There is increased political gridlock (if possible).	Consumer demand is proven; massive change toward only buying from positive social and environmental brands.
There is business uncertainty about voluntary programs.	Environmental regulations are weakened.	Occupy Wall Street movement returns, is organized, and leads to structure changes in income inequality.
Income inequality is accepted.	Additional conflict in the Middle East pushes oil higher.	Middle East conflicts drag U.S. and Russia in. China and Japan stop exporting to one another.

Specifically, be sure to ask the following questions:

- What are the global and local economic dynamics that impact across market sectors?

- How are demographics shifting?

- Where is our industry headed?

- How will politics affect the situation depending on who is in power?

- What are our biggest potential vulnerabilities?

- What's definitely going to happen, what is likely, and why?

- What is totally out of your control but could severely impact your operations? How can you best mitigate that risk?

Lessons Learned

The following are key takeaways from "The Business Case" chapter:

- Huge market opportunities exist for meeting new market forces and regulations around sustainability.

- More than 45 separate studies demonstrate that there is money to be made on sustainability and companies can increase profitability, reduce risk, meet stakeholder expectations, and improve brand value by incorporating it into their practices.

- When making the business case for sustainability, you will want to vary it depending on who you are talking to, so be sure to demonstrate top-line revenues to the CEO, bottom-line savings to the CFO, risk reduction to Investor Relations and Legal, recruiting benefits to HR, and consumer issues to Marketing and Branding.

- Companies that have ESG criteria in their management outperform those companies that do not; SRI investments have outperformed the S&P 500 for a decade.

- Not only are employees considering sustainability in their job decisions, but Gen X and Gen Y employees are expecting it. They are showing a willingness to take a pay cut, and now that the economy is improving, they are showing a readiness toward leaving companies with poor social and environmental practices.

- Sustainability can be your competitive advantage and differentiator, especially when price, performance, and quality are similar. But it's an advantage only if you use it.

- As the value of companies increasingly is reflected in terms of intangible assets, a company's value is more at risk from social and environmental issues than ever before.

- Use the Protecting Your Brand exercise to get ahead of the next crisis—whether that is financially, socially, environmentally, consumer, or politically driven.

2

Defining Sustainability

hat do we mean when we say the word "sustainability"? How one person thinks about it might be very different from how another person thinks about it. Therefore, your first step in any sustainability plan is to define sustainability—why your company is doing this, what it means to your company specifically, how it adds business value—and settle on a common definition and language that all employees and stakeholders can both understand and get behind.

Why Are We Doing This?

Too often as I've engaged with companies, there has been a wide gap in understanding as to why the company is embarking on sustainability and to what end. And as you can imagine, this leads to a predictable gap in employee enthusiasm and acceptance of the idea.

Employees will have questions and will want to know the following:

- Is this a business driver or are you just trying to save the planet?

- Is it about saving money or brand differentiation?

- Are we doing this to appeal to younger, more socially and environmentally conscientious millennial consumers?

- Is this about having a stronger connection with our community and other stakeholders?

- Or are we just trying to do our part because we believe it's the right thing to do?

Executives and management must answer these questions and explain the "why": Why are we doing this, what is our company's story around sustainability, what do we want to accomplish, and how can each employee play a part? They must communicate how all these actions around sustainability woven together will improve its social, environmental, and financial performance at the same time.

Defining Sustainability for Your Company

The most common definition of sustainability is from the 1987 World Commission on Environmental Development (Brundtland Report), which states, "Sustainable development is development that meets the needs of the present without compromising the ability of future generations to meet their own needs."[1]

And there are literally dozens of other definitions out there. Some will resonate with your company whereas others will not. Therefore, while you are explaining the why, you need to define sustainability in a way that is true to your organization and is easily understood by all your employees, customers, and other stakeholders.

Depending on the nature of your business, sustainability could have a social, financial, or environmental bent:

- If you are a retailer, sustainability might mean offering your goods and services at the lowest possible price so that all consumers can afford it. Or it might mean that all of your products are organic, fair-trade, local, non-GMO, and so on.

- If you are like many companies that are just coming up for air after the financial crisis and the great recession, sustainability might just mean keeping the lights on and staying in business.

- If your company mind-set is more focused on the environment, sustainability might mean saving money and the environment at the same time. Or it might be defined as producing the highest-quality products and growing the company while reducing your environmental footprint. Or it could mean greater profits while producing zero waste and zero emissions. It can be all over the map.

- Or if you are a family or privately held business, sustainability might simply mean passing the company down to the next generation.

What Does This Mean to Your Employees?

Now that you've tailored your sustainability message to your organization, you need to take the even more critical step of helping your employees understand what it means to them and their jobs, and put it in language they understand.

Don't speak Greek! Or Geek, for that matter. How you talk about sustainability and the language you use is just as important as what you say. You have to put sustainability into terms that people can understand and relate to. Instead of thinking, *This is really important and they need to know this!* flip your mind-set and ask yourself, *What does this person care about and how can we talk about sustainability in a way that they can relate to both personally and in their job?*

Use the old MBA acronym WIFT—or what's in it for them. Think about what is in it for the listener, not just what you want to convey.

This has been one of the major problems with the environmental movement over the past 25 years; it has often had the mind-set of trying to tell people what they should care about and why, rather than listening to people's concerns, finding common ground, and communicating in a language they both understand about issues they care about.

For example, look at the Pacific Northwest salmon. For years scientists have been screaming about the potential catastrophic consequences to the salmon if we don't change our practices. The problem is that regular consumers don't care about farmed salmon weakening the genetic diversity of wild salmon, but they do care about how it tastes, what chemicals and dyes are used, and how it affects their health. These taste and health concerns are all impacted by the same root cause that scientists are worried about, so rather than engaging consumers around issues of genetic diversity, they should engage consumers on the issues they care about most.

Or to use a more recent business example, remember when the iPhone 4 came out? The first version was a huge bestseller, but there was a problem with the antenna if you held the phone in your right hand. Too often when you were making a call, the call was dropped. So when I went in to buy one, the salesperson was telling me all about the new features of the phone, including faster data, new apps, and a better camera, but the only thing I truly cared about was whether I could make a phone call without it being dropped! I kept asking about the antenna, but the salesperson kept talking about all the other benefits. He was not listening to my concerns nor was he framing the conversation around the thing I cared about.

It is no different when talking about sustainability. For whatever reason, people forget to ask themselves, *Why would this person or organization care about what I am trying to tell them?* Now, there isn't a businessperson in the world who will tell you that he or she enjoys polluting, generating waste, or threatening the biodiversity of our planet for their children. In fact, most people will tell you that they wish they could do more, but it's just not in their job description.

That's why tailoring both your message and your language to the person you are talking to is so important. If you want to be successful in getting your employees and co-workers to care about sustainability, think about what's in it for them, and explain how integrating sustainability into their job will help these people be more successful in their day-to-day lives and deliver improved performance for their company overall.

Your primary role might end up being that of a translator, explaining the same concept in numerous ways throughout your company. If the language you are using isn't getting through, you might have to tailor your message and utilize different words because whatever you are saying makes sense to you but not to others.

Table 2.1 Tailoring Your Language

Person/Department	Explain How Sustainability Will:
Accounting and Finance	Save and make the company money
Facilities	Make operations more efficient and save resources and costs

Person/Department	Explain How Sustainability Will:
Fleets	Save on fuel and delivery times
Investor Relations	Answer SRI/CDP investor questions, shareholder resolutions
Office Manager	Make the office more efficient
Travel Coordinator	Reduce business travel and costs
CEO	Improve her or his own legacy and peer reputation
PR and Marketing	Create brand value and positive press
Sales and Business Development	Generate new leads, products, and sales opportunities
CSR and Green Team	Become corporate culture
Logistics	Improve efficiency
Human Resources	Attract better talent and improve retention
Supply Chain	Lead to a better understanding of opportunities in value chain
Legal and Issuance	Reduce risk and improve resiliency

Eli Reich, the CEO and founder of Alchemy Goods, believes that you need to "teach your employees, help them understand the language, help them understand the opportunity, and then let them make decisions."[2]

Dawn Danby, the sustainable design program manager at Autodesk, adds that you need to "feed information back in a language employees and stakeholders care about and understand. When you do this, be sure to address both their fears and opportunities! Package it in a way that they get it."[3]

For example, when dealing with executives, you cannot be heavy-handed, grandiose, or too "big picture" with your language. If they believe that their competitive advantage or purpose is based on technology, price, performance, or customer experience, you need to talk about sustainability in this context as well.

Another example is that of the engineer. If you are talking about sustainability in a general way and the engineer wants a specific technology solution, your language won't work. Or if you are talking to a product designer who thinks from a customer/user perspective, making the business case won't be as important to the designer as showing how the design solution will make for a better customer experience.

If Your Message Isn't Getting Across

Sometimes it could also be the mode or medium that's the problem. Realize that some people prefer to hear the message in person or face to face, so an e-mail or a Web site isn't going to work for them. Others don't grasp things verbally and they need to have it written down, so that might be the best format. Ask people how they prefer their communications and have multiple ways to communicate your sustainability message so that you can meet their needs.

Lastly, it could be the wrong person delivering the message. Maybe the person is too corporate and doesn't connect with the everyday employee. Or it could be the opposite and the person has too junior of a position to get the attention of the Board. Sometimes you just need to change the person who is delivering the message.

Create a Common Language

The last step is to develop a common language or lexicon within your company. Just like people understand margins, ROI, payback, and other common business lingo, it's important for your company to use common sustainability language and even consider creating a "data dictionary" of sustainability terms internally so that everyone can be on the same page. There will likely be cases, beyond the word *sustainability*, where one person uses a term very differently from how another person uses it, so be aware of that and work to find common language.

One of my clients has actually been very successful in deploying a data dictionary. Not only are people on the same page, but in situations in which a person leaves or a task is assigned to someone else, there is continuity of terms, words, and understanding, which minimizes confusion and increases the efficiency for everyone involved.

The Sustainability Elevator Pitch

In the business world, it's commonly understood that you need to be able to describe what your company does in about 10 to 15 seconds, roughly the equivalent of the time it takes to ride up an elevator six floors. This is called the elevator pitch because you need to be able to get someone's attention and explain your message before the person tunes you out!

The same is true with sustainability. Develop an elevator speech that reflects what your company is trying to do on sustainability and embed it into your company culture. You want it to be short and sweet; something that your employees, volunteers, and Board understand; and easy enough to remember so that employees are able to communicate it with confidence when talking to stakeholders. This is especially helpful in situations in which there are new people or there has been turnover; being able to explain the company's shared vision for sustainability will help continuously drive the message home and ensure that the torch is carried on. Table 2.2 gives you a few ideas on how to get input for your pitch.

Table 2.2   Employees and Sustainability

Surveying Employees about Sustainability
One of the easiest ways to ensure that your sustainability message is understood by all your employees is to start by asking. Getting employee input from the very beginning can be an invaluable source in defining sustainability for your company. Many companies find that using a survey is typically the best way to reach a large group. Here are a few potential questions to ask employees: ■ What does sustainability mean to you? ■ What does sustainability mean to our company? ■ Have you had any ideas for innovation and sustainability or improved company efficiency? ■ What do you think the company could do to reduce carbon emissions and/or environmental impacts? ■ Are you doing anything at work or at home related to climate change or sustainability that you'd like to share (i.e., printing double-sided, never idling your vehicle, making your own biodiesel, shopping at the farmers' market, etc.)?

The following are topic areas usually covered in HR surveys, so add sustainability questions to surveys going out about them:

- Training and skills needs
- General work environment
- Employee satisfaction
- Opportunities for professional growth
- Motivational levels
- Ways to make the office more efficient or problem solving
- Management responsiveness toward employees' work needs
- Effectiveness of communication among staff and management
- Levels of service quality and products offered by the business
- Service delivery systems

Lessons Learned

The following are key takeaways from the "Defining Sustainability" chapter:

- Make sure everyone knows why you are implementing sustainability.

- Define sustainability and tailor it to your organization.

- Make it easy to understand and simple for people to grasp.

- Put your sustainability questions, opportunities, and actions into your audience's language and use terms and words that the people you are talking to are familiar with.

- Realize that you might have to be a translator at times.

- Creating a common vocabulary within your company culture is essential.

- Develop your sustainability elevator pitch and make sure that others can recite it easily.

3

Understanding Your Stakeholders and What Is Material to Them

Befrore companies charge down the path of sustainability, they should figure out what is material to their business and what their stakeholders care about. Too often, organizations make the mistake of skipping this step because they are in a rush to "get something done" or they are responding to an external request from a customer, shareholder, or supplier. This Ready-Fire-Aim approach misses a crucial step if you want your sustainability efforts to be successful, and that step is stakeholder engagement.

A company should first determine what aspects of sustainability are material to its business. Then it needs to understand what its various stakeholders care about, prioritize actions based on this feedback, develop best practices, and then communicate what it plans to do for all involved. By doing this and engaging your stakeholders, not only at the beginning of your efforts, but repeatedly along your sustainability journey, you'll be better able to anticipate their concerns and meet their expectations.

This is essential because different external stakeholders will have divergent perspectives on sustainability issues and might be able to shed light on your blind spots and provide potential solutions to the issues you are facing. So stakeholder engagement is about both risk management *and* innovation.

In fact, there is an old African proverb that rings true with sustainability and stakeholder engagement: "If you want to go fast, go alone. If you want to go far, go together." Along your sustainability journey, be sure to bring your stakeholders along with you!

Why You Need Stakeholder Engagement

Even though CEOs recognize that stakeholder engagement is a critical step in implementing sustainability, few businesses are actually doing it as well as they could be. In fact, according to a Havas Media Lab survey, only 17% of survey respondents really engage and collaborate with customers regarding corporate social responsibility activities. Moreover, respondents said they engage business partners and community members only 23% and 20% of the time, respectively, around CSR and sustainability issues.[1] This represents a major missed opportunity to find out what your stakeholders care about and ensure that your sustainability efforts meet both your company needs and your stakeholder needs. Without it, you might end up spending precious time, money, and resources on the wrong things!

Specifically, when you reach out to stakeholders, you want to be able to accurately answer three questions:

1. What do they care about in regard to your business (what is most material)?

2. How do they define sustainability? (This might be different from the way you think about it.)

3. What is important to them (socially, environmentally, and financially) and what is not?

For most companies, their *primary key stakeholder* groups are these:

- **Customers:** Corporate and individual consumers.

- **Employees:** Current employees, executives, and entry-level employees.

- **Suppliers:** Vendors throughout your value stream.

- **Investors:** Current shareholders as well as potential socially responsible investment (SRI) investors.

- **Community partners and donor recipients:** All organizations that have benefited from your company's philanthropic (cash and product), volunteer, and pro-bono efforts.

Secondary stakeholder groups include media, government, NGOs, creditors, industry associations, and other groups relevant to your company.

If you want to make sustainability stick and realize its full potential within your company, you need to find out what they care about socially, environmentally, and financially, and then as you take action, you'll want to bring your stakeholders along with you. They will help you:

- Identify issues that need attention and give you a heads-up on things to avoid

- Discover new product/service opportunities

- Uncover unmet needs

- Recruit your biggest clients/stakeholders to be an influence on your behalf

- Plant seeds for future collaboration

- Find advocates for your company that you didn't know were there

One common concern for CEOs is the worry that if they do a stakeholder engagement, they feel as though they will have to tackle everything on sustainability at once and open themselves up to criticism if they don't. The opposite is actually true.

More often than not, companies can address and diffuse environmental and social issues with stakeholders by better managing their expectations. Critics typically want to air their concerns, see that you are taking them seriously, and know that their issue is going to be addressed at some point. Therefore, if you communicate with them and explain your priorities and why you are tackling certain issues before others, with a plan to address their concerns, you'll find that they are usually more understanding and more likely to work with you to help you solve whatever issue they are bringing to the table. In fact, you might end up strengthening a relationship that could otherwise have become hostile and turn them into an advocate on your behalf.

This has been proven numerous times as companies are embracing the very same NGOs (nongovernmental organizations) that used to pick on them or protest their practices. Many companies are realizing business benefits from being proactive, reaching out and bringing them into the fold. For example, in the investment community, SRI firms and pension funds are taking a more active approach to working with companies toward a common objective versus divesting. Instead of walking away, they are working with companies to encourage the type of behavior and action they want to see socially and environmentally.

BUSINESS CASE: PARTNERING WITH CRITICS

For example, we all remember the controversy surrounding Nike and its poor working conditions within its overseas factories back in late 1990s. After news broke that Nike factory workers were being treated poorly and both human rights and labor violations were being committed, the company knew it had to act in order to prevent a catastrophic attack on its brand. Nike worked with the NGOs that were originally protesting the company to have these organizations inspect the factories and publicly report their findings.

By partnering with the "opposition" to find a solution, Nike was able to address stakeholder concerns head on, be transparent, work directly with the NGOs to correct the problem, and now has industry-leading practices.

In terms of supply chain, a similar trend is emerging as companies are reaching out to their suppliers and taking time to foster the open lines of communication and explaining why they are engaging on sustainability to gain buy-in, rather than just dictating new rules. Instead of just abandoning or exiting factories and looking elsewhere, they are trying to encourage the changes they want to see socially and environmentally. Of course, there are always exceptions and you cannot please everyone, but both of these trends are more positive and focused on collaboration toward a shared objective and creating stronger partnerships to last for the long term.

Materiality and the Process for Determining It

Determine what is most important to your stakeholders and figure out what sustainability issues need to be addressed, in that order. This is called "determining materiality." A useful tool to help you determine your materiality and the importance of each aspect of sustainability (both internally and externally) is the materiality matrix example shown in Figure 3.1.

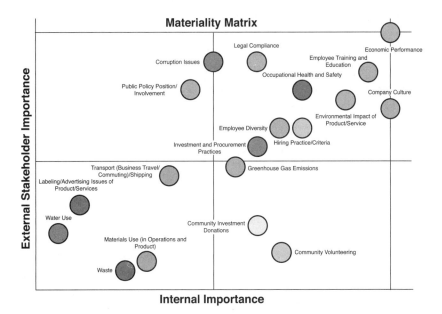

Figure 3.1   Materiality matrix.

Too often people try to make each issue a global issue. But the reality is that not every issue is material to your company or stakeholders. Not everything will end up having a direct impact on polar bears or will impact the two billion people who live on less than $2 a day.

The Process

Before starting, you'll want to diagnose your current and existing outreach efforts so that you can build off the existing channels of communication when engaging around sustainability.

Ask yourself these questions:

- How do we currently interact with customers, suppliers, vendors, and employees?

- How often do we do this and in what form?

- What are our stated issues? What are the hidden ones? Where are there similar values among these groups?

- What do our stakeholders have to gain or lose from each of these in regard to sustainability?

Then, before you seek stakeholder input on exactly what you should be doing on sustainability, be sure they fully understand why your company is pursuing sustainability. As mentioned earlier, share your definition of what sustainability means to your company so that everyone is on the same page and is using common language.

Then make sure to involve the right people in the process. You cannot just engage friends and clients who like you. You need to invite the people who will also expose your warts and tell you the "uncomfortable truths." These will be the most valuable because they'll make you aware of your blind spots and risks.

When you convene these conversations and focus groups, be sure to inform participants of the desired topic and let them know what you are trying to accomplish, and that it is an open conversation, with no incorrect answers so there is no fear of discussing controversial issues. This will help you develop a deeper understanding of key perceptions, mental models, aspirations, and barriers, both emotional and rational, to help your company truly understand what's on people's minds.

Table 3.1 and Activity 7 will help guide you through the materiality process and help you develop the questions that you'll want to modify to determine what is most important to your stakeholders and your company.

Table 3.1   Creating Your Materiality Matrix

Stakeholder Materiality Process
1. **Project planning.**   ■ When we say "our company," what is the boundary that we are drawing around our impacts?   ■ Who should be accountable for engaging each group of stakeholders?

2. **Determine and prioritize stakeholders.**
   - Who affects the organization? In what ways?
   - Who is influenced by our actions? In what ways?
   - Who is directly responsible for the decisions on these issues?
   - Who runs organizations with relevant interests in the area (NGOs, industry associations, etc.)?
   - In what ways are our stakeholders most influential on these issues?
   - What stakeholders have been engaged on these issues in the past?
   - Who has not been involved, but should have been?

   Customers/clients/consumers

   Employees

   Suppliers/business partners/vendors

   Investors/shareholders

   Communities in which you operate and from which you take materials

   Community leaders

   Nonprofits/philanthropic recipients

   Media

   Governments

   Debtors/creditors

   Other

3. **Identify issues.**
   - What are the issues most important to our company and business?
   - How does our organization define sustainability (environment, community involvement, people, philanthropy)?
   - What are our stakeholders' main concerns (perceived and actual)?
   - Do we have a "sustainability issues" map to help guide efforts?
   - Are there any environmental/social issues that could sink us as a company?

4. **Draft questions.**

5. **Determine techniques and the best way to engage.**
   - How do we currently communicate with customers, employees, investors, and other stakeholders?
   - How do we communicate our sustainability efforts to each of these stakeholder groups?

- In what ways could we better align our sustainability messaging with our other communications efforts? How can we leverage these?
- Are we fully engaging with all of our stakeholders (customers, investors, employees, suppliers, partners, NGOs, governments, communities, etc.)?
- What is the best way to conduct the engagements (surveys, focus groups, summits, invite people onto Board/committees, other)?
- Is a third-party facilitator needed?

6. **Design logistics and agenda to meet objectives.**
   - What logistics and rules must be in place?
   - Who will invite the participants and how will this be done?
   - Where, when, and how will the engagement take place?
   - How will results be tabulated?

7. **Provide stakeholders with background information.**
   - Do we have the right background information, materials, and training to inform stakeholders so that they can maximize their ability to provide frank input and feedback?

8. **Engage.**

9. **Review results and process.**
   - What are the outcomes?
   - Did we find out what we set out to understand?
   - Was the engagement successful based on our criteria?
   - Was the medium selected appropriate/correct for each stakeholder group?
   - How often is the appropriate number of times to communicate with them (annually, biannually, quarterly)?
   - What happens after the engagement? What are the next steps?
   - Do we need further sessions or clarification?

10. **Share results internally and externally.**
    - How can we be sure the results reach the right internal decision makers?
    - In what ways can we respond to these results?
    - What is the best method for following up from the session?
    - Which suggestions will we be acting on immediately, or in the future, and which ones need further research or deliberation?

11. **Repeat annually. It should become as automatic as lather, rinse, repeat!**

The following are sample questions you can use to help determine materiality around sustainability with various stakeholder groups. Use these questions to build out and tailor questions for these and the remainder of your stakeholder groups (government, NGOs, creditors, industry associations, lobbyists, donors, etc.). Of course, who the primary and secondary stakeholders are will vary by company and industry.

Customers and Consumers

- What social/environmental issue(s) are most important to you with regard to our company?

- How aware are you of our existing sustainability efforts?

- What aspects do you like? What should we do less of?

- What specific activities make you want to buy/use our goods and services?

- Would you be more/less likely to buy our goods and services if we improved our social/environmental performance?

- What should we be doing that we are not?

Employees

- What social/environmental issue(s) are most important to you with regard to our company?

- How aware are you of our existing efforts?

- What aspects do you like? Where should we take a leadership role?

- How important is it to you that our company pursues environmental or social initiatives?

- Which specific initiatives would you like to see our company participating in or putting more resources toward?

- How involved are you in environmental issues outside of work? Do you currently volunteer in your community outside of work?

- How involved would you like to be in social/environmental initiatives sponsored by our company? (For instance, how much time each month would you like to devote to such initiatives?)
- Would you be more excited to work at our company if it made sustainability a priority?

Vendors and Suppliers

- What social/environmental issue(s) are most important to you (community, human rights, employee workplace conditions, etc.)?
- If we add sustainability criteria to our purchasing guidelines, how would these affect you?
- Would these influence your decision to sell us your products/ service at the same price?
- Are you being asked by anyone in your value chain about similar issues?
- In what ways could you help us improve our social/environmental performance?

Investors/Shareholders

- In what ways are you benchmarking or comparing our sustainability performance against other companies? How do we stack up?
- What do you think are the biggest sustainability issues (risks and opportunities) that will impact our company?
- In what ways would you like to see us improve on our existing performance?
- What social/environmental activities should we be doing that we aren't?
- Is there anything we should stop doing?
- Are there shareholder resolutions that you have heard about that we should be prepared to respond to?
- In comparison to financial performance, how important to you is our sustainability performance (more, equal, less, way less, not important at all)?

Community Partners

- In what ways are our employees and company visible in the community to you?

- What community and environmental activities does the company do that we should do more of?

- What activities are you aware of that are of lesser importance? What should we focus on less?

- In what ways could we be more effective with our community, philanthropic, and volunteer efforts?

- How could we better leverage the work we are doing/could do with you and others?

Best Practices and Common Delivery Mechanisms

There are many ways and mediums to consider before reaching out and engaging your stakeholders, so before you do so, be sure to determine which is the best method to reach each stakeholder group successfully. I have detailed the five most common ways that companies do this and have highlighted the pros and cons of each method on the following pages, but the most important things are to engage the right people, in the right way, using the communications medium most appropriate and applicable to them.

For example, younger generations prefer social media or electronic communications, whereas baby boomers or Generation X stakeholders might want in-person focus groups, printed communication, or hard copy reports. Also, be sure to ask them when is the best time to contact them to elicit their feedback (time of day, day of the week, etc.) and then adhere to those preferences as well as you possibly can.

Ask Your Frontline Employees

Through all of our work, we've found that the best place to start is with your frontline employees because they are a potential gold mine of information. Whenever we ask our clients' frontline employees for their input on improved social and environmental performance, they inevitably come up with more efficient ways to do things, new product ideas, and potential new revenue streams. Some of these ideas are unique to the company and others are pretty ubiquitous across corporations. By engaging frontline employees in this way, companies will discover new opportunities, uncover risks, and get the pulse of their employees as to what they would like to see the company do.

Asking Your Customers

You want your customers to be able to tell your story and how your product or service helped them. The winemaker Yellow Tail, for example, got feedback from customers that they wanted a wine that was, according to Chris Laszlo, the coauthor of *Embedding Sustainability,* "easy to drink, easy to select, and fun."[2] By working to eliminate the complexity of the wine selection process, Yellow Tail enhanced their brand and attracted many non–wine drinkers, including those who previously favored beer.

BUSINESS CASE: SUSTAINABILITY ACTIONS CUSTOMERS AND EMPLOYEES CARE ABOUT

Ross Freeman, the former environment and sustainability manager at the Ski Resort at Stevens Pass, Washington, surveyed his employees who felt bad about all the food that was being thrown away at their mountain restaurants. Although food is not as big an impact as the water used to make snow or as the energy to run the lifts, it was visible waste that customers could see. So Stevens Pass created a pilot project with Cedar Grove composting to separate trash from food waste with the goal of reducing landfill waste and cost. The result was that the resort was able to downsize its garbage contract and find a way to put food waste back into productive use as compost.

According to Freeman, "Customers loved it, employees felt good about it, and it was positive for Cedar Grove in that it gave them great exposure. And, after I ran the numbers, the cost ended up being the same, not extra."[3] This was an example of working with stakeholders to create a truly win-win-win.

Supply Chain

Suppliers are essential to engage because they can significantly and positively impact the value chain. In fact, for many industries this may be one of the largest opportunities for sustainability improvement. Because suppliers have a vested interest in keeping your business, they should take your sustainability concerns seriously just as they do in making your logistics run as smoothly, efficiently, and cost-effectively as possible.

The reality, though, is that suppliers and their subsidiaries form one of the toughest barriers to implementing sustainability. According to a report from the UN Global Compact, "While 91% of suppliers and 88% of subsidiaries agreed that sustainability should be incorporated into their work, only 59% and 54% (respectively) acknowledged it had been."[4] This differential provides an opportunity for companies to better engage their supply chain and positively influence the social and environmental aspects of their products and services, especially overseas where language, culture, and business mind-sets might be different.

Involving Your Industry Association

Some of the challenges your company will face around sustainability are bigger than what one company can take on. These issues are beyond your immediate stakeholders and require whole changes to the system and industry. This has happened in the energy industry where companies such as Duke Energy, AEP, and DuPont have proactively asked for carbon regulation at the federal level. They know they need to act, they want to act, but they can't afford to do so if it will put them at a competitive disadvantage; so they became members of an industry association pushing climate legislation. Issues like climate change transcend countries and even industries, so companies have been forced to find ways to work with their competitors and industry associations to take meaningful actions.

The good news is that more and more companies are finding ways to engage their key stakeholders and industry associations to tackle these larger issues when trying to do so as a single company won't suffice. One of the best examples of this was in the outdoor retail industry. Many of the companies (Nike, REI, Patagonia, Timberland, etc.) were trying to find ways to measure and communicate the environmental benefits of their products. However, no single standard or set of metrics existed, so consumers, designers, and industry executives had no way of knowing which product truly had a better environmental footprint than another.

Therefore, a group of individuals from these leading companies formed the Eco-Working Group (EWG) within the Outdoor Association to do just that. Together, they were able to create a set of key environmental metrics that all companies in the industry could follow. They developed the methodology, metrics, and reporting criteria that were soon adopted by the Sustainable Apparel Coalition. This is an example of where working with competitors in an industry toward a common goal enabled each company to accomplish its own goal in a much faster, cheaper, and more collaborative approach than going alone. These companies engaged their stakeholders around issues most material to their products and involved their industry association to tackle global issues that they never could have on their own. Don't worry; they still compete on products, just not on the measurement criteria to determine those environmental attributes.

This collaborative approach is not limited to apparel, because most industry associations have launched some type of environmental/ climate/sustainability program or working group. A few of the biggest are listed next, but look at your company and find out what your industry associations and/or trade groups are doing on these topics. You will likely find free information and resources available.

- The Sustainability Consortium
- American Sustainable Business Council
- Electronic Industry Citizenship Coalition
- Sustainable Packaging Coalition
- Sustainable Food Trade Association
- Beverage Industry Environmental Roundtable
- The Better Cotton Initiative
- And many more

Five Common Ways to Engage Your Stakeholders

There are a various ways to reach out and engage your stakeholders. Five of the most common ways are listed in Table 3.2, with the various pros and cons of each. Choose the appropriate ones and tailor them to your company and each stakeholder group that you are reaching out to.

Table 3.2 Types of Stakeholder Engagement

1. Surveys	*Pros*
Embed sustainability questions in surveys that are already being sent out to stakeholders—whether customers, suppliers, or employees. In fact, one of our preferred methods for doing this is by combining it with existing customer-service or employee-satisfaction questionnaires. That way you can also elicit ideas and solutions to social and environmental issues the company is facing at the same time.	Large reach. Inexpensive. Easy to create and tabulate results.
	Cons
	No face-to-face interaction. Hard to understand context behind answers, no ability to read body language or mood. One-way conversation. No trust is built; therefore, only surface ideas are delivered.
2. Focus Groups	*Pros*
When conducting focus groups, it's important to select a broad reach of people from each of your different stakeholder groups. If you can, conduct one for each type of stakeholder, independent from the others. Be sure to not only select participants who are expedient and can attend, but choose people who are both supporters and contrarians, because you'll probably learn the most from the latter group. If you cannot get access to multiple groups, pick one with an issue that needs urgent attention and conduct one focus group to prove out the value of the whole.	Ability to interact with participants and understand context of statements. Ability to ask clarifying questions, know who is saying what. Leaders can emerge. Trust can be built through deeper conversations and information.
	Cons
	Time, cost, and resources to perform nationally or globally. Must have diverse group in room and a trained facilitator to avoid bias taking over from one person or a sub-group within the participants. Difficult to repeat and scale.

3. Summits	Pros
This is an effective way to bring a wide variety of stakeholders together all at once to share what the company is doing and use the combined cross-functional knowledge of the different groups to solve challenges (more eco-friendly solutions, workplace hour and age requirements, etc.). You can explain and teach in-person the "how" and "why," and develop accountability and feedback mechanisms right then and there!	Effective way to bring everyone together in one place.
	Teams are often formed to find solutions to expressed issues or opportunities. Solutions can come straight out of the summit.
	Attendees can ask questions and raise concerns that they and others might have.
	Larger purpose can be seen through camaraderie (we're all in this together).
	Accountability, everyone has been told and trained all at once. There are no excuses for lack of compliance.
	Cons
	Cost prohibitive, extremely time-consuming for staff and attendees.
	If you have one loud group that is skeptical, there is a danger that they could bring other stakeholder groups to their side.
	Finding a time and place that works well for everyone is difficult.
4. Scorecards	Pros
Scorecards are typically used by companies that have an expansive supply chain and are especially important in the retail industry. This is a way to ask stakeholders both quantitative and qualitative questions. Scorecards put issues into categories for the user, which can help organize thoughts and compare answers.	Quantitative data to act on and compare performance over time.
	Everyone can see what the company is tracking.
	Cons
	Does not have a conversational element to it.
	The questions need to be worded specifically or this might not have as much utility, especially when sending internationally because things can get lost in translation.

	If someone sees a category that their company does not speak to, they tend to ignore it, resulting in a loss of diversity in responses. Suppliers and customers are beginning to experience "scorecard and questionnaire" fatigue and might not engage. There is no space for creative input.
5. Other This includes anything else: community meetings/open houses, newsletters, feedback boxes (at facilities and online), social media (blogs, Facebook, Twitter), etc.	*Pros* Each offers alternative ways to reach out to these groups. *Cons* May be skewed generationally or geographically.

Communicating It Back to Stakeholders

After you have performed your engagement, you need to communicate the results back to your stakeholders. This is an essential step and requires developing a feedback mechanism that is tailored to the methods, styles, and mediums they prefer:

1. **Use visuals and put issues into words and terms that each different stakeholder group uses.**

   Keep your message concise and to the point rather than providing all the details.

   For example, one of our government lab clients needed an easier way to communicate sustainability information and progress to stakeholders. It identified which data points and areas were of most concern, and then used easy-to-understand graphics, such as up and down arrows that were color-coded red and green, so that customers and employees could track performance over time and understand how the organization was progressing.

   When you are showing areas of concern, the colors of a stoplight seem to work really well because people can identify with that very easily in the U.S. Red can indicate a problem area that needs immediate attention, yellow signifies an area of caution, and green means things are going well or are under control. People already see this in other aspects of their life and the concept is easily understood by everyone.

2. **Make it digestible.**

Don't create a big report and just assume that someone will read it.

For example, when a large retailer began communicating with its stakeholders about its sustainability efforts, the company was asked not to give a big report or to have information pushed onto them. If the company was going to provide something, the stakeholders wanted something they could read and engage with.

3. **Inform them subtly.**

One method you come across on a frequent basis, but probably don't even recognize anymore, exists in almost every hotel room in the country. Hotels put their environmental message right in front of consumers—on the bed or in the bathroom via small placards—and invite their stakeholders (guests) to help them by reusing towels and sheets in the hotel's quest to be more sustainable. This is a good example, because hotels are in a situation in which they are wondering how best to engage with 200 new guests every night. Take a page from what hotels already do and see whether there is a way you can apply this approach to your business.

Implement a Feedback Mechanism

Too often companies ask their stakeholders for feedback, implement a few items, and then never report back to them. This is shortsighted because you want your stakeholders to know what you've done, what you still plan to do, and what you did with their feedback so that they feel as though their time and energy were of value to you.

Therefore, before you have a survey, focus group, or summit, be sure to create a feedback mechanism that will report the results, share how information will be used, let the participants know what specific actions you'll be implementing, and be honest with them about other comments or issues brought to light that you might delay, study, or choose not to do and why. This will demonstrate responsiveness and accountability and also keep their expectations in check so that you don't overpromise and then underdeliver.

Create this feedback loop and be sure that it is both formal and informal. In fact, create a system in which you don't have to rely on annual or semiannual formal engagements, but rather have a more frequent feedback mechanism in which stakeholders are free to provide more informal feedback to you. For example, between formal, annual stakeholder engagement sessions, be sure to have informal phone calls, e-mails, and conversations with each of your stakeholder groups. This way you can receive frank feedback continuously, in a timely manner, and can take action as things come up.

Remember if your stakeholders have a positive experience, they will be more likely to continue to participate and support you in the future, and you'll better manage stakeholder expectations over the long term. Bring your stakeholders along with you throughout this journey and their experience will enable you to make the necessary changes to make sustainability stick for the long term.

ACTIVITY 8: FEEDBACK/GRIEVANCE MECHANISM

A feedback mechanism probably already exists in your company, whether by policy or by informal problem solving and recognition. Some sample questions to ask yourself when developing communication and feedback mechanisms around sustainability include these:

1. What kind of feedback are you looking for (constructive, ways to improve, etc.)?

2. Who will respond?

3. When will they respond?

4. What type of response should people expect and what will it look like?

5. What have you done with feedback in the past?

The Goal of the 5 Touches

The ultimate goal of all this stakeholder engagement is that you want each stakeholder to not only understand what you are doing on sustainability but also be an evangelist of your message. So during the feedback process, when you share your message with your stakeholders, be sure to say it in a way that they can run with it. Your goal is for each stakeholder to achieve what I call "the 5 touches on sustainability." You can massively leverage and multiply your message through this human component if every stakeholder were to share your sustainability story with the following:

- One friend

- One family member

- One professional colleague (work, industry association, rotary)

- One neighbor

- One community member (church member, volunteer group, parent from your kid's sports team, and so on)

Lessons Learned

The following are key takeaways from the "Understanding Your Stakeholders and What Is Material to Them" chapter:

- People jump down the path of trying to implement sustainability before figuring out what stakeholders care about. If you have done this, be sure to go back and find out where you need to focus your sustainability efforts.

- Use a materiality matrix to determine those issues most important to your business and stakeholders.

- Customers and employees tend to care about things they come into contact with, things they can touch and see every day. So pay attention to not only the big impact areas, but also those smaller ones that stakeholders come into contact with most frequently.

- By bringing your stakeholders into the mix, you'll find new allies and people who will give you the benefit of the doubt if you fall short of your goals or mess up.

- There are multiple ways to conduct stakeholder engagement, each with its own pros and cons. Be sure to tailor yours to your unique situation and stakeholder groups. Realize that the method and medium of communication might be just as important as the message.

- Create a feedback mechanism back to your stakeholders and develop a process that will continually gather information over time.

- If you are hearing information that you already know, that means that you aren't asking tough enough or the right questions. The point is to find out things you didn't already know!

4

Baselining Sustainability to Measure What Matters

ou can't know where you are headed unless you know where you are!

I use this sailing metaphor often because you can't know where you are going or how you are doing over time unless you first conduct a sustainability baseline.

So before you decide to lose a bunch of weight, be sure to step on the scale!

Measure What Matters

As Peter Drucker so eloquently said:

"What gets measured, gets managed."

You have to measure your social and environmental impacts so that you can determine the risks and opportunities to your company, then prioritize and take action on the issues most important to the company and its stakeholders. The baseline is important because it allows your company to know where it stands, manage your performance over time, and close the gap from where you are to where you want to be.

Sustainability initiatives need to be tracked, with hard data that shows progress over time, both positive and negative.

The sustainability baseline will help you do the following:

- Know where you are having the biggest impacts
- Identify your hot spots

- Understand where your greatest risks and opportunities exist

- Determine low-hanging fruit so that you can take action

- Identify your barriers to implementation

Drawing Your Boundary: What Is "Your Company"?

The first step in any baseline assessment is getting clear on what exactly you are talking about when you say "our company." How big and wide are you drawing the boundary around your company? Are you just including the things you have financial control over, which includes only those things you own or co-own due to a joint venture with another company? Or are you taking a position on things that you have operational control over, which includes things you don't own but you impact on a daily basis through your company operations? These are important to clarify before getting started so that you know what you are going to include and exclude from your baseline.

For example, if you want to include your supply chain, are you including only your impacts with your Tier 1 suppliers, or are you going all the way up the value chain to the very extraction of the raw materials found in the products?

Are you including your products? If so, at what stage do you draw the line and say it's outside of your control? After it's sold to a customer? When it is disposed of or at the end of its life cycle?

These are all crucial questions to answer before getting started so that you can *ensure materiality, completeness, and accuracy. Moreover, this will help you determine when and where it's worth the time to track down difficult data versus using proxy data or industry averages.*

Also, when determining your baseline, put yourself into the minds of your stakeholders and ask yourself, "What information would they want to know?" And then ask, "Where are our blind spots—where we don't know what we don't know?" This will further help you determine what to include in your baseline.

This is also an important exercise because how stakeholders interact with your company varies considerably across industries. If you have a consumer product, chances are stakeholders will care most about what's in it, the packaging, and how/where it's made, versus your company's social and environmental impacts at your offices. If you are a service-based business, it's more likely stakeholders will care about how you deliver your business and in what format. Or if you have franchises (such as restaurants/coffee shops), customers will want to know what's in your product *and* they'll care about the franchise operations.

Therefore, before starting, take these steps:

1. Get the right people in the room.

2. Explain why the baseline is important.

3. Ensure that participants understand the outputs and what you are trying to do with the final result.

4. Determine your boundary, what is in and what is outside of "your company."

5. Delegate tasks and assign responsibility for data gathering.

6. Let participants know this won't be a one-time exercise so that they start building processes for gathering this data the first time they look for it.

7. Make sure you get support and approval from the key decision makers so that data isn't delayed by middle management.

Be Inclusive

For many companies, the first time they perform a sustainability baseline, they make the mistake of drawing their boundary too narrow for fear of seeming "too fat" or having too big a number. This is exactly the opposite of what they should do. Draw it wide. Capture the issues most material to your company and realize that there are opportunities all over the business landscape.

Calculating the baseline the first time might seem daunting, but you want to capture the most accurate snapshot of your company and the impacts you are making so that you can take corrective action where necessary. Be sure to look holistically, because the more you look at and include, the more you'll find.

Begin with the End in Mind

Begin with the end in mind. Know what you are going to do with the information after the baseline is completed. Are you planning to report your information to your Board or externally to a reporting agency such as the Global Reporting Initiative (GRI),[1] the Climate Registry,[2] or the Carbon Disclosure Project (CDP)?[3] Are you going to share it with an investor who has an SRI screen or with a customer who has a specific supplier scorecard? Each one has different data requirements, so don't make the mistake of overlooking exactly what information you'll need in the beginning for your desired output.

Think about the possible decision criteria and metrics the reader will want to know about at the end of the process. Don't just conduct the baseline and forget to have it tie into metrics for your existing business decision processes. Moreover, think through the type of questions management will ask after the baseline is completed. A common one is, "How does our baseline stack up against our leading competitors?" So research your competitors through the CDP, Climate Registry, Climate Counts, CSR Hub, and industry publications, as well as their websites and CSR reports, because you will definitely be asked this question by management. To sum up, determine the following:

- Who will use this information (customers, management, external reporting groups)?

- How will this information compare against our competition?

- What metrics would assist decision making?

ACTIVITY 9: SUSTAINABILITY BASELINE: QUESTIONS TO ASK WHEN GETTING STARTED

Before beginning your sustainability baseline, consider the following questions to set you in the right direction.

Starting Out

- What are your main business goals for conducting your sustainability baseline?

- What outputs/metrics will you need/want to communicate about your sustainability performance?
- Which year is your base year? What was the reasoning?
- What will be your policy/threshold if you feel that you'll have to recalculate your baseline (i.e., structural changes, changes in methodology, improvements in accuracy of emission factors or data, errors, etc.)?

Organizational Boundaries

- What is your company's legal and organizational structure? Is there shared ownership? Do you own any subsidiaries or joint ventures?
- Which will be your organizational boundary?

- **Control Approach:**
  1. *Operational Control:* Full authority to introduce and implement its policies at the operation level (includes subsidiaries with full operational control) where you don't own everything (facilities, office leases in which you operate but don't own the property).
  2. *Financial Control:* Ability to direct financial and operating policies of the operation with a view toward gaining economic benefits from its activities.

- **Equity Share Approach:**

  Percentage ownership of the operation (subsidiaries, affiliated companies, nonincorporated joint ventures, partnerships where partners have joint financial control, franchises). (For example, if you own a percentage share of a joint venture, such as 50%/50%.)

Operational Boundaries

When deciding on your operational boundaries, be sure to use the following reporting principles, which are based on the GHG (greenhouse gas) protocol:[4]

Relevance	Ensure that the baseline appropriately reflects the sustainability impacts of the company and serves the decision-making needs of its users (internal and external).
Completeness	Account for and report on all impacts, sources, and activities within the chosen inventory boundary. Disclose and justify any exclusion.
Consistency	Use consistent methodologies to allow for meaningful comparisons of emissions over time. Transparently document any changes to the data, inventory boundary, methods, or any other relevant factors in the time series.
Transparency	Address all relevant issues in a factual and coherent manner, based on a clear audit trail. Disclose any relevant assumptions and estimations. Make appropriate references to the accounting and calculation methodologies and data sources used.
Accuracy	Ensure that the quantification of your impacts (GHG, water, energy) is systematic and that uncertainties are minimized as much as possible. Achieve sufficient accuracy to enable users to make decisions with reasonable assurance as to the integrity of the reported information.

For example, when determining your boundary for your GHG inventory, address these questions:

- What Scope 1 (direct) emissions will be reported (i.e., natural gas, furnaces, fuel burned by vehicles, owned and controlled boilers, etc.)?
- What Scope 2 (direct) emissions can be identified (i.e., purchased electricity, heat, or steam)?
- What optional Scope 3 (other indirect) emissions will be reported (i.e., purchased materials, business travel, supply chain, commuting, etc.)?
    - Describe your value chain and its associated GHG sources to help determine which Scope 3 categories are relevant and should be included.
    - How were these determined? What was excluded and why?

Although each organization is comprised of many multifaceted sustainability issues, Table 4.1 includes all of the areas to consider for your sustainability baseline.

Table 4.1   Ensure That Your Baseline Incorporates Each of These Important Areas

Corporate Vision and Governance on Sustainability	Environment
Governance Management Support and Commitment Budget for Sustainability Sustainability Goals and Vision Sustainability Investments and Banking	Energy Greenhouse Gas Emissions (GHGs) Waste, Recycling, Compost Water Business Travel Employee Commuting Paper and Other Supplies Hazardous Waste Operations: Other, Procedures, etc.
Employee Engagement and Evaluation on Sustainability	**Product Design and Responsibility**
Employee Education and Training Employee Hiring and Promotion Integration of Sustainability Across the Company Employee Evaluation and Compensation Aligned with Sustainability	Product Responsibility Compliance with Regulations and Industry Standards Product Take-Back and Reuse Toxins and Restricted Substances Industry Collaboration Packaging
Vendors and Suppliers	**External Reporting**
Freight and Third-Party Shipping—Fed Ex, UPS, Other Supplier Reporting and Auditing Sustainability Guidelines and Engagement	Stakeholder Engagement Reporting and External Communication
Social Policies and Community	**Fleets and Field**
Employee Benefits and Safety Philanthropy and Community, Volunteerism, Diversity and Inclusion	Fleets Field Employees and Work Environment Systems and Procedures

Know the 80-20 Rule

The Pareto principle[5] in business is an old axiom that 80% of your profit comes from 20% of your customers. The idea is that you should focus your attention on that 20% of your customers because they are the most important. It's no different when it comes to sustainability, because you'll find that a disproportionate share of your impact comes from just a few areas within the total operation of your company. Therefore, it's essential that you focus on the areas of greatest impact and opportunity. Too often there is a misconception about where you can make a difference, and people tend to concentrate on the things that they are most familiar with or that are right in front of their faces. Doing this can sometimes lead to focusing on the wrong issues.

"Be aware that with limited resources you need to focus on the big things instead of small things! Focus on what matters to the environment and the consumer,"[6] says former Starbucks Vice President of Global Responsibility Ben Packard.

This is especially true with manufacturing and retail clients. Although your employees might want to focus on efforts to "green" your offices because that is where they work every day, that isn't going to be where your biggest impacts are coming from. They will be from the manufacture, shipping, and distribution of your products, areas that employees at your corporate headquarters are not likely to see on a daily basis.

For example, consider greenhouse gas emissions. Table 4.2 shows the areas of highest impact according to greenhouse gas emissions from my clients' experiences.

Table 4.2   Common Emissions Sources

Company Type	Biggest Sources of Emissions
Retail	Product Manufacturing, Shipping
Mining, Oil, Gas	Extraction, Shipping of Fuel Source
Banking	Paper, Commuting, Business Travel
Marketing/PR	Business Travel, Energy, Commuting
Real Estate (Brokers)	Broker Driving, Energy
Logistics	Shipping, Energy, Waste
Legal	Business Travel, Commuting, Paper
Online Retail	Shipping, Energy
Accounting	Paper, Energy
Government Agency (Parks Dept)	Energy, Fleets, Water
Architecture Firm	Energy, Business Travel, Commuting
Entertainment Company (Radio Stations)	Energy, Commuting, Paper

I highlight these because too often companies choose to focus on the low-hanging fruit, and they miss the bigger opportunities for mitigation, sustainability improvement, and cost savings.

BUSINESS CASE: FUEL EFFICIENCY

When we conducted a baseline for a small real estate company here in Seattle a few years back, immediately the conversation turned to how to best reduce paper usage since their office was overflowing with documents related to mortgages. But after we performed the baseline analysis of their impacts, it turned out that their biggest impact area was in their agents driving clients around all day to see houses. They needed to be focused on fuel efficiency and route optimization of their agents, not paper, which ended up being less than 5% of its environmental impact.

In fact, after the baseline, the organization surveyed its agents to find out how many of them were driving around with roof racks on their car year-round. It turned out that most of them were, even though they maybe were going up to the mountains only a handful of weekends each year.

The real estate firm then instituted a policy that its agents remove their roof racks when they weren't using them. This not only saved emissions, but improved the fuel efficiency of the agents' vehicles by over 3%, which also saved on fuel costs. They then took the next step and also asked their agents to properly inflate tires every two weeks and replace air filters on time, which, according to the EPA, can improve fuel efficiency by an additional 2%, for a 5% increase overall. They targeted their biggest areas of impact and set their policies to address them accordingly.

For example, a church diocese client wanted to meet the requirements of the Genesis Covenant of the Episcopal Church. This was an older church where you could literally feel the heat being sucked out of the building, so they obviously wanted to focus on their energy usage. What we found from the baseline was that their best opportunity for environmental improvement wasn't internal but lay externally with their parishioners. So, in addition to making recommendations for how the church itself could reduce its environmental impact, we provided a list of ideas for ways the parishioners could reduce their impact beyond the one to two hours a week they spent at church. This list was made up of numerous ideas to improve their environmental behavior at home, at school, and in the decisions they made in their offices at work. This hadn't been mentioned in conversations before the baseline was established.

Baseline Your Supply Chain

Understanding your supply chain and its impact on your company is an essential component of your sustainability baseline. Not only will this help you round out your understanding of its true impacts, but often many of the larger global social and environmental issues play out in your supply chain in a bigger way than your own internal operations. In fact, your supply chain might be where your largest opportunities for improvement, efficiency, and cost savings lie.

ACTIVITY 10: CREATING OR RESPONDING TO SUPPLIER QUESTIONNAIRES

There will likely be other questions depending on the industry you are in, but this is a summary of the type of questions you will likely be asked in order to prepare for these questionnaires. Or you can use them to ask questions of your own value chain.

Energy and Climate

1. What policies are in place to measure environmental impact and what are the criteria?

2. Do you measure your energy use and GHG emissions?

3. Do you have an energy-use and GHG-reduction strategy? What are your targets and how do you plan to get there?

4. Do you use renewable energy? If so, what and how?

Transportation/Shipping

1. Do you measure the environmental impacts associated with shipping and transportation?

2. What policies are in place to minimize the environmental impacts and costs of shipping and transportation?

3. Do you have shipping and transportation environmental impact reduction targets? If yes, what are they?

4. Does your packaging consist of recycled or biodegradable content? If so, what percentage?

Waste, Water, and Material Efficiency

1. How much waste does your business generate on- and off-site?

2. How much water does your business use on- and off-site? Please include a description of the breakdown by potable water use and gray/black water disposal.

3. How much water is used by your individual facilities and how do they compare to similar facilities?

4. Do you have a waste and water-use reduction strategy? What are your targets and how do you plan to get there?

Sourcing and Toxins

1. Do you have sustainability guidelines for your purchasing? If yes, what are they?

2. Do you use any third-party certification or verification for your own or your business partners' sustainability efforts? If so, what are they?

3. Do you verify the toxic safety of your products? Is so, how?

4. If there are toxins used anywhere in production, do you know how much ends up in your products or impacts your workers?

5. How do you verify that no conflict minerals were used in your products?

People and Community

1. Do you know where your products are produced and by whom?

2. Do you have a policy to ensure labor and human rights?

3. Do you invest in the communities where you source your products?

4. Has your company ever been cited for a noncompliance issue? If so, what and when?

5. Has your company been fired or cited for a workplace violation within the past three years? If yes, please explain.

6. What procedures do you have in place to ensure that no human trafficking is occurring through your supply chain?

Governance and Corruption

1. Who within your company holds ultimate responsibility for sustainability?

2. How is your executive team/board evaluated on social and environmental issues?

3. Describe your company's anticorruption policy. Has your company been fined for any corruption or bribery charges within the past four years?

Following are examples of supplier sustainability scorecards or questionnaires:

Walmart Supplier Sustainability Assessment:[7] www.bpaww.com/ Bpaww_com/HTML/iCompli/Downloads/2012/CSR/Walmart_ Sustainability_Assessment.pdf

Philips Supplier Audit Tool:[8] www.philips.com/shared/assets/ company_profile/downloads/Philips-Supply-Sustainability-Audit-tool.pdf

Arizona State University Supplier Sustainability Questionnaire:[9] www.asu.edu/purchasing/forms/sustainability_IA.pdf

Greenbiz, "10 Key Questions That Focus on Supplier Sustainability":[10] www.greenbiz.com/blog/2009/10/06/10-key-questions-focus-suppliers-sustainability

We have all heard stories of companies that have suffered PR disasters or hits to their brand from workplace issues associated with their supply chain. It's bad for business and a controllable risk. We're all familiar with the sweatshop labor issues of the 1980s and the recent troubles in Bangladesh, but it extends globally. As stakeholders and customers become increasingly sophisticated, the number of potential supply chain risks around social and environmental issues continues to grow, so baseline your supply chain and be sure to do the following things:

- Map out your supply chain to understand where your products are coming from and where they are made/grown/processed.

- Find out the names of suppliers and determine whether any of them could put you at risk.

- Share what you find out with people throughout the organization.

One way to show your supply chain is through an illustration such as Figure 4.1.

Mapping your supply chain will also help everyone involved in your business visualize their contribution and value.

According to Claudia Capitini, the former eco-maven of Eco-Products, baselining helped "change the discourse about our supply chain. Just knowing where our impacts were helped drive a better understanding of our product and can help our sales staff differentiate our product."[11]

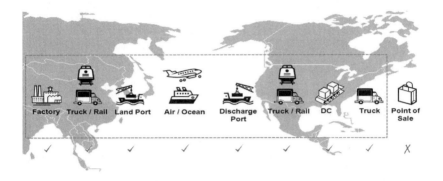

Figure 4.1   Example of a supply chain map.

"Additionally, sharing supply chain information with people throughout our company helped bring dialog around sustainability to the front,"[12] said Capitini.

Baselining Your Products

This seems like an obvious statement, but I can guarantee you that with at least 75% of the products/services you come into on a day-to-day basis, nobody within the company that produces them knows exactly what is in their products. With all the consumer sentiment and upcoming regulations around specific chemicals and toxins in products, this is a potential risk to any company.

That's where a product baseline comes in. I'm a big proponent that for all but some service-based organizations and educational institutions, it is important to baseline your key products.

This is primarily done through a screening Life Cycle Assessment (LCA), which shows the environmental impacts of all the inputs and outputs of a product through all stages of its life, from cradle to grave.[13] This means from the extraction of raw materials through processing, manufacturing, distribution, use, and then either disposal or recycling. This is an effective way of truly knowing everything that is going on with your product throughout its life.

A full LCA is expensive and very time-consuming, so most companies are moving to the quicker "screening LCA" because it typically is about one-tenth the cost, takes one-third the time, and gets you about 90% there in terms of identifying the hot spots with your products.

In fact, I've been in rooms where a CEO asks, "Okay, so you want to make our product greener—what specifically should we focus on and how much greener will our product be?"

Answering this question is important, but also difficult, especially if you are a retailer with hundreds or potentially thousands of products, in which case this will be too costly and time-consuming to be practical. Therefore, if you fall into that category, try to find a few products that are representative of your brand, measure those, and then use them as representative examples for the rest of your products. This will help you figure out where to focus your time and attention.

BUSINESS CASE: EXTRAPOLATING PRODUCT INFORMATION

For example, when we were working with an apparel client that had hundreds of different footwear and apparel options, they performed an LCA of their top-selling shoe and two different pieces of apparel whose life cycles would be indicative and representative of the rest of the company. Although it didn't provide a 100% accurate analysis of all of its products, this was sufficient to provide the company with a snapshot as to which aspects of their products' lifestyle—primarily the chemical makeup, manufacture, and shipping of the footwear—had the largest environmental impact. The company changed its focus to those areas instead of the typical assumptions of packaging or end-of-life disposal.

Sustainability Consortium and Higg Index

Due to the time and resource commitment required for a LCA, groups such as the Sustainability Consortium and Sustainable Apparel

Coalition (SAC) are banding together to collaboratively create tools that will enable companies to more accurately and quickly quantify the sustainability of their products. This will better inform decision makers at a fraction of the time and cost.

The two ways in which these groups are doing this are through the consortium's sustainability measurement and reporting system (SMRS) and through the SAC's Higg Index. The consortium's SMRS, which includes Category Sustainability Profiles (CSPs), summarizes the best available, credible, and actionable knowledge about the sustainability aspects related to a product over its entire life.[14]

The Higg Index, which was created by the Sustainable Apparel Coalition, provides guidance on sustainable practices in manufacturing supply chains. It is an outgrowth of the Outdoor Industry Association's Eco-Index and Nike's Apparel Environmental Design Tool. It has been designed to enable apparel companies to "evaluate material types, products, facilities and processes based on a range of environmental and product design choices."[15] I highlight both of these efforts because these organizations are trying to help companies baseline their products' impacts and be proactive about social and environmental issues on the front end of product development.

After you create your product baseline, be sure to do the following:

- Provide your suppliers with sustainability procurement guidelines for your products.
- Institute a restricted substances list.
- Provide your designers internally with a digital prototyping solution that can show a designer in real time both the costs and the sustainability impact of each raw material as it is being designed online.

All three of these approaches should complement your baseline work and help you get a better handle on the sustainability components of your products before they are produced. They should also help enable you to meet new industry requirements, especially as environmental product declarations become standardized and required in the future.

Using the Gap and SWOT Analyses

Two existing business tools that many companies use during their strategic planning process are actually quite helpful when baselining a company's sustainability performance: the Gap and SWOT (Strengths, Weaknesses, Opportunities, Threats) analyses. Both tools help you gain a better understanding of where the company currently stands with its sustainability efforts versus where it wants to be. Moreover, by incorporating sustainability into these tools, it can also help with resiliency planning.

The Gap analysis takes what you've learned from your baseline assessment and compares actual performance against the desired sustainability state of your company. It will detail the company's social and environmental efforts to date and explore the company's operational, governance, HR, and procurement policies/practices (both internal and with vendors) to gain a better understanding as to where it can improve and identify areas in which the company can influence its value chain (suppliers, vendors, customers).

A sustainability SWOT (sSWOT) is different from a traditional SWOT in that it is tailored to addressing challenges specifically around implementing sustainability. It is designed to identify your company's strengths, weaknesses, opportunities, and business risks around social and environmental issues in a way that you might not have been aware of using a traditional lens.

Activity 11 is a sSWOT tool created by the World Resources Institute (WRI) for corporate sustainability.[16]

ACTIVITY 11: WORLD RESOURCES INSTITUTE'S SUSTAINABILITY SWOT (SSWOT)

Ask the following questions to help identify your company's strengths, weaknesses, opportunities, and business risks around social and environmental issues.

Environmental Challenges and Big Trends

1. What (or whom) do you want to inform?
2. What do you and others see changing?

Opportunities and Threats

1. Where are social/environmental challenges creating broad threats to future business value?

2. Where can we create new solutions for social/environmental challenges? What can we stop doing?

Strengths and Weaknesses

1. What are unexpected ways we can apply our strengths to these challenges?

2. Who else has similar weaknesses or faces similar risks from social/environmental challenges?

Act and Prioritize

1. Which issues or insights will influence our CEOs, CFOs, directors, or other decision makers, or keep them up at night?

2. What can we do in the near term, midterm, and long term to mitigate against these?

There is nothing too complicated about using these tools, but they will help round out your baseline to better inform action steps and a strategy for moving forward.

ACTIVITY 12: SUSTAINABILITY GAP WORKSHEET

The sustainability Gap analysis example shown next provides various "current states" because each company differs in where they currently find themselves. Think through your current and desired sustainability state and determine what is missing in order for your company to achieve its goals.

Category	Current State	Desired State	Gap
Operations	Strong operationally, no environmental or social focus other than compliance.	Sustainability intertwined into all that the company does.	

Category	Current State	Desired State	Gap
Policies	We recycle paper, but no other environmental policy. Minority, Women, Disabled Veteran (MWDV) owned criteria established by law.	Environmental and social criteria incorporated into all operational, decision-making, purchasing, and philanthropic policies.	
Facilities	When making upgrades, already consider energy efficiency and choose longer-lasting products, but have no policy.	Sustainability added to decision criteria for all facility decisions. LEED standards for any new buildings or retrofits.	
Governance	Executives discuss these issues annually, but no formal governance or evaluation procedures on social/environmental issues.	Executives are evaluated and compensated on community and environmental performance along with financial performance.	
Technology	Externally: The company trails competitors with website and mobile applications. Internally: A large investment was made in technology but employees underutilize and continue to rely on paper.	Externally: Technology that competes with/equals large-sized competitors. Internally: Employees fully utilizing benefits of technology.	

Category	Current State	Desired State	Gap
Vendors	The company tries to use local vendors/customers whenever possible.	All vendors/suppliers are educated on the company's goals around sustainability. They step up their game to provide the company with the same high-quality services, using more local and environmentally friendly products/providers.	
Employee Workplace and HR	Award-winning place to work. No environmental benefits or PTO for volunteering. Employees don't know whether their focus should be sales or service.	100% employee satisfaction. Employees see community and environmental improvement as part of their job. Employees understand their roles and leadership decision making. Remain an award-winning place to work while being recognized for diversity and sustainability!	
Training	Employees are not getting specific sustainability training, but every employee gets ethics and diversity training.	Employees are 100% trained in their job around technology, company culture, and sustainability. All wrapped into one comprehensive training.	

Category	Current State	Desired State	Gap
Customers	Customers love the friendly community approach. They aren't asking about our environmental performance yet.	Increase in customer retention, new customers attracted by the company's sustainability plans. Customers espouse all the company's sustainability work.	
Products	Products have no sustainability attributes other than recycled packaging.	Offers cutting-edge, green/sustainable products that customers value. Regenerative products that actually improve the environment.	
Environment	Currently not doing much more than energy-efficiency upgrades at facilities. Lacking the most basic areas, such as recycling, paper, the use of online meeting software.	The company becomes known as "the sustainable benchmark" in its region and certainly in its communities. The company achieves carbon neutrality and employees have the means to be more sustainable at work.	
Leadership of Organization	Very strong leadership. Just getting started on understanding climate change.	Leaders are modeling sustainability for the entire organization and employees know how to participate. Recognized as leaders by industry.	

Category	Current State	Desired State	Gap
Communications	Great at traditional media but trailing on social media. Community doesn't know all that the company does. Missed opportunity.	All stakeholders understand what the company is doing and why. They spread word to their family and friends and through social media. All communications integrated and free press weekly from sustainability efforts.	
Community	Strong community connection. Seen as excellent steward for education, healthcare, and the arts.	Seen as #1 business asset in each community it operates in. Community and environmental actions perfectly align with company business objectives.	

"Your baseline assessment is important because you are learning what people are doing and how they are doing it before you implement all the changes necessary to get you to your desired state."[17]

Baselining Supports Other Business Decisions

One of the most surprising and beneficial aspects of conducting your sustainability baseline is how often the findings support other business decisions. You'll uncover efficiencies, opportunities to innovate, ways to cut costs, and new ways of doing things. The good news is that from my experience, about eight out of every ten ideas will support your existing business efforts.

BUSINESS CASE: BUSINESS TRAVEL AS A TOOL FOR BEHAVIOR CHANGE

One of our financial institution clients asked us to conduct a GHG inventory during the financial crisis of 2008, and we were able to find ways to save the company money while lowering their carbon footprint. Interestingly, you'd think that with its being a financial institution, they might need to focus on paper. However, one of the largest portions of their GHG emissions was coming from business travel—specifically, the air travel for board members and mileage from monthly branch member meetings.

Therefore, the company implemented teleconferences for three out of the four branch manager meetings per month and also decided to move all board meetings to its home state to eliminate air travel. The result was that the company not only saved money during a down economy, but got its board and managers involved in truly walking the talk. They reduced GHG emissions by over 40 metric tons year over year, which was a 75% reduction.

When we completed a sustainability baseline for another financial institution, they wanted to focus specifically on paper. Now, this was a very strong and well-capitalized bank, but they had file cabinets and paper stacks literally everywhere in their headquarters and executive offices. So they obviously thought that they needed to crack down on their internal paper usage. As it turned out, 97% of their paper usage was tied to their customer statements, which further reinforced their need to incentivize and emphasize e-statements, online banking, and mobile applications. They already knew some of what they needed, but the results from the baseline helped reinforce these efforts and helped to kick our client into gear!

You'll be amazed at how many ways sustainability supports business decisions to help you save money and find waste where you weren't looking, especially when you start tackling energy, fuel, travel, and materials usage.

Managing Your Sustainability Data

Data management is the most difficult aspect of recording, measuring, and reporting your sustainability performance. Most of this lies in the fact that the majority of information required for external reporting has not been captured in traditional financial accounting or enterprise resource planning (ERP) systems.

According to Patrick Drum, Senior Portfolio Manager at UBS Wealth Management in Seattle, this is the biggest challenge. When he tries to compare one company's sustainability performance against another, "less than 20% of participants currently offer good data sets."[18] To avoid a bad data set, companies should move to a sustainability data management system as soon as possible.

The reality is that most companies start by using what they have, often tracking data in Microsoft Excel. Then as they mature in this space, they might seek out a data management system that can range from GHG reporting software to more robust Environmental Management Systems (EMS) to full sustainability packages, which include social and environmental criteria.

I'm not about to make a recommendation on a particular piece of software or tracking method, but I will say this: After you have completed your first baseline, invest the time and resources to automate the process. It is an investment that pays off in spades because instead of tracking down data, your Corporate Social Responsibility (CSR) Director and green team can focus on implementing and making change versus data gathering.

When you are selecting your system, realize that most off-the-shelf software will not be able to track every single piece of sustainability data that applies to your company. Some will be very close, but since this is such an emerging field with new questions and guidelines being issued regularly, it's important you have a system that works for you, is scalable, and is adaptable.

Display Your Data Visually

A picture says a thousand words, and nowhere is this truer than in a sustainability baseline. When we started assessing companies years ago, we'd do months of work and write very detailed analyses, but in the end the CEO would see the pie chart in the executive summary and she would say, "We need to focus on these two pieces of the pie!"

So, although it's great to have a system that can slice and dice sustainability criteria into actionable minutiae, it's more important that your system and your report have a way of displaying results in a visual way that people can understand. I cannot stress that enough. Realize that although 50% of the people will read the results, a full half won't. They will just look at the visuals, so make sure you have something to appeal to those individuals as well.

BUSINESS CASE: MAKE IT VISIBLE

Visuals have a way of making the data "real" for people in a way that numbers do not. For example, we worked with a retail client to show how much paper they used in comparison to the height of the Columbia Tower (the largest building in Seattle). For another with a major presence in Chicago, we compared how many cans of Coke they consumed in their offices and stacked them up against the Sears Tower (now called Willis Tower).

Improved Data over Time

It's important to understand that no company can capture every piece of data the first time around. It's just like anything else; if you've never been asked to track something before, it takes a while to put in place the processes and procedures to do so effectively. Usually, the data exists in various formats and in different parts of the business, but the key is figuring out a streamlined process for getting the data and improving each year.

When you are working with a third party, such as a supplier, explain exactly what you need: what data is needed, why, by when, and in what format. This will facilitate the process and make it much easier the next time around. But be sure to let them know you will require this requested data annually going forward.

Lastly, when you are done with your baseline, look for areas where you can get more accurate data next year. Then be sure to create an inventory management plan (IMP) to establish the data collection process, and record responsibilities so that when you go back next year you'll know who to turn to. That way, if something happens or a person leaves the company, there is a road map for how to continue to move things forward.

The following road map gives you an idea of what to expect with your data collection:

- **First year:** You'll receive 70% to 90% of the data. The process will take longer than you think it should, and some of the data will be incorrect, incomplete, or in the wrong format. This is a word to the wise: Even if your company is data intensive and you are highly motivated and organized, expect it to take twice as long as you think it will. Budget your time accordingly.

- **Second year:** Closer to 90% to 95% of the data will be collected, it will be of a higher quality, and processes will have been established to streamline the process. You'll find out if anything was missing and catch any mistakes from the previous year.

  We discovered this with a retail client. It wasn't until year two when we had something to compare the data against that we realized that the data from one of their overseas facilities in China the first year was incorrect. We were able to go back in and revise the baseline to improve its accuracy.

- **Third year:** Processes and procedures should be in place. Data will be strong, but you'll likely go back and determine whether there is anything else you need to include since business conditions will usually have changed in three years. This could be because of merger, acquisition, spinoff, or better data availability.

Go into the baseline process knowing that it will be a process of continuous improvement and refinement over the first three years, but find solace in knowing that your data quality and management will improve over time.

Lessons Learned

The following are key takeaways from the "Baselining Sustainability to Measure What Matters" chapter:

- Be inclusive. Choose the issues most material to your company. And remember, it's okay to have a large number the first year or to be "big and fat." You will improve performance over time.

- Use a Sustainability SWOT and Gap analysis to help uncover your hot spots, where the biggest risks and opportunities lie. Baseline your supply chain, products, and services, too.

- Begin with the end in mind. Think about what you are going to do with the results before you get started.

- Baselining supports other business decisions so be sure to track money saved, money earned, and the business potential if measures are implemented.

- Know the attention span of your decision maker. Show things visually through an infographic or a pie chart. Rarely will anyone want the massive amount of data collected, but keep it close so you have it just in case.

- Report back to everyone after your first assessment is completed with results so that they understand why you asked them for everything. Let people know when you'll be contacting them (again) next year so that they'll be ready for it.

- Seek to automate the process as soon as possible so that your time and money are spent on implementing and not on data gathering and calculations.

5

Goals/Vision and Your Sustainability North Star

Most of us have been part of a company that has made a commitment to a new initiative or program only to see it be put on the back burner when times get tough or busy. To avoid this, sustainability needs to have an aspirational or "North Star" goal so that everyone understands where the company is trying to go, and so the idea is anchored in both good and bad times. Sustainability needs to be integrated into the goals of the company, tied to key performance indicators (KPIs) and business metrics, and the responsibility and accountability for meeting the sustainability goals need to be at all levels—corporate, departmental, and individual.

As Daniel Pink states in *Drive*,

"Sustainability is something you strive to get to or master, but something you can never quite reach. It is a journey, a goal whose point keeps moving as we study and learn more! The benefits and joy are in the pursuit, not the frustration of never attaining it!"[1]

The North Star

People change, and short-term goals can change, but for a company to know where it is going, it needs to have a North Star to help guide it. Sustainability is journey that will be full of twists, turns, successes, and setbacks along the way. Therefore, the only way to stay true to where you are going is to have a North Star that can serve as a constant reference point for knowing where you are in terms of your end goal.

The North Star needs to be clearly articulated and it needs to be strategic, not some stand-alone effort. It doesn't necessarily have to be aspirational, but it does need to be inspirational. Trying to be "less bad" is hardly motivational; you want the North Star to give employees something to strive for. Additionally, your North Star needs to be tailored to your company. Don't just have it be what others are doing because it's fashionable. Make it your own.

Whether it is a long-term aspiration or a mile marker just down the road, your company and its employees need to know what you are trying to achieve and why.

As Ben Packard, the former VP of global responsibility at Starbucks, says, "Ask if this is a me-too or industry-leading play. Are we doing this just to not get caught or in trouble? And how far away is our North Star? Is it out in the galaxy or 100 yards down the road? If it is the latter, then you need to ditch the aspiration goal and tailor it to achieve the goal of 100 yards."[2] Ask the tough question early on: "How serious are we?"

In fact, this is one of the most common mistakes that sustainability managers, CSR directors, or green teams make: They fail to ask the most fundamental questions at the front end of this project, including, "Where are we trying to go?"

For example, let's say you are a new CSR director at a firm or have recently taken over these duties, and you see numerous opportunities for your company to implement sustainability into your operations, products, and services that will both make your company money and enhance the brand. You're likely going to be champing at the bit.

This is great and it's what is needed to truly make the change that the world needs. However, in order to have long-term success and to bring the rest of the company along with you, everyone needs to be in alignment as to where the company is trying to go.

ACTIVITY 13: DETERMINING YOUR NORTH STAR

Before creating your North Star or aspirational goal, ask yourself and your company these questions:

- Are we trying to be an industry leader? Or are we just trying to be a fast follower? The strategies for reaching these goals are different.

- Do we want sustainability integrated into everything we do? Or are we doing this just to stay in compliance, to stay out of trouble, or just because our stakeholders are requiring us to?

- Do we want to be a "me-too" brand around sustainability? Or do we want to do business in a new way that will create a competitive advantage for us?

- Is our North Star aspirational? Or do we need something more realistic, practical, and short-term?

- Should our North Star be 20 years away or not too difficult to achieve?

Jim Collins has a great story in *Good to Great* that he uses when talking about the foundation for setting a North Star. In 1950, George Merck II set forth his company's philosophy, which I'll paraphrase as, "Let's remember that the medicine is for the patient. The profits will follow if we do our job correctly."[3]

Figure 5.1 can help companies understand how they compare to other organizations considering different types of sustainability efforts. Each company listed has a significant sustainability mission, yet they all fall in different areas.

It's also important to factor in the mind-set of your CEO when initially considering what your North Star should be. You want it to last. And one thing to know about CEOs is that their personalities can end up playing a huge role in driving sustainability and in whether it's successful. Typically, the more entrepreneurial the CEOs, the less likely they want to be bound by a plan, and the more likely they want flexibility.

For example, entrepreneurs who are in the CEO seat tend to get excited about chasing the next shining thing. Then when reality hits or something more interesting appears, they simply want to change the goal or create a new North Star. This isn't how you get people to commit and buy in. You need one that is designed to last.

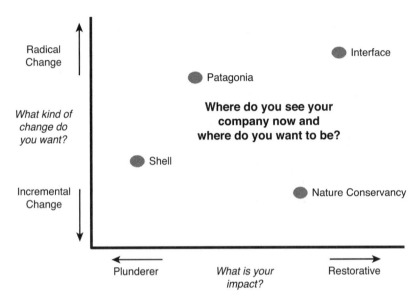

Figure 5.1   Type of sustainable company.[4]

What Not to Do

Back in 2006 and 2007 when climate change was on the cover of every major magazine and people had been moved by Al Gore's *An Inconvenient Truth,* it was trendy to set a North Star goal of carbon neutrality. Unfortunately, as most companies soon realized, this is a goal most companies can never achieve without spending a ton of money to purchase renewable energy credits (RECs) or carbon offsets. And many, including Nike, have backtracked from that goal.

One of my clients and I actually had a knock-down, drag-out argument about this (which I eventually lost). Their CEO had heard a competitor declare at a conference that they were going to be "Carbon Neutral by 2015," so when the time came for my client's CEO to speak, she got up and stated that they were going to do this by 2012! She was going to show them!

This was back in 2007, so I'm sure my client's CEO thought that they had five years to figure it out. But the reality is, and was true back then too, that there was no way the company could get there even within ten years without 100% changing their business model, something they were unwilling to do. Moreover, after the financial crisis hit, the idea of spending scarce resources on carbon offsets did not seem appealing anymore, so they backtracked away from this goal.

Do not set something that you'll have to change or backtrack from, because that might end up doing more harm than good. As with any plan, you don't immediately set the highest aspiration and go bounding 100% full-force straight there without first surveying the pitfalls, chasms, and swamps that lie in your path.

Integrate Your Goals

As stated by Lorinda Rowledge and Cynthia Figge in *Igniting the Core:* "Sustainability is most powerful when fully integrated into the overall business strategy, rather than as an initiative or functional responsibility on the side. The target...is every employee having a 'line of sight' understanding of how their work contributes to achieving the organization's vision, goals, and objectives."[5]

Sustainability goals have to be integrated with the corporate goals and the day-to-day operations; otherwise, you are destined to fail. Too often I've worked with companies that have tried to create sustainability goals in a vacuum without understanding how they could support the overall goals of the company. When this happens, the goals become siloed and have little chance for success.

There needs to be strong alignment between the sustainability goals and the business's sources of competitive advantage. For example:

- A competitive advantage can come from innovative, loyal employees, so how can sustainability promote employee effectiveness, creativity, and commitment?

- With product innovation as a means of competition, how can environmental and social performance support the delivery of desired benefits for customers?

- If operational excellence distinguishes you among competitors, where does social and environmental performance aid in discovering new and more efficient ways to operate?[6]

Although this might sound difficult, it is actually easier than you think because sustainability is so effective at supporting traditional business metrics. It isn't just about being a better community or environmental steward; it is about saving money, reducing waste, being leaner in your operations, and being smarter with your employees' time. And you'll want to integrate it across the company through its systems, policies, procedures, and company culture as detailed in later chapters.

Goals Need to Be Corporate, Departmental, and Individual

Sustainability goals need to hit at all three levels within a company—corporate, departmental, and individual. Each company is different in how they lay out their organizational chart, so for the course of this book, I'm going to use the term *department* to generically encompass department, business division, facility, etc. Goals can be distinctive for each level by considering the following:

- **Corporate:** This gives the big picture so that everyone knows what the company is striving toward.

- **Departmental:** Managers or department heads need sustainability goals of their own that they are evaluated against.

- **Individuals:** They need to know how sustainability applies to their job.

Middle Management Needs to Be Onboard

For sustainability goals to take hold and reach everyone throughout the organization, they must filter down to the departmental and individual level, and not get blocked or sidetracked by middle management.

From experience, this is most often the sticking point. The executives, CSR, or green teams set out great goals for a company around sustainability, but implementation doesn't fully occur because middle management doesn't get behind it. If middle managers or department heads are not being evaluated, being rewarded, or having their budgets at least partly affected by their sustainability performance, they will never be fully onboard. They have to be held accountable.

It is the responsibility of the C-Suite that middle management delivers on sustainability!

Make Goals Material to Each Department

Goals also need to be specific and material to the job functions and operations of each department. Aspirational goals of zero waste, zero toxins, or carbon neutrality might work at the corporate level, but they generally don't work at the departmental level.

For example, how does a 50% GHG reduction goal play out in finance or accounting? For the most part it doesn't. Employees in these departments might not see the immediate connection to their jobs because this issue is usually more applicable to the facilities, risk management, and investor relations departments.

That being said, every department does have a role to play. Their goals just need to be in their own sphere. For example, the finance department could focus on finding socially responsible investment options that also meet their financial return criteria. And accounting could work with procurement, because they already have a relationship based on billing and price negotiations, to add social or environmental requirements to their vendor agreements to force the issue up and down the supply chain.

At the Individual Level

Employees want to know how sustainability ties into their job and whether/how they will be evaluated on their sustainability performance. This is an area where most companies attempt to shortcut the process by hoping that with a little bit of education employees will "get it and get onboard." The reality is a little more complicated than that.

I'll describe the specifics of how to do this in Chapter 8, "Engaging Employees Around Sustainability," but it starts with understanding the goals and how they relate to each individual's day-to-day job.

Set the Right Goals

Your sustainability goals need to be targeted toward what matters to your company. They need to work toward solving the areas of biggest potential impact, addressing your greatest opportunities or addressing areas in which you have the most influence or control.

You want your sustainability goals to work in conjunction with your overall business objectives to reach your North Star. And you want to be a little more specific than the cartoon shown in Figure 5.2.

Figure 5.2 Miracle cartoon.

Keys to Setting Your Sustainability Goals

There are a few things to keep in mind when setting any goal, and the same holds true for sustainability goals. The following list should be a helpful reminder of what to think about when setting your goals:

- **Clarity:** Clear, concise goals with one unified vision that people understand.

- **Strategic Intent:** Determine focus areas, make a commitment, develop metrics for success.

- **Alignment:** Goals aligned across all departments—internally, collaboratively, and diagonally.

- **SMART:** Need to be Specific, Measurable, Actionable, Results-oriented, and Time-specific.

- **Listening:** Engage skeptics, listen to issues, and anticipate obstacles.

- **Accountability:** Who's responsible for achieving the goal?

- **Reinforcement:** Goals need to be constantly communicated and reinforced.

- **Implement:** Can the goals be implemented or are they likely to be pushed aside?

- **Report back:** Think of what and how to report back to management.

A good example to follow is Interface's "one mind at a time" approach. The company communicated their strategy within the metaphor of climbing seven faces of "Mount Sustainability," clearly defining the path, establishing metrics, setting challenging yet achievable goals, and assessing and reporting on progress "up" that path.[7]

Three Methods Companies Use for Setting Goals

As I've worked with companies on setting their goals around sustainability over the years, I've found that companies tend to have three distinct methods for approaching this task:

1. **Set aspirations and backcast:** Companies throw out a North Star and work backward from there, as in the example mentioned previously.

2. **Incremental, fear-based approach:** They set only short-term goals they are likely to reach.

3. **Magnitude-of-order goals:** Companies set something that will require groundbreaking thinking.

Method 1: Setting Aspirations and Then Backcasting

Most people are comfortable setting immediate goals and then building on those, but I have found through my work that backcasting from the North Star is more effective. If you first create a North Star, short-, medium-, and long-term goals can be developed in support. The benefit is that when you set your sights high, you are likely to accomplish way more than you thought possible and definitely more than if you set your sights only to what you know is attainable.

One of the most interesting aspects of setting sustainability goals versus generic corporate goals is that people tend to see only the crisis or issue right in front of their face, and although they know that major change is needed to address an issue like climate change, they are often unclear about what lies in between. Backcasting is usually easier for people to understand and grapple with than starting from where they are and trying to determine all the steps from A to Z.

ACTIVITY 14: USE BACKCASTING TO GET YOU FROM WHERE YOU ARE TO YOUR NORTH STAR

To backcast, start with the ideal vision and then map the steps needed to bring your vision to reality. The idea is to flip the timeline. First find true north and then figure out the steps, working backwards from that ideal vision to the present. Ask yourself these questions:

- What is your North Star?
- How can you get there?
- What are the major steps and milestones along that path?
- What is the timeline for short- and long-term goals?
- Who will be accountable for these goals?
- How will we measure success?

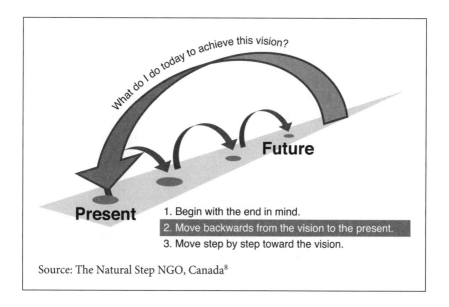

What do I do today to achieve this vision?

Future

Present

1. Begin with the end in mind.
2. Move backwards from the vision to the present.
3. Move step by step toward the vision.

Source: The Natural Step NGO, Canada[8]

Method 2: Setting Goals That You Know You Are Likely to Meet

This second method for goal setting is usually found in larger publicly traded companies. It is fear based, minimalist, and incremental. This is usually because the culture of the company is so performance based that managers and directors have learned not to set goals that they cannot meet. I've been shocked at how common this is, but who can blame these individuals for not wanting to stick their neck out and risk a poor evaluation or firing, when the safer course of action is to set a goal they know they can meet.

I experienced this firsthand when we were pitching a carbon footprint proposal to a Fortune 500 insurance company. I told them that after they had the baseline and knew where their largest impacts were, they should get a goal that everyone could get behind, engage their employees, brainstorm ideas for carbon reduction, and then put in place all the policies and steps to be successful.

Their response shocked me. They said: "No way; we only set goals around here that we know we can meet. And you can forget about involving employees and brainstorming ideas, because what if people find out we had an idea and didn't act on it?" This type of timid approach doesn't work. We didn't win the contract, which was fine with me because five years later the company still has made little progress.

Method 3: Setting an Order-of-Magnitude Goal

A third method is to set stretch goals—ones that will require such an order-of-magnitude shift in how business is done that people will have to think differently, be creative, and be innovative, and will have to design and deliver products and services in a new way.

According to Blue Ocean Strategy, the best approach is to create "a leap in value for buyers and your company, thereby opening up new and uncontested market space."[9] Rather than making products either cheaper or more unique, they focus on creating unique customer value. This can be done with sustainability because there are still so many market opportunities to be had.

I tend to agree with change-management practitioner Terra Anderson, who advises, "Don't choose little goals because people will just keep doing what they're doing! We need to be part of something worthy of the sacrifice we will be making, and that is usually not small stuff."[10]

ACTIVITY 15: CREATING ASPIRATIONAL ORDER-OF-MAGNITUDE GOALS

If your method of creating your North Star or aspiration goal is to challenge your company and yourself, then ask the following questions:

1. How could we move from sales to a service business model?

   Think about what Interface did or consider what Apple did first when it unveiled iTunes and then applications for the iPhone. It moved away from just selling hardware to subscription services in which customers came back over and over, opening up a giant revenue stream.

2. How could we be more like a Formula 1 pit crew for our operational goal?

   If you think about it, when you take your car in to have a tune-up, it is probably in pretty good working condition since you drove it there, but you drop it off for a number of hours because that is what is required in order to do all the diagnostics and repair work. Just imagine if they applied the same thinking, diagnostics, and action as a Formula 1 pit crew, which does all this in a pit stop in less than 12 seconds? That is asking for an order-of-magnitude change.

For example, Deloitte put out a paper about how a healthcare provider wanted to know how their emergency room could be more like a Formula 1 pit crew. This forced the hospital to reexamine everything and come up with a whole new process for triaging, diagnosing, and admitting patients that was fast, more effective, and less costly.[11]

3. How could we trim our design and testing time in half? How could we be 50% more efficient in our service delivery? How could we eliminate waste entirely?

   These are not simple, incremental goals. They are stretch goals that require a different type of thinking and actually a different type of question.

4. What would have to change in order to do this?

This is also a great time to explore the cause-and-effect relationship using the "5 Whys,"[12] which can help you get to the root cause of a problem or uncover what major changes are necessary.

Things to Consider When Setting Your Goals and Determining Which Method to Employ

The following list will help ensure that your goals are successful:

- If goals are not realistic or reasonable, employees will tune out. They can't be too pie in the sky.

- Goals cannot be too far out in the future from a time perspective. A goal for 2030 will be met with a shrug of "not my problem—I won't be here in 25 years."

- You need broad buy-in, so after you have your goals and strategy session, ask your employees to help prioritize because the goals cannot be held by management or the green team alone.

For example, a leadership team cannot just go away on a retreat and then come back with a sustainability plan. They need to get frontline feedback and input. People will have buy-in only if they are consulted and help to shape the process. As faculty and lead for leadership and personal development courses John Koriath points out, "If executives go away and come up with the new law of the land, the employees will rebel!"[13]

Aspirational Goal Examples

Here are some examples of aspiration goals from some leading companies:

- Patagonia's mission is to "build the best product, cause no unnecessary harm, and use business to inspire and implement solutions to the environmental crisis."

- In 2005 the former Walmart CEO Lee Scott outlined three broad environmental goals:

  - To be supplied 100% by renewable energy

  - To create zero waste

  - To sell products that sustain our resources and the environment

Focus on What Matters

As mentioned earlier, your sustainability goals need to be material and matter! Who cares if you reduce something that makes up less than 1% of your footprint? When setting goals, it's important to make them meaningful so that if you achieve the desired results, there is a recognized positive benefit.

My company, Sustainable Business Consulting, is one example. Since we are a smaller, service-based firm that does not create products, we opted to set goals outside our internal sphere because we realize that our opportunity to have the largest impact is with our customers. Even if we reduced our own impact to zero, this still wouldn't matter much in terms of the big picture, so our focus is in helping other larger organizations make changes within their operations and supply chains. In fact, we have a goal of managing and reducing emissions from our clients by 10,000 times our own carbon footprint. This by no means indicates that we aren't taking aggressive action to reduce our own (in fact, we are), but it is a constant yardstick and reminder that we need to focus on what matters.

Several times when we've worked with clients, we've performed their baseline sustainability assessment and conducted a carbon footprint, and then they've turned to us and said, "Great, what should our goals be?" Companies have to develop the goals themselves based on what matters most to the company and its stakeholders, from both a sustainability and a business perspective.

Plan for Ups and Downs

When creating goals, factor in that there will be ups and downs with both your company's business cycle and the economy. For example, instead of committing to something like a 2% reduction in greenhouse gases year over year, it's safer and more realistic to commit to a 10% reduction over a set period. We had a marketing client who tried to go the former route. They easily made their goal in 2007 and 2008 when the economy was heading into recession and the company was cutting jobs and all business travel. But after business picked back up in 2009, hiring returned, and budgets opened up for travel again, it became impossible to reach the 2% reduction goal that year. Be sure to factor this into the equation. Be bold, but be smart and plan for the ups and downs.

Absolute versus Intensity Goals

There are two types of goals around sustainability: absolute and intensity. Absolute means that the company will grow or reduce its impacts by a certain percentage by a certain time; for example, we will achieve 10% overall growth within three years or a 20% reduction in GHG emissions by 2020.

Intensity goals differ in that they measure how you are performing in relation to business conditions that you normally track; for example, all of our products will use 10% less energy per dollar of revenue or per product shipped. Intensity goals need to be aligned with business metrics that make sense to your company and that you already follow.

It's important to make sure what type of goals you want to commit to. This is especially true when it comes to publicly held or fast-growing businesses. Executives and companies don't like to be boxed in, and very few CEOs have the courage to commit to absolute energy, GHG, or waste reductions if they are expecting to grow over the next few years. They are much more comfortable picking an intensity goal.

Therefore, if you are trying to set goals that will define you as a leader in this space, you will want to choose an absolute goal, especially around an issue like GHG reductions because of the work that this implies. However, if you are in a company that is just getting started, or is in a fast growth spurt, then using an intensity target might be a better fit for you in the short term.

Ditch the Five-Year Plan

Five-year plans are passé. The reality is that things change. Although it's true that the Soviets and Chinese were very good at five-year plans, they don't really make sense anymore in the business world, especially since the average employee tenure is just over four years. Whatever you put on paper beyond two to three years will definitely change. Go with a three-year plan.

Don't Write a Novel

Too often companies get so wrapped up in writing a detailed plan that it ends up taking forever, is too long, and inevitably ends up on a shelf. Don't let this be you.

If you assign responsibility and people know what they are going to be held accountable for, then lay it out in as basic and simplistic a format as possible. Moreover, after you have written the plan, distribute it as quickly as possible. Don't spend all your time planning and reporting. Minimize these and focus on action!

Hidden Benefits of Goal Setting

Sustainability uses a different lens than what people are used to, so it will enable you to look at how you currently operate and uncover and attack things that you might not otherwise see because they are embedded in your culture.

BUSINESS CASE: TARGETED GOAL SETTING

For example, one of our small retail clients had offices around the country. They were an incredibly collaborative organization, but this meant that employees felt they needed to be in the room whenever an important meeting or decision was being made. This resulted in huge travel expenses and emissions associated with the time people were traveling instead of using video- or teleconferencing solutions—something the company already had in place.

After they calculated their sustainability baseline, they realized that their largest impact was business travel and it forced them to relook at their travel practices and their culture of always needing to be "in the room" for meetings. They set a goal to reduce their travel, which helped make it culturally acceptable for internal meetings to occur virtually and saved the company thousands of dollars in travel costs and an equal amount in productivity, GHG emissions, and employee wear and tear, since employees were spending less time in airports and on planes.

Align KPIs and Sustainability Goals with Corporate Goals

Creating key performance indicators (KPIs) around sustainability will enable decision makers to better understand, forecast, and communicate your performance throughout the company on a regular basis so that corrective action can be taken, just as you would when sales or revenue metrics predict shortfalls. They become the buzzwords for executives and managers to quickly assess how they are doing the same way they use financial metrics such as net income, gross revenue, or store sales.

In one example, we were asked by one of our outdoor retail clients to help them develop metrics around GHG emissions and energy that could be integrated into their traditional corporate KPIs. So we performed in-depth market research and worked closely with their team to uncover examples of industry-leading metrics in these two categories. We determined what would be most material to their company and then facilitated a session with a cross-functional team to develop KPIs that worked for them, and could be measured and integrated into the company's overall set of KPIs. These were adopted and are now tracked quarterly and monthly.

There literally has been an explosion in the number and variety of metrics that companies can use for their sustainability KPIs. There are ones from the Global Reporting Initiative (GRI), CDP, and Walmart Scorecard, as well as those from financial analysts such as Bloomberg Sustainability, Patrick Drum of UBS-Seattle, and Bob Willard's "Gold Standards."

Table 5.1 shows a comprehensive list of potential sustainability metrics and key performance indicators to draw from with the ones applying to each disclosure method shaded. The most important thing is that you create metrics that work for your company. These TKR metrics are what we use at my firm Sustainable Business Consulting. TKR stands for Tauschia, Kevin, and Ruth, who all helped create the metrics internally.

Table 5.1 TKR Metrics

Type of Comparison		Total Impact	Against Others	Compared to Sales	Total Impact	Against Yourself	Compared to Status Quo
	TKR	Gold Standards	Carbon Disclosure	Bloomberg	IFC	GRI	UN Global Compact
Environmental	Water						
	GHG (scope 1, 2, 3)						
	Waste						
	Material						
	Toxins						
	Travel						
	Green building						
	% Renewables						
	Biodiversity						

TKR	Gold Standards	Carbon Disclosure	Bloomberg	IFC	GRI	UN Global Compact
Social						
Health and safety						
Job satisfaction						
Turnover						
Diversity						
Age/gender						
Open hiring process						
Stakeholder engagement						
Incidents and results						
Volunteering						
Philanthropy						
Feedback mechanisms						
Living wages						

	TKR	Gold Standards	Carbon Disclosure	Bloomberg	IFC	GRI	UN Global Compact
Governance	Diversity						
	Corruption						
	Transparency						
	Trainings (executives, supplier, employees)						
	Supply chain						
	Goals (frequency of evaluation)						
	Purchasing (local, sustainable)						
	Products issues						
	Product % take-backs						
	Audit/compliance						
	Level of CC/sustainability awareness						
	Sustainability policy						

	TKR	Gold Standards	Carbon Disclosure	Bloomberg	IFC	GRI	UN Global Compact
Qualitative	Risks and opportunities identified in these areas						
	Do you disclose? How?						
	Resources given to political parties/lobbying						
	R&D resource allocation for sustainable alternatives, methods						

Assign Responsibility and Accountability

Accountability is truly what puts meat on the sustainability bone!

Assigning accountability is essential to making sure not only that goals are established, but also that someone will be rewarded or held responsible if the goals are not met. Accountability for sustainability requires the following:

- Designating a leader

- A governance structure

- Leaders with authority, budget, and control over what they are trying to accomplish

As Ben Packard recommends, "First, figure out where accountability lies. Define and understand who the ultimate decision maker is on your sustainability efforts. Is it the executive's or VP's role? If so, make it known!"[14]

Although the ultimate goal is to have the responsibility of sustainability integrated into everyone's job description and function, typically responsibility and accountability for sustainability efforts mirror the five steps shown in Figure 5.3 and often depend on how long the company has been pursuing sustainability efforts internally.

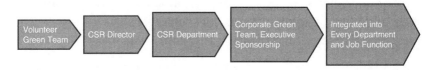

Figure 5.3 The typical five-step progression of responsibility within a company.

Step one is where most companies start, with a volunteer green team; then in step two they hire a sustainability director/manager. By step three they have hired an additional two to four people and have created a CSR department, have created a global green team, and have executive sponsorship; however, executives aren't being held accountable for performance results yet.

At step four, executives are now responsible for their own division's and department's performance, as well as the company overall. The eventual goal in step five is for the CSR department to dissolve and go away because sustainability is integrated into everyone's job. However, until that point, you want the CSR director to have the authority to delegate all the work and data gathering to the appropriate departments and individuals with their role focused on coordination.

For example, Proctor & Gamble has clearly articulated sustainability goals and strategy, as well as mechanisms to inform and enroll all 135,000 employees in achieving its strategy. It has a cadre of more than 500 self-selected "sustainability ambassadors" who have a passion for sustainability. The manager who owns each network seeds it with ideas, blogs, and discussion threads. The ambassadors are then given information and asked to help spread awareness and build enthusiasm, especially among younger employees. This helps generate enthusiasm as well as show who is responsible for what.

There Have to Be Consequences

The final aspect, and one of the most important aspects, of assigning responsibility is that there need to be consequences if goals aren't met. At first you don't want the measures to be too punitive or you might scare people away. But in general, "the more aspirational the goal, the less accountability, so there is less of a performance bonus implication," says Kevin Hagen, the former director of corporate social responsibility, Recreational Equipment Inc. (REI).[15]

Tie it to their jobs and you have to come to a happy medium where, culturally, if a goal isn't met, people are held accountable.

Think about it: How seriously would you take a goal if there was no consequence if you didn't meet it? Would you bust your butt to make it happen? Most people will try, but if or when the going gets tough or they meet resistance, they'll say, "Oh well, I tried." Just as with anything else, there have to be consequences for your goals to be taken seriously.

Lessons Learned

The following are key takeaways from the "Goals/Vision and Your Sustainability North Star" chapter:

- Have a North Star. Don't copy someone else. Make it your own and make sure it is material, meaningful, and true to your company.

- Ask the uncomfortable questions early on, including how far are we trying to go?

- Understand the mind-set of your CEO and leadership team when setting goals.

- Sustainability goals need to be integrated with your corporate goals.

- Set the right goals. Focus on what matters—your biggest impacts and areas you can influence most.

- Plan for ups and downs and ditch the five-year plan.

- Choose between absolute goals and intensity goals.

- Goals need to cascade down to departments and individuals.

- Create sustainability KPIs that work for your company.

- Assign responsibility and hold people accountable.

6

Management Support Is Essential

E very company I've ever worked with has been full of bright, intelligent, and passionate people who want to find ways to operate more sustainably, but they are held back by a combination of things—time, resources, budget, and authentic management support. Employees need to see management walking the talk in a sustained and consistent fashion, backing up their words with actions, decision making, budget, and time.

People Need to See, Hear, and Feel Leadership Support

I'm often reminded of a story about W. Edwards Deming when the quality movement was taking off in Japan in the 1970s and early 1980s. A CEO once asked Deming to speak to his leadership team and educate them on ways to increase the quality of the company's processes and products.

The CEO introduced Deming to his leadership team and told them that he wanted them all to listen to what Deming said, buy into what is being taught, and then be ready to implement it next week. Then the CEO walked out of the room.

Deming paused and then walked out after him.

In the hall the CEO asked Deming, "What are you doing?" To which Deming replied that the CEO had just undermined the importance of the whole thing by walking out. In fact, Deming told the CEO that he refused to give the training unless the CEO turned around and went back in. Which he did.

I think the Deming example is important because the same is true with sustainability. Management cannot just say that sustainability is important; it has to demonstrate its commitment through its actions.

Employees will become disillusioned if they feel as though they are being asked to do something but leadership won't provide the time or resources or show the commitment necessary to be successful!

Therefore, if management is claiming to give you full support but in reality they aren't, show them a different issue within the company that is a priority, and then compare and contrast the level of engagement you are receiving to show them the gap between their actions and words.

There are multiple ways for management to demonstrate that support, and according to Dawn Danby, the sustainable design program manager at Autodesk, "There is a big difference between 'thou shalt do' from the CEO and 'you have management's blessing.'"[1] Either way, it's important for management to show support for sustainability by doing the following:

- Showing up and making themselves visible
- Providing budget
- Providing time and resources
- Walking the talk and reinforcing their message
- Incorporating sustainability into decision making
- Providing "air cover" so people can prove things out

One of my favorite examples of management showing support is that of Lyell Clarke, the CEO of Clarke, a leading product provider for the large-scale building cleaning industry. The company was about to embark on their sustainability journey and Lyell wanted to create a moment that his entire management could galvanize around. He wanted to acknowledge that they didn't know 100% what they were getting into, but that they were going to do it anyway. So at his leadership meeting, he had his entire management team jump into a pool at the same time. This provided a camaraderie-building moment that employees related to, as management was literally jumping in with its own two feet around sustainability.

Budget

We've all heard the phrase "Put your money where your mouth is!" It's true. If you are serious about sustainability, you need to fund it.

Companies that succeed not only create the positions and give authority to their green team and sustainability managers, but provide them with budgets to actually get things done. Budgeting is truly where the rubber meets the road. A company cannot say that sustainability is a priority and then give it a measly budget. If a company wants to implement sustainability and make it stick, it cannot be an unfunded mandate.

Just as one cannot expect the sales and marketing departments to be able to drive new business without a budget to pursue new leads or ideas, companies cannot expect much to get done without a budget for sustainability. I like to say to executives, "You can't have champagne taste with only Bud Light money!"

For example, one of my best friends had a sales job at a multimillion-dollar outdoor retailer and was also given the title of sustainability manager when the company realized it needed to take action. The problem, though, was that he was only given a budget of $10,000 and was told that he could spend only four hours a week on sustainability. What kind of message is being sent? Probably something like, "We'd like you to do all that you can, and, even though it's really not too much of a priority for us, we still expect you to deliver results." Needless to say, not much has progressed in terms of sustainability.

What to Do When the Budget Is Less Than You Need

As with most initiatives, the reality is that at first you probably won't have all the funding you want to accomplish all that you need to do. So what do you do when the funding is less than you need? Get creative, be entrepreneurial, bootstrap, and find allies. I've found that working in this space requires people to be innovative and sometimes scrappy because you must be able to work across the company to find areas of common ground with other departments. For example, if you are a sustainability manager and you cannot get funding for a CSR report, but you know you need to deliver one for a certain stakeholder group, then you might have to reach out to the following departments for help because they might share your interest and have the following motivations:

- **Human resources:** They want to highlight sustainability in their recruiting efforts, especially with millennials.

- **Investor relations:** They need to respond to SEC guidelines and shareholder resolutions and respond to questionnaires from to SRI funds.

- **Marketing and public relations:** They want to tell their sustainability story for their brand.

- **Supply chain:** They might want to influence and inform their value chain.

- **Sales:** They respond to customer or vendor questionnaires, such as the Walmart scorecards.

The Battle between Budgets

One of the trickier budget issues you will run into is what to do when one department's actions impact another's budget. How do you navigate a situation where an action helps your department but may end up negatively impacting someone else's?

Or what should you expect if you ask someone to make an investment from their operational budget this year and the payoff isn't going to show up until next year or the year after? Even though this might make sense for the company overall, they are going to be hesitant because this might make their department look bad and they might suffer because of it.

Mary Kay Chess has experienced that "asking people to think about the business and getting them to think more broadly about other departments and the rest of the company is very difficult. The larger the company, sometimes the harder it is to get people to do that, especially if it hits their budget directly and that's what they are being evaluated on."[2]

This will be the case, so be prepared for it. First look for ways to get sustainability improvements and actions built into the capital budget so that both of your departments can reap the future rewards of potential better operating margins when the benefits start occurring. But if you cannot do that, as mentioned previously, try to find common areas of interest and look for opportunities where your budget and actions can positively impact what others want to do in their departments. This will build allies.

For example, the CSR director at one of our retail clients, who had been struggling with a skeptic in the company's facilities department, found out that this individual's main concern was that he didn't want to give up any part of the budget for fear of getting a lower budget the next year. The CSR director found a way to use some of the sustainability budget to help fund some facility improvements that would help "green up" their headquarters and generate an operating savings for this individual's department. This turned the skeptic from being one of the biggest roadblocks to being the director's biggest cheerleader and supporter.

Make It Part of the Normal Business Cycle

Getting sustainability initiatives into the normal business cycle and budgeting schedule is also key.

From experience, I'd say for the majority of my clients, sustainability is usually a bit of an afterthought when it comes around to budgeting in their first or second year. Just like anything else, sustainability needs to be included in the normal budgeting cycle. As companies mature around their sustainability efforts, this will become second nature; however, it is something to be aware of when just getting started.

Developing Your Own Internal Fund

Another way to protect the budget of future sustainability projects is for the company to create an internal revolving fund.

The idea is that sustainability gets funded with initial seed money and the savings from these projects then funds future investments. This is a self-sustaining way to ensure that projects continue to move forward and aren't prone to the annual budget battles at headquarters or management's shifting priorities.

For example, Harvard created a revolving Green Loan Fund that has been quite successful. It is a $12 million fund that "provides upfront capital for projects that reduce Harvard's environmental impact." Projects pay back the loan from their savings within five years. It has funded 192 projects, loaned out over $15.1 million, and has achieved $4.8 million in savings with a median ROI of 29.9%.[3]

If you do this, make sure that the fund is hands-off to other departments, so that your savings don't get raided, and you can continue to make investments over time.

Dedicate Time and Resources

Although having the budget is incredibly important, surprisingly it's a lack of time and resources that most of my clients have cited as the roadblocks to actually getting the job done. Since the financial crisis, employees have been working longer and harder than ever before. Many people have been working the equivalent of one-and-a-half or two jobs while employers have been slow to hire. This has been to the detriment of many motivated individuals or companies because people simply haven't had the time or energy to work on sustainability issues.

Even for the no-cost low-hanging fruit, like adding sustainability criteria and questions to your vendor agreements or having your IT department set all the printer and copier defaults to double-sided, employees just didn't have the time or go-ahead from supervisors to pursue them.

A common theme I hear with firms, especially as they are just getting started on sustainability, is that they have the support of their boss "as long as it doesn't take time away from their current job." This kind of thinking is unrealistic because how can someone work on something but only if it doesn't take time away from their existing work? This means they have to work on it after hours, during lunch, or on their free time.

This is not management support. In fact, it is exactly the opposite: It's confusing and it sends mixed signals. Managers cannot give support to measures and then not allow employees to have the time or resources to implement them.

Of course, in the short term, employees can work extra hours and pull heroic efforts, but eventually their energy and enthusiasm will begin to wane and they will burn out or lose heart. Half measures will only produce half results; resources need to be dedicated.

Provide Time to Innovate

Companies need to provide the time, space, and "air cover" necessary for people to innovate, try new things, and occasionally fail when trying to come up with new solutions. At 3M, for example, "technical staff spend 15% of their time on projects of their own choosing and initiative."[4] This was the type of thinking that led to the development of Scotch Tape and Post-it Notes. I'm not saying that you have to devote 15% right off the bat—you might want to start with between 1% and 5%—but this is the type of time investment that can be very beneficial and applicable toward innovation around sustainability.

Prove It Out. Small Wins Build Momentum

You don't have to bet the farm all at once. Prove it out first!

If you are struggling to gain management support, develop a pilot project or prototype to prove out your ideas. I can honestly say that when we try to build management support with each of our clients, one of the first concerns executives have is about making a radical change that will alter their business model, company culture, or way of life.

For example, when I first met with one of our contractor clients, right off the bat the client asked, "If we start down this whole sustainability journey, are you going to want to turn us into a bunch of Prius-driving vegetarians?" Of course we weren't, but this was the client's fear. So we had to start small and prove it out to create buy-in.

BUSINESS CASE: VIDEOCONFERENCING

Many service-based clients use a ton of air travel to meet with their customers. When we broached one of our clients about trying to use videoconferencing for some of their customer meetings, they immediately went to the worst-case scenario and worried that by trying to be more sustainable, we were telling them that they could never again fly to meet with a customer face to face—something that would totally ruin their relationships and value to their clients.

We assured them that this was not the case and put them at ease by trying to do a small pilot with one of their more progressive customers, who shared our client's desire to improve the company's environmental impact. They piloted having every other meeting virtually to prove out the concept in a nonthreatening way that made both business and environmental sense. It worked and the customer saw no decrease in value. In fact employees felt as though they could actually meet with their customers more frequently and for shorter periods, since they could just dial them up through a videoconference.

Telecommuting is another common "prove it out" example. For most service- and office-based businesses, one of their largest environmental impact areas is the emissions generated from employee commuting. Companies typically first look at offering benefits such as bus passes or van pools, but the biggest opportunity, often at the lowest cost, is to offer telecommuting or WFH (working from home) as an option. This can require the biggest mind-set change from management for two reasons: (1) they simply cannot get past the worry that employees are slacking off at home; and (2) although the manager might generically support a program, when it comes to the manager's department, often it is a belief that "my employees need to be there every day." The unfortunate reality is that managers typically empower and trust their best employees around the office, but for some reason, that trust doesn't always extend to employees when they are working from home.

BUSINESS CASE: WORK FROM HOME

Sometimes you need an event that enables you to prove out a sustainability initiative to gain management support. For example, a marketing client of ours had a work-from-home option, but it was not being fully utilized. So when its corporate headquarters went through a full remodel in 2011, they decided that the most effective way to stay open and minimize disruption was to force employees from various departments to rotate out of the office and work remotely for up to three months at a time. Of course, they still came into the office for meetings when necessary, but for the most part, employees worked from home. The client's fears of work quality suffering and productivity going down were never realized and the idea of working from home was proven out.

In fact, there are a number of case studies that support this, such as these:

- "Deloitte LLP offers most of its 45,000 employees nationwide the option to telecommute as many as five days a week. As leases came up for renewal, the consulting firm was able to reduce office space and energy costs by 30%. In fact, Deloitte saved $30 million in 2008 after redesigning facilities to accommodate mobile workers who don't need permanent desks."[5]

- At Cisco Systems, with 65,000 employees in 92 countries, $1 billion was saved in 2.5 years through videoconferencing, but their real payoff is considered to be retention due to increased work-life balance and decreased traveling and thus decreased time away from families.[6]

Small Wins Build Momentum

Small wins help build momentum and demonstrate the possibilities that sustainability can bring to your organization. Just as in baseball, while everyone wants to be the home run hitter and swing for the fences right off the bat, realize that if you hit a few singles first, that will better set you up for home run opportunities later.

When trying to gain management support for your sustainability ideas, first figure out the business benefit. The actions that save or make money *and* also have sustainability benefits will gain acceptance more quickly than others with less quantifiable benefits.

Dave Low, the director of sustainability practices at Kidder Matthews, confirms that small wins are essential to building management support. "You have to do more than show an anecdote. If you can win business and bring revenue to your company through sustainability, that will help to gradually shift the culture of the organization. Nothing makes the case better than results."[7]

Ross Freeman, the former environment and sustainability manager of Stevens Pass, agrees. He has seen that the best way to build that momentum is to pick two or three programs, make them work, look good, "and make sure you inform management of the success and beneficial outcomes."[8] Then if any of your successes are press worthy, he's a big supporter of communicating success externally to get positive media coverage from your efforts.

Small wins help breed success because they begin to make what might seem like unattainable goals more reachable. As Chicago Mayor Rahm Emanuel says, it's important to "get points on the board" when you can.

Lastly, when you have small wins, be sure to document what occurred and why. Kevin Hagen experienced that at some point, "a common myth will be born as to why success occurred, with most people thinking it was obvious or the work of smart people, and will overlook the barriers that needed to be overcome and how this occurred."[9] Be sure to write down what happened so that you can build off of those successes and speak the truth years later as to what things it actually took to be successful and how the eventual whole was initially made up of a number of small initiatives.

ACTIVITY 16: MANAGEMENT SUPPORT CHECKLIST

The following questions can show you potential barriers or areas that need attention.

Here are the questions to ask to determine whether management is onboard:

- In what ways does management walk the talk on sustainability? In what ways does it need to improve?

- Do you have resources (human and financial) dedicated to sustainability efforts?

- Do your managers mention sustainability to people other than you?

- Do your managers see sustainability as an opportunity rather than a challenge?

- Does management have sustainability embedded into its decision-making criteria?

- Has management asked you about situations in which sustainability could be applicable that you have not brought up yourself?

Lessons Learned

The following are key takeaways from the "Management Support Is Essential" chapter:

- People need to see, hear, and feel leadership's support because half-hearted support leads to half-hearted results.

- Fight for a dedicated sustainability budget.

- You must dedicate time and resources as well. Employees need the time and management approval, and should not be expected to work on sustainability after hours or after everything else gets done.

- Find easy and fun ways in which management can walk the talk. Don't start with the toughest, most painful stuff at first. Be patient and realize that it takes time to bring along the whole management team.

- Start with a pilot project if you meet resistance. Don't bet the farm; prove it out first.

- Underpromise and overdeliver. It's always better to overdeliver than to come up a few dollars short and fall short of expectations.

7

Understanding Change Management to Guide Implementation

hange is tough. Nobody likes to be told to change how they do things, whether it's at work or in their personal life. Don't believe me? Cross your arms in front of you. Now cross them the other way. This feels weird, right? Now cross them back to your normal way again. Feels better and more natural, right? This is what you are up against. People are comfortable in the way they do things and even the smallest, simplest behavior changes run up against both real and perceived barriers.

It is no different with sustainability, where you might be asking employees to act or think differently. You will run into barriers that will need to be overcome, especially from employees who have done their job a certain way for a long time. You need to have a compelling vision of the future and a good rationale as to why the new, more sustainable way will be better. This is going to require a ton of heavy lifting, so you need to explain why it is worth doing.

Kevin Hagen, the former corporate social responsibility director of REI, says it best: "A sustainable business will outperform a traditional business; it's the change required to make the shift that is most difficult."[1]

Therefore, before attempting to implement sustainability across your company, it's important that you first truly understand how your company and employees manage change within its operations, processes, and culture. Only after you have that understanding of behavior change can you break down barriers, engage the skeptics, and set your company on a path toward sustainability that will last for the long term.

Change Is Tough and Nobody Likes to Change

Think back to the last time somebody looked at the way you did your job and suggested that you do something differently—how did this make you feel? Probably not too good. Your first thought probably was, *Why is this person trying to tell me what to do?* This was likely followed up by the thought, *I've been doing my job successfully for a long time. Who are they to tell me to do it differently?* These are very real emotions that everyone has, which can create a natural resistance to any suggestion toward change, however logical the idea is or regardless of whether the person believes she needs to make a change.

Then there is the rational level. Think about the last time you were introduced to a new piece of technology or your firm upgraded its computer operating systems. Even though the new system was supposed to be better and provide productivity improvements, your comfort level with the existing system wouldn't be the same and there would definitely be a learning curve that you probably didn't feel that you had time for.

Suggesting behavior change around sustainability is just like anything else. Even though it shouldn't be tough, it is. The common misconception that many environmentalists had over the decades was that if people just understood the facts, they would jump to acceptance and change their behavior. This was naïve and is at the core of why so many change efforts are unsuccessful.

The reality is that we all see and relate to the world through our perceptions. As John Koriath, a leadership professor at the Bainbridge Graduate Institute, states, "None of us are seeing the world as it is. We're seeing it through our own beliefs and our emotional response to events. This is fundamental to understanding change. Nothing can change if we only see things the way we've always seen them. If we only see things the way we've always seen them, we can only go where we've already been. And, with sustainability, we need to take a new path."[2]

Change Brings Emotion

Change has a direct and significant impact on people. "Not every employee will have the exact same response to every initiative, but by acknowledging the different ways that employees respond to change, you'll be better positioned to understand their reactions and how to best move forward,"[3] says Mary Kay Chess, the change management lead, Bainbridge Graduate Institute.

"Additionally, you have to show how the adoption of a new way is attractive and will be better for them. It can't come across as, 'Do this just because the boss or company says so.'"[4]

The diagram shown in Figure 7.1 illustrates the progression of emotions when one is trying to implement change within organizational change.[5]

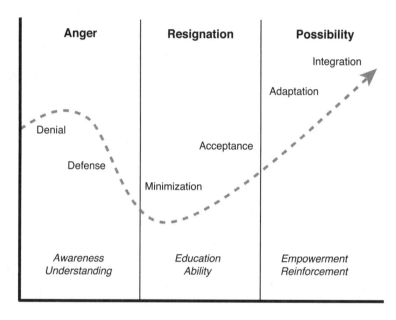

Figure 7.1   Stages of change.[6]

For example, when you talk to a skeptic about climate change, sure, some of them don't believe the science. However, the underlying psychology is that there is a fear that they're going to have to change and that you are going to be telling them what to do and taking away things they care about.

Your role as a change agent on sustainability is to facilitate with your employees and skeptics how the new way will be better. Show them all the business benefits outlined earlier relating to cost savings, lowering risk, the ability to attract more customers, enhancing the brand, and attracting new employees, but be sure to demonstrate how the change will be better for them individually as well.

Change Is a Phased Approach

As your company embarks on sustainability or as it tries to regain momentum that it might have lost, it is helpful to realize that change is not linear. As much as a strategist would like to map it out on a flow-chart, change is a process. There will be people who "get it" right away, whereas others will take more time. People move along at their own pace, and even those who get it might understand something entirely different from what is being presented by the company or leadership.

There are varying levels of idea adoption, as illustrated in Figure 7.2. There will be first movers, fast followers, the middle majority, and the naysayers. They will adopt and accept change at a different rate.

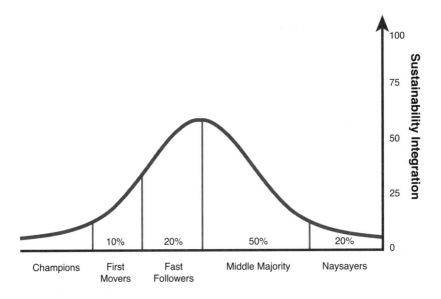

Figure 7.2   The Sustainability Adoption Curve (SAC).

The first thing you want to do is identify the first movers. Leverage their passion and expertise to bring the fast followers along, because they'll move into the adaptation and integration phase relatively easily and this will build momentum. Next, your efforts need to focus on the middle majority, on moving them from the resignation phase to one of possibility as soon as possible. After they are engaged, your ability to make sustainability stick will greatly improve because this is the largest group to try to shift. The naysayers and skeptics will take the most time and potentially drain your energy, so you don't want to start or focus there. Deal with them last.

Change Is a Constant

After the change process has begun, it is important to take into consideration that this will require "multiple attempts at a process because with each change there will be ripple effects," according to Chess.[7] The reality is that when you try to implement change, even benign actions will have consequences, both good and bad, on other aspects of the organization. So realize that when you push on one point of the star shown in Figure 7.3, it will tend to put other things out of balance.

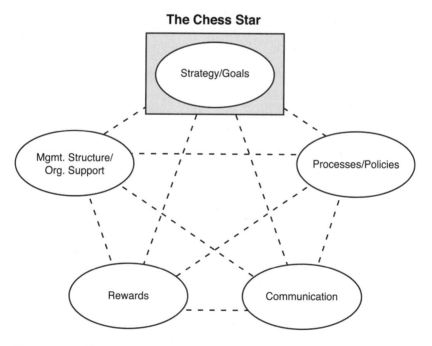

Figure 7.3 Change management star.

The goal is to make sure that all five factors are internally consistent. When this occurs, you will enable effective behavior and have the greatest chance for successful implementation. And remember, sustainability change is not much different from other change; it is just that the language is different for most people.

The Hagen-Wilhelm Change Matrix

There are a number of different diagrams out there to help companies understand where they are in their sustainability journey. However, none truly captured what I felt companies wrestled with as they moved from one phase to another in their adoption of sustainability. It turned out, though, that a few months into my writing of this book, both Kevin Hagen and I had started on new matrices that provided more detail, context, and the characteristics of change as companies implement sustainability. So we combined efforts and created the Hagen-Wilhelm matrix illustrated in Figure 7.4. This is designed to visually help a person or company understand what the dominant characteristics and drivers are in each stage of sustainability implementation.

Ultimately, the objective is to get the company all the way to phase five, and by having a map of the journey and what is involved in each phase, this should facilitate the process and help companies to avoid the pitfall of skipping a step or stalling out. I've detailed the information in Table 7.1 about each phase and described the unique characteristics to help you identify where your company is along the journey and the challenges you will face.

The goal of Figure 7.4 is to demonstrate the different types of change that occur, who predominantly leads the change, the unique characteristics, and the financial drivers of each phase as they differ as the company matures with its sustainability efforts. As you can see, at first the costs and environmental and social impacts increase as you grow, and then once sustainability becomes more embedded in everything you do, the environmental and social positives increase and lead to greater value creation and growth, and the negative impacts subside.

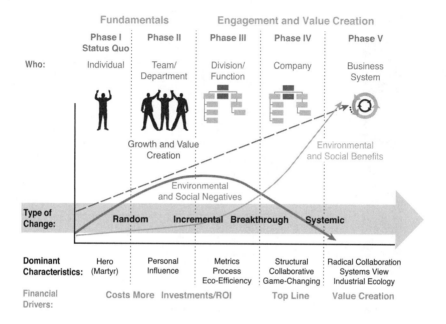

Figure 7.4 Hagen-Wilhelm Change Matrix.

Main Points of the Matrix

Next I want to highlight some key points about the matrix, especially about the skills and competencies required to implement change successfully.

Table 7.1 Hagen-Wilhelm Matrix Phases and Skills

Muscle and Skills to Develop				
Phase 1	**Phase 2**	**Phase 3**	**Phase 4**	**Phase 5**

Skills

	Phase 1	Phase 2	Phase 3	Phase 4	Phase 5
Leadership	Status quo. Typically mavericks, or martyrs, are working independently trying to make things happen.	Strong personality, probably at/near the top or with endorsement of CEO. Begins to be a team effort. Need the ability to lead without budget or full authority. Leader needs to give credit to others.	Moved from charismatic leader to execs. Need to make them think it's their idea because it helps them make better business decisions. Lead without recognition.	Leadership no longer accepts compromise. Tension arises because innovation is required. Leadership now means outside the walls—leading industry work, collaboration with NGOs.	Radical collaboration with industry and stakeholders is required for company to take next steps. Policy agenda is aligned with company outcomes on sustainability. Engage with networks of nontraditional partners on key issues (e.g., Starbucks joins BICEP).

Muscle and Skills to Develop					
	Phase 1	Phase 2	Phase 3	Phase 4	Phase 5
Data	Raw data might be around utility bills but not organized. Just starting to ask about social and environmental data. Not tracked well.	Baseline work of gathering and tracking social and environmental data. Likely in Excel. Begin to match cost and savings to these issues. Build confidence in data accuracy.	Develop systems beyond Excel. Metrics and KPIs are developed. ROI and cost-saving info required. Metrics become forward-looking tools.	Sustainability integrated into ERP systems. Metrics completely shift from historical to future forecasting and planning.	Data is essential to management and long-term planning. Part of business decision process.
Processes	None.	Processes discussed and begin to be introduced. People are encouraged to look at things holistically.	Processes launched, procurement guidelines created, etc. Cross-silo functional teams used to attack key opportunities and risks.	Processes in place. They work independently of CSR/green team. Processes enforce actions.	Culture. Just how things are done. It would be foolish not to use this way of thinking now—it delivers better results. Embedded in strategic and business-development conversations.

Muscle and Skills to Develop				
	Phase 1	Phase 2	Phase 3	Phase 4	Phase 5
Mind-Set				
Prevailing Mind-Set	Business as usual.	Do less bad instead of do good. Cost mitigation and bottom-line focus. Start showing solid ROI with solid rigor.	Leaders begin to see little trade-off between sustainability and financial benefits. Attitudes shift to innovating and delivering new solutions. Focus begins to be on top line. Company has the data to make public statements with confidence.	Challenge to the business model and value proposition of company's products/services. Long-term thinking is "let's choose to do things with positive side effects" (e.g., the textile mill that makes clean water; the soda bottling plant that is restorative to its watershed).	Let's change the world! Think like an ecosystem. Industrial ecology is used. Regenerative products and services. Let's outperform the competition because we have an inherent competitive advantage.

Muscle and Skills to Develop				
Characteristics	Phase 1	Phase 2	Phase 3	Phase 4	Phase 5

	Phase 1	Phase 2	Phase 3	Phase 4	Phase 5
HR	Benefits not part of formal sustainability policy or strategy. HR not involved with green team. Employees have no pride of being in an organization that cares about what they care about.	Some benefits such as commuting incentives/wellness added. HR rep on green team and CSR/sustainability directors hired. Sustainability skills become needed for key roles (e.g., LEED AP for real estate or facilities team).	HR formally involved. Begins to show up in evaluations and compensation. CSR dept. and HR start hiring sustainability expertise in all departments as these skills become part of job descriptions. Recruiting gets easier—people want to work for this company.	Sustainability incorporates everyone's compensation, job description, and evaluation. People join the company to be able to bring their whole selves to their profession and to be part of something bigger than themselves. Concern begins that people might try to "game the system" by setting easy-to-achieve goals.	Sustainability fully embedded in HR. "Gaming" concern is resolved.

Muscle and Skills to Develop					
	Phase 1	Phase 2	Phase 3	Phase 4	Phase 5
Accountability	Individual responsibility. No corporate goals. Random acts occur by individuals.	Green team established. Shared responsibility with CSR director. Corporate goals created but no teeth.	Responsibilities begin to be delegated. Corporate and department goals are given teeth. Top leaders participate in annual sustainability goal setting as part of strategic planning process.	Goals trickle all the way down to individual level; they are embedded in company expectations and results.	Everyone is accountable.
Rules	Maverick is challenging the mind-set. People believe this person is getting away with things. Or this person dies trying.	Employees are operating within the company norms and trying to get sustainability done where they can.	More permission given to make change, encouraged to do so in role. Testing of rules begins.	Rule breaking occurs. Employee engagement starts to spike. Leaders give permission to fail so that innovation and new ways of doing things can be adapted faster.	Sustainability and innovation are the new rule.

Understanding the Table

- The company moves through phases in a cluster, not in lock step—there will always be folks ahead of, and folks behind, the main curve. The practitioner has to be able to recognize where folks are at any time and keep the masses moving in the right direction.

- Each phase has things you must learn in order to be successful in the short term and long term. Each phase has paybacks and merit. You can deliver measurable value to the organization in each phase.

- You don't check a box and move from one phase to another; it will be more of a cultural and operational shift that everyone will recognize.

- Although the lines are smooth, expect small dips in productivity between each phase reflecting the necessary learning, realignment of processes, inevitable confusion, and just natural variation of people repositioning themselves for change.

- When you get to that trade-off conversation in Phase 3 and tensions mount because people are starting to become backed into a corner, that's when innovation and rule breaking occurs because they might need permission to knock down a wall.

- Start working with NGOs and industry partnerships early because you'll need these relationships later, especially in Phases 4 and 5.

- Be warned that the dominant behaviors of the leader that are needed for success in one phase can be derailers in the next. As the leader, be self-aware and recognize it if you're the barrier to next-phase success.

Skills and Competencies

- There is a set of individual skills and competencies that go along with this process. A company builds them over time, the same way an athlete builds muscle. You might not need every skill in every phase, but you'll want to build that muscle for later phases, where you'll need it. If you don't build it earlier, it will stop you or slow you down when you need it.

- Moreover, the skills, people, and competencies that were necessary for one phase might be different from what you'll need at another phase. This will be difficult especially if you were successful in the preceding phase. Getting people to change or think differently will be tougher in the next phase. Ask, "What needs to be changed to get to the next phase?"

People

- As Kevin Hagen says, "The job of the leader is to know how much to invest in skills and competencies in each phase. You can't spend all the resources in Phase 1!"[8]

- "Executive sponsors need to adapt, learn, and move with the organization as well. They have to move to deemphasize what worked in that first 'hero phase' and move to a new stage."[9]

- Everyone likes to be recognized, so remember a famous quote that is often attributed to Harry Truman: "It's amazing how much you can get done when you let other people have the credit."

- From that point, realize that it might take time for a CEO or manager to understand what is needed in a phase, so plant a seed in their head well ahead of time, and then ask questions about it. You'll be more successful if they think it is their idea when the time comes.

- The characteristics of the people who helped you get started in the hero stage will be essential early on, but as you move into later phases, you'll want to rely less on individual heroism and more on process and systems. For example, creative employees might do great in one phase but struggle in the next phase when operationalizing the idea requires a different skill set.

Arguments Worth Having

- Although there is always a cost to getting started and beginning implementation, it's also important to ask and calculate the cost of not moving to the next phase. Be sure to ask, "What cost savings and efficiencies are we leaving on the table? What opportunities are we not capitalizing on?" Too often the conventional wisdom focuses on what things will cost to "do"; be prepared to show the cost of not moving!

BUSINESS CASE: FREIGHT EFFICIENCY

A retailer was between Phase 2 and 3, and its CSR team was looking for a way to lower the emissions from their freight transport. With almost everything manufactured in China and Southeast Asia, a major portion of the retailer's carbon emissions came from their shipping. It turned out that the freight team was looking for a better deal on freight, too. Therefore, the two teams started working together to find a solution that could lower freight costs and emissions. They soon realized that if they worked with their freight forwarding company, they could use a longer water route, which would take more time, but would cost less and lower emissions. However, this ran up against opposition with sales, merchandising, and inventory, which were focused on time delivery and the ability to order whenever they needed it.

The breakthrough that was required was for the company to change its inventory system and order further in advance to meet sales objectives. And later, as they moved into Phase 4, they ended up actually partnering with a competitor to find a way to share a cargo container coming from overseas to reduce further costs and emissions for both companies.

Understand Your Company

Any change initiative is going to be messy. How do you best prepare for this? You want to first assess your company culture and identify how your company best handles change.

When assessing your company culture, you will want to look broadly across your company at your services, products, customers, finances, processes, history, and internal policies. This is because you'll realize that your culture is embedded in each of these. As intercultural solutions specialist Cecilia Utne, of Shepell.fgi, states, "Culture is in how we communicate, the words we use, and the way we think."[10]

Don't minimize the role that culture can play when trying to implement change. It can play a powerful role when the behavior you want to change is in alignment with your existing corporate values and goals and isn't something that is radically different. Operate from within a cultural language and framework that people in your company can relate to, or it simply won't work.[11] Therefore, be sure to assess and know your culture before launching behavior change.

Beware of the "Initial Nice"

Claudia Capitini, the former sustainability maven of Eco-Products, said about working with one of her former companies that "when you first get started, a lot of people are initially nice, but the authentic culture does not become apparent to you for months after those initial meetings."[12] People might voice support or nod in agreement early on, which might give the impression of perfect alignment, but the reality might be quite different after they are asked to allocate resources, budget, and staff.

How Your Company Manages Change

Company cultures are as varied as the employees themselves, and each company handles and manages change differently. Here are a couple of basic questions to ask to determine how your company best manages change:

- How do policies and procedures normally take root? Is it a top-down approach or more of a grass-roots movement?

- Do you have a command-and-control structure in which people wait for approval before trying something new, or do you have a creative structure in which people innovate and tend to ask for forgiveness rather than permission?

- How competitive are you as an organization? Are people motivated to win? For example, will people or departments be more likely to embrace change if they can "beat" someone or a group within the organization?

Table 7.2 displays the four methods for managing change according to the National Environmental Education Foundation.[13]

Table 7.2   Change Management Methods

Collaborate Oriented	Control Oriented
Facilitate group brainstorming sessions	Understand relevant regulations and associated risk exposure
Develop or improve the employee suggestion and feedback system	Analyze or audit existing processes and environmental impacts (e.g., life cycle analysis)
Develop an online internal collaboration platform	Review existing policies for procedural inefficiencies and opportunities for sustainability
Create Oriented	**Compete Oriented**
Use social media and crowdsourcing to generate new ideas faster	Establish goals, objectives, and measures based on company vision and standards
Create a training program to cultivate creative thinking	Benchmark performance against initiatives of key competitors
Empowered intrapreneurs	Use competitive means for project idea generation, such as a contest between individuals and teams

Understanding how your company handles change sheds light on how change can be implemented. In some cases the structure might vary on the timing or type of initiative, so it might be a combination. Therefore, it's prudent to first figure out the best method for implementing that change and apply the appropriate structure to give it the best chance for success.

Change Takes Time

Sustainability is a complex issue. It requires systemic, long-term thinking and hundreds of small actions, not just one big one. Change is a triathlon. You need time to train and build muscle. You're not going to wake up and do it all tomorrow. For even small changes to take place, it is reasonable to expect that it takes two to three months to understand, to tweak, and then to incorporate new approaches. As Mary Kay Chess says, "For large, complex organizations with multiple changes underway, it might take almost a year for ongoing, conscious or unconscious modifications to processes and communication."[14]

Get Comfortable with Uncertainty

There are going to be instances when there is no guideline, playbook, or path to follow. In fast-moving markets you might be innovating or making things up on the fly. Don't let this scare you. Remember that ambiguity and contradiction are inherent in what you're doing, because it's complex; don't cower from that, but embrace it.

Stay positive and realize that with sustainability, persistence is key. Change takes time and you will lose battles along the way. Keep perspective and remember what change-management practitioner Terra Anderson says: "There will be scary times, but the difference between a loser and a winner on these issues is that the winner gets up one more time."[15]

Understanding Your People

As mentioned, people will be at different points on the sustainability adoption curve. That makes it essential that you make an extra effort to understand the people within your organization.

Understand not only their opinions about sustainability, but their different personality types, speaking styles, and learning styles. You cannot apply a one-size-fits-all approach to your sustainability implementation plans.

You will need to tailor your message and education of your employees using various methods and techniques based on how they see the world and what they care about. As Steven Covey is fond of saying, "First understand what the other person cares about, and then try and talk to them about that."[16] Don't start trying to talk to someone about sustainability and change without knowing what the person on the other end cares about.

This will be more difficult within larger organizations, but this work is essential. Dawn Danby, the sustainable design program manager of Autodesk, states from her experience that "some people are effective at being collaborative. Others need to be told what to do and work better under a more authoritative manager. Some are driven and self-directed. Others need education and want a safer route with a plan and formula."[17]

The style you use will depend on the culture of the company, and it's important to realize that your change efforts will need to reach both extroverts and introverts, as well as visual and auditory learners. Each type of person has different ways in which he or she wants to learn and embrace new initiatives.

For example, I've found that most CEOs with whom I interact are extroverts. Because of their time constraints, they learn best from short, succinct, summarized reports with easy-to-understand visuals. Because this works for them, they sometimes think this is the best and only way to reach all of their employees. Nothing could be further from the truth.

Having a fair understanding of these stylistic differences will open the door to assorted methods to reach your employees, expand your reach, and ensure that you will be appealing to all cross sections of employees and not to only one group. This requires some nuance but it is doable.

The Culture Outside of the Office

Understanding your people means also considering the culture outside of work—what the norms are in their lives, in their community, and in the communication styles of their culture. This is especially important with multistate and multinational companies.

Different offices from around the globe will be home to employees with different cultural norms. For example, North American employees tend to be more individualistic, talkative, pragmatic, and goal oriented, and believe that their destiny is in their own hands, whereas in Japan or the Far East, employees are more group orientated and listeners. Here, a 20-second delay to listen and think through an idea is commonplace.

You need to recognize these cultural norms, because if you are suggesting sustainability ideas in a boardroom in the Far East and "hear no objections," you'll think you've nailed it, when the reality is that maybe people are just being polite. Similarly, if you aren't used to direct communication and you present an idea to someone from Germany or the Netherlands (where they tend to speak more directly), when they start intensively asking you questions, you might take this the wrong way if you aren't prepared for that type of communication style. They might simply be asking questions and are in total support.

Culture norms are the things you are doing and the way you are doing them, without knowing you are doing anything at all. For example, Table 7.3 shows the differences between the aforementioned individualistic and group-oriented cultures that you'll need to be aware of when talking sustainability with your employees.

Table 7.3 Behavior Styles

Individualistic	Group Oriented/Collective
Doer.	Collaborator.
High-context communication style.	Provide little context when communicating.
Give feedback: verbally, nodding. Uncomfortable with silence.	Prefer silence. Don't offer verbal or physical cues.
Direct.	Indirect.
Assertive.	Passive.
Explicit.	Implicit.
Skeptic.	Optimist.

When you're working toward change within an organization, it is 50% about learning about other people and their cultural norms and 50% about inflection/learning of your own. So before you try to talk to your employees about sustainability and why they should care about it, understand both your culture and theirs and ask yourself, "What emotions and expectations am I holding? Do I have an anticipated outcome or am I open to any occurrence?"

Connecting Personally First

One technique I use when talking with someone about sustainability for the first time is that I don't try to get into the technical aspects of the work before I connect with them on a human scale. So rather than asking people about what they think about sustainability, I start by asking them where they are from because we all are from somewhere. I look for some type of shared connection or shared cultural experience (whether it be a travel experience, knowing someone from there, rooting for the same sports team, etc.). This then helps smooth the path into talking about sustainability, because when we get to that point of talking about change, you will have made a personal connection and won't be seen so much as "that green/sustainability" person.

ACTIVITY 17: ORGANIZATIONAL CHANGE ACTIVITY

Following are questions to answer internally when you are trying to figure out how best to approach a change initiative within your company, as sustainability will likely involve change for at least some of your employees:

1. How does your company manage change: collaborate, control, compete, or create?
   - What does this mean for how you should handle change within your organization?
   - What elements work best for achieving your goal? How will these play in your road map to implementing sustainability?
   - What are the needs and self-interests of your staff?

2. Where is your company on the Hagen-Wilhelm Matrix?
   - What does that mean for your company in terms of trying to get to the next phase?

3. What roadblocks and constraints should you expect?
   - How will you handle denial and resistance (business as usual, focusing on the past, anxiety, anger, etc.)?

4. What other change initiatives has your company implemented (diversity, affirmative action, etc.)? And what were the keys to making this successful?
   - What worked and why?
   - What motivated your staff?
   - How did you communicate this new vision?
   - Who were the empowered players in the process? Who needs to carry out the vision for the change?

5. What parts of your existing culture already support sustainability?

6. What initiatives have you tried and failed? What were the specific reasons behind the failure and what could be done this time to mitigate those issues?

7. Is management onboard with changing the institutionalized legacy and culture of the organization?

Breaking Down Silos and Coordinating across Departments

Organizational structures have long been set up with silos to create specialization and focus. Although this worked well in the 20th century with managers concentrating on their own stovepipe and rarely looking up, down, or across the company, this will no longer work in today's fast-paced, information- and consumer-driven economy.

Companies need to get away from the silo mentality because coordination across departments is where the greatest opportunities lie to create efficiency, drive change, incorporate sustainability, and harness the power and ideas of all of your employees.

Most large companies still work with siloed departments, in that each one has little to no idea what another is doing. Someone might be driving the sustainability program in one department, but other groups like marketing, public relations, philanthropy, sales, business development, R & D, operations, logistics, and community relations might be implementing their own efforts, usually without communicating with each other, and rarely aligned.

This typically happens because people are evaluated and incentivized by what they do for their boss and within their department, not for how they help the company's overall efficiency, productivity, or success. Therefore, five things have to occur to help break down silos and increase collaboration around sustainability:

1. Ensure that information flows across, up and down, and within departments.

2. Priorities need to be aligned—the company versus the department.

3. Decision making should be coordinated across silos.

4. Create a team that looks across the company. They should be skilled leaders with credibility to identify opportunities and drive change, including key people who could block things later.

5. Find examples in the past—whether they be a product, process, or service—where cooperation between departments led to success, and build off those instances.

The goal in breaking down silos is not to destroy a department's autonomy, but rather to eliminate the issues that caused conflicting priorities, lack of information flow, and duplication of efforts and resources.

How many times have you come up with an idea at your company, only to find out that another branch or department is working on the same thing? At one point when Kodak was trying to get into the digital camera market, it had seven separate initiatives taking place across the company.

Let me give you two examples that illustrate two different siloed approaches: first, where silos were plain as day and led to inefficiency and a lesser work product, and second, where sustainability was used as a means of breaking down the barriers between various silos and a new process was developed that led to a new product and a new revenue stream.

The first scenario was with a utility company. We had been working with their green team on a variety of issues over the course of a year, and it got to the point where the team decided that it wanted to create a CSR report. Then after weeks of working with the team and talking through the best stories to share, we drafted the beginnings of a C-Level GRI report. But about six weeks in, a communications person joined the conversation and blurted out in frustration: "I don't know why we keep talking about this; we have an environmental report at the printer right now. My department has been working on this for months!"

We were all dumbstruck. Nobody on this fairly high-level green team knew that this was already in the works. In addition, after reading the report, we all found it full of fluff and it seemed that it was likely to do more harm than good. The siloed approach of this company's communication department wasted energy and resources of all those involved. It resulted in the group feeling burned by the process, and it made them less inclined to help the next time around.

What you want to do is use sustainability to break down silos. Take, for example, the second scenario with Cascade Designs, the maker of the popular Therm-a-Rest mattress. It was looking for ways to reduce its waste costs associated with the disposal of excess foam from its mattresses. In a traditional siloed organization maybe the manufacturing, facilities, or designers would have tried to come up with a solution on their own that could reduce waste disposal costs. However, what Cascade did was bring together a cross-functional team to look at this issue, and they found that the excess foam could be used as the raw material for new camping pillows, something that its customers had been requesting. So they took what was waste and turned it into the raw materials for a new product, thus reducing waste costs and increasing topline revenues at the same time. It took what was an expense and turned it into productive revenue on the income statement, all while meeting customer expectations and lowering their environmental impact.

This is an example where sustainability can turn what was once thought of as business as usual onto its head, inviting innovation, collaboration, and excitement into any organization as long as the people are willing to adopt a new way of thinking. This can make any type of change initiative feel more empowering and less daunting.

Don't Rest on Your Laurels

There is a tendency at some point within any initiative to feel as though you've made it and you can begin to relax. For any of us who have ever tried to diet, we've gone through this same cycle. After you lose the weight and feel good, at some point you want to reward yourself ever so slightly. It's a snack here or there, and soon you stop getting on the scale. Then because the changes are so slight, you don't notice them until it gets bad enough that you feel as though you need a drastic change again. In the same way, companies get started on sustainability, make progress, feel good, and then lose momentum and have to reenergize their efforts over and over. Because the feedback and measurement for social and environmental issues are usually not immediate, the steps backward are less visible. Be careful to avoid this step.

When you are doing great, have a budget, and have engaged employees, don't take your foot off the gas; step on it with all your might!

Engaging the Skeptics

Throughout life, we have all run into skeptics or naysayers about something we're trying to do, whether it is at work or in our personal life. The natural tendency is to get annoyed and try to disassociate yourself from skeptics. Don't do that in this case. When trying to implement sustainability, engage the skeptics early on. They are the ones who will identify the land mines on your path. And it's better to find these out and figure out how you are going to address them before you get 80% of the way down the path.

Skeptics can be one of the greatest resources you can have with any implementation project or change initiative because they are the ones who have concerns, see potential hiccups, notice blind spots, and think they know what's wrong with your idea. They might know the answers to the unspoken questions. And remember, not all naysayers or skeptics are ill-intentioned. As Terra Anderson is fond of saying, "The cynic is the one whose heart has already been broken."[18]

Go to your skeptics and ask these questions:

- What's going to go wrong with this plan?
- Can you think of something that would work better that will address your concerns? If not, who should be asked?
- What has to happen for this to work? What would you do?

Then, repeat this process at every major stage of work flow.

As with all things, the key here is timing. You don't want to engage skeptics fully and try to address all their concerns before you've even started, or else, in shipping terms, you might never leave port. The best time to engage them is when you are 20% in. This is where course corrections can be made easily before too much time and resources have been spent, and it allows for heightened engagement because they can help shape the effort. If you wait until you are 50% or 75% of the way there, it will require much more time and work to undo things, cost more, and be demoralizing to the people involved.

Find Common Ground

When you run into resistance, ask questions differently to find out what is behind their resistance, and try to seek common ground.

When we started working with one of our retailer clients, the sustainability director had cooperation from most of the people she worked with but not all. There were a few people who viewed sustainability as a distraction and therefore weren't fully supportive. In a heart-to-heart discussion with these individuals, she realized that the sticking point wasn't that they didn't believe in the idea of enhanced sustainability across the company, but just that they were already stretched thin and were worried about how the costs were going to show up on their own department's profit and loss (P & L) statements.

To alleviate this problem, she pulled money from her budget and used some of it to create an internal fund to support internal projects. Then she reached back out to one individual who had the greatest reservations about "this whole sustainability thing" and used that money to fund an energy-efficiency project for this individual's line of business. It was a win-win for both of them and the skeptic was happy because it did not negatively impact his department's P & L.

The result was that now they are working together and looking for other high-value projects where they can partner again in the future.

Group Discussion versus One-on-Ones

There are times when you are trying to get things worked out and you want all the decision makers and affected parties in the room so that there can be agreement. Realize that it is actually very rare when you need to have everyone in the room. Most of the time it's best to have little side meetings offline, where you can work out the uncomfortable issues ahead of time and quietly rather than in front of everyone. If someone is showing true resistance, often it isn't what they are saying in the big room that is the reason. There usually is something more fundamental that is bothering them—they might be afraid of being "on the hook" if things don't work out right, and they don't want to be the fall person. In these instances, rather than trying to convince them in front of everyone, try to meet up with them one-on-one and hash out the issues privately.

Sometimes an Outsider Works Best

If you cannot make any headway, sometimes a solution is to bring in an outside consultant or facilitator. They can do the research independently and provide a report to management or the skeptic. This can have a way of providing an opinion outside of the company that they haven't heard from before. I've seen this be successful a number of times, because it changes the dynamic between you and the skeptic. It is no longer about you or your opinion; instead, the discussion can be about the report, what the expert said, and the information instead of the personalities involved.

ACTIVITY 18: WORKSHEET ON HOW TO ENGAGE DIFFERENT NAYSAYERS

Following are a number of comments you can expect to hear from naysayers, along with some tailored responses. I've outlined them as "expected barriers" and "strategic responses." In each category, feel free to add others, and identify the naysayer, their likely issue, and a potential response that is specific to what they care about. There is also a space for this at the end.

If the responses don't match up exactly with the mind-set of the person at your company, develop questions or strategic responses that ask: "How could we use this sustainability initiative to make our jobs easier and provide value to the stakeholder?"

Investor Relations	
Expected Barriers	**Strategic Response**
We need to maximize shareholder value.	Focus on new SEC guidelines that require disclosure on climate change, etc.
	Show how the Dow Jones Sustainability Index has actually outperformed the S&P 500 over the past 11 years.
This money could be better spent elsewhere.	Demonstrate the ROI for sustainability initiatives to support your argument.
	Identify intangible benefits like increased brand value, competitive advantage, and goodwill that are improving shareholder value.
Not everyone reports.	The reality is that more of the Fortune 500 are reporting to the CDP than not. If you are in the "not" category, this may raise a red flag to investors.
Shareholders aren't demanding sustainability over other issues, especially during economic uncertainty.	Maybe not, but it prepares you for the future and is a smart risk management strategy.
Other barriers.	Enter your own.
Finance/Accounting/CFO	
Expected Barriers	**Strategic Response**
This is going to cost more.	Use activity-based costing and total-cost accounting to demonstrate the financial benefits and show where it will actually cost less.
We need to see a quick payback.	Ask what other projects are held to such a quick payback period. Ask what payback was required for diversity and sexual harassment education.
We want both short-term and long-term ROI.	The business case shows both short-term and long-term ROIs. Show low-hanging fruit opportunities in the short term, like energy efficiency.

There is a lack of information and no way to track progress easily.	Work with operations, HR, logistics, and finance to look for solutions using your existing ERP and accounting systems. All you have to do is build in codes and line items into your chart of accounts for ways to track the things you typically haven't been tracking. Eventually you'll want to move to an automated system.
We don't understand the information by anyone right now.	Put everything into normative, easy-to-understand factors and terms that you already use to make decisions.
We are not being asked to generate this information.	Investor relations, marketing, or sales will be asking soon, because stakeholders are demanding to know what you are doing.
There is a cultural legacy of sticking with the status quo.	Acknowledge that it's always easier sticking with what you know. But in this case, by not improving your data and financial systems to capture this information, "you don't know what you don't know!" And you might be at risk.
There is no business benefit.	Firms that demonstrate stronger ESG performance have a much higher market capitalization than those that don't.
Other barriers.	Enter your own.
Operations/Facilities	
Expected Barriers	**Strategic Response**
This is too expensive to implement.	Start with no-cost and low-cost investments, and then move to bigger projects and potential savings. The earnings from the small changes can help pay for some of the costlier, bigger changes.
It will take too much extra time to make this work.	Highlight case studies that saved money and actually made things easier and more efficient.
There is limited accessibility to renewables.	Focus on efficiency first, second, and third, and then on renewables.
	Work with industry association and academic institutions to find green alternatives.

It's too difficult.	It doesn't have to be. Start small and focus on efficiency that is core to what you do.
This requires a cultural change and that is difficult.	Yes. But you can accomplish this by a few measures. Update policies, procedures, and systems to incorporate sustainability. Set up a realistic time frame and let them know that not everything will be expected overnight.
	Enact a structure to help support sustainable decision making.
There is a lack of communication between facilities/departments.	Create cross-departmental/facility meetings where groups share best practices and concerns. This leads to cohesiveness, collaboration, and creative problem solving.
We have a way of doing it, and it works. Don't mess with it! We understand our operations, so don't try to tell us what to do!	True, but we need you to look at things with a sustainability lens. You might be missing things just because you haven't thought of them in that regard.
This is only extra work and doesn't help me or my business unit.	Show them where the organization is heading and how their actions can be part of that change.
We've done everything we can.	Ask yourself, "Where are we normal?" Those are the places you can start to work on.
	It is important for every department to try, even if they can't change much.
Other barriers.	Enter your own.
Legal	
Expected Barriers	**Strategic Response**
Will this put us more at risk?	Sustainability is good financial and risk mitigation. By paying attention to new areas and keeping track of new potential social and environmental regulations, you might actually be reducing your risk over the long term.

We don't want to disclose risks if we don't have to.	You don't have to disclose, but you should track. It's a risk-mitigation strategy.
If people aren't asking, let's not volunteer information.	Don't be afraid to show the good you've done. If you are worried about being attacked, engage an NGO or friendly stakeholder to provide "air cover" for you.
You can't write that.	If you're afraid of public commitments, keep things internal. Set caveats that will allow you to use statements such as "best to our knowledge" so that you can be transparent.
Will this make us "contractually" bound in some way? We don't want to set a precedent.	Show best intentions and maintain the right to restate and clarify if new information becomes available. You're not contractually bound to report or continue reporting if you choose to stop in the future.
Will disclosure make us liable?	Legal experts suggest that disclosing risk lowers liability by creating a more defensible position: "We told you."
Philanthropy and volunteerism are sustainability.	No, this is how sustainability used to be thought of. You need to evolve your thinking because stakeholders have higher expectations.
Other barriers.	Enter your own.
Supply Chain	
Expected Barriers	**Strategic Response**
Our suppliers don't get what we're trying to do.	Invite them to a supplier conference where you can explain your goals/vision. Ask them to share in your vision.
	Ask them to suggest solutions rather than listing problems.
There is a language/ cultural barrier.	Use internal team members who are native speakers/fluent, or use a trusted third party to explain things in their language/dialect.

We're not a big enough fish to influence change.	Partner with others in your industry. For example, many outdoor retailers use the same factory in China; together they could create a critical mass.
	See who among your peers are having the same issues, band together, and call your suppliers on the same day!
	Work with industry associates to create new guidelines for your industry.
Don't just give us another questionnaire.	Offer support in responding to the requirements/questionnaire.
	First offer to engage, educate, and help, but communicate a "two or three strikes you're out" policy.
	State how you need to do this to meet investor or customer demand.
Other barriers.	Enter your own.

Human Resources

Expected Barriers	Strategic Response
Policies	
We don't have a policy.	Create one or draft one. Realize that when you start, you don't have to have the perfect policy for everything that matches your vision right off the bat.
We can't afford to do this.	Highlight low- or no-cost things you can do; for example, switch to double-sided printing, e-statements, and internal intranet sites so you don't have to create HR manuals.
Sharing Information	
We can't get employee information.	Add sustainability questions to annual employee surveys that already exist (satisfaction, commute trip reduction).

We can't afford sustainability benefits.	Audit what benefits employees are currently using. You might be able to replace some that aren't being utilized.
	You could also create an opt-in or trading system where you could provide a suite of benefits. Then based on costs, employees could trade one for another. (For example, younger employees could trade away life insurance for wellness or gym membership benefits.)
We have to deal with the union, and we don't want things like bus passes incorporated into the next union contracts.	Offer it as an incentive or a reimbursement, not something that is included in their actual contract.
Benchmark Benefits and Compensation	
We can't compete with Google's benefits.	You don't have to. Do what you can that will support your sustainability goals and that your employees will appreciate.
How can we know this will help with retention and recruitment?	Demonstrate how millennial/Gen Y and Gen X employees expect this, and show case studies of other companies.
There is no hard data about retention and recruitment. What is this going to cost?	There is a ton of data out there on the cost of losing a good employee, costing between 70% and 200% of current pay. Perform a cost-benefit analysis of the cost of the sustainability benefits to employees.
	Highlight studies where changes were made, resulting in tangible benefits such as improved morale and enhanced customer relations. This should be a win-win for employees and the company.
We can't afford to train everyone.	The more people you train, the more opportunities you'll uncover and the more money you'll save. Explore low-cost training or online classes by Hunter Lovins and Kevin Wilhelm.

We can't offer these new benefits to everyone.	Then create competitions and offer up things as prizes for the sustainability idea that saves the most money. Use these savings to pay for the benefits.
Other barriers.	Enter your own.

Sales, Marketing, and Public Relations	
Expected Barriers	**Strategic Response**
There is no market.	Show them the market and LOHAS (lifestyle of health and sustainability) market statistics about the preferences of younger consumers.
The market is unproven.	Maybe, but that provides an opportunity for first-mover advantage and a way to build out top-line revenue growth.
This is a fad (everyone seems to be doing this).	Show them Chapter 1, "The Business Case."
This requires a lot of effort for little return.	Actually, it is not that difficult and there is an opportunity for differentiation and/or competitive advantage.
Current customers are not asking for sustainability.	Tell your story to a select group of customers; see whether your sustainability efforts resonate with them. They might just never have thought of your company or your products/services in that light. Few will see it as a negative; the majority will react positively.
This takes away from our core brand message (which is premier products, comfort, performance, price, etc.).	It doesn't have to. It can actually support and strengthen your message. People may assume that "premier or performance" are the ones that meet their needs and are green, too.
We don't know how to talk about it or how to message it to new customers.	Talk with your younger employees, and look at your competitors' Facebook/social media pages to see how they are talking about it. Seek input from your green team.

We don't want to overpromise or greenwash.	Don't. Just be authentic and communicate only what is true.
	Apply for awards; these can actually do your marketing for you.
Sustainability will mean lower margins.	Maybe, but it might increase brand loyalty over time.
Other Skeptics	
Expected Barriers	**Strategic Response**

Lessons Learned

The following are key takeaways from the "Understanding Change Management to Guide Implementation" chapter:

- Change is tough. Do not expect it to be easy or quick. Accept that it takes time. Change is scary for most people. People will go through various emotions during the change, from anger to resignation to realization of possibility. If you ask people to change, you have to show them how the new/sustainable way will be better for the company.

- Change is not linear. People, departments, and offices will not move in lockstep.

- Deliver. After you tell people you are going to change, you have to do so. Nothing is more demotivating than having an employee with a passion who offers something but nothing is done!

- Before starting on incorporating sustainability, understand your people and how your company deals with change.

- Know where you are on the Hagen-Wilhelm matrix and realize that the skills and competencies required in one phase might be inadequate or you might need new ones in order to move through the next phase.

- When you experience success, push the advantage while you have the momentum.

- There will always be skeptics. Rather than dismissing them, engage them. Find out what their concerns are, and then address them.

- Look at past change initiatives that have been successful, such as introducing sexual harassment policies, work from home, or diversity. Identify what the keys to success were and replicate them.

8

Engaging Employees Around Sustainability

E mployees are most effective at their job when they can engage their head, their heart, and their hands. This chapter is designed to help you understand the benefits of a fully engaged workforce, and why sustainability is one of the best ways to achieve that, and then to describe the various intricacies required for sustainability to be fully embedded in your workforce.

Engaged employees are more productive and enthusiastic and will carry the mission and goals of your company forward. The most productive employees have high job satisfaction and find purpose at work outside of financial gain. I emphasize this because although there are a number of technical aspects of sustainability implementation, it will never reach its full potential unless employees are engaged, trained, and brought into the process.

Numerous studies show that employees are the least engaged they've been in a generation, so that's why I'm going to lay out why sustainability is the best way to engage employees, the specifics for doing just that, and how it ties back to both innovation and your bottom line.

Introduction to Employee Engagement

How is employee engagement best defined? I think it is when employees do the following:

- See their talents, values, and aspirations aligned with the company's mission and goals

- Are emotionally attached/committed to their work and to the organization

- Are motivated to contribute and put forth discretionary effort that furthers organizational success

These factors are important because, as Daniel Pink says:

"Companies need to move past their outdated reliance on carrots and sticks. For creative, 21st-century work, companies are better off ensuring that people have ample amounts of autonomy and that their individual efforts are hitched to a larger purpose."[1]

Unfortunately, there are a number of barriers that are keeping this from happening around sustainability at various companies, including the following feelings by employees:

- They are overworked, have no time, and already have too much on their plates.

- This is just another thing they have to do.

- They lack training and don't know exactly what is being asked of them.

- They are not empowered.

- Their boss doesn't support time away from their "real job." It is acceptable to work on sustainability only after work or during breaks.

- Past efforts failed, so they are apathetic this time around.

- Middle management and department managers don't see how business objectives are tied to sustainability.

- This is management's "fad of the year."

These are common statements that employees express all the time. Therefore, it's important to remember that when you engage employees on sustainability, you first need to make sure that the fundamentals are in place, which were outlined in Chapters 1–6:

- Defining sustainability and why the company is taking action

- Making the business case

- Setting the company's North Star on sustainability

- Demonstrating stakeholder interest

- Ensuring management support

- Conducting your baseline

Obviously, the easiest solution is to incorporate sustainability into every job description and include it in every new employee orientation and training. However, the reality is that most, if not all, of your employees have already been trained and have been working off of their existing job descriptions, so how do you change your employee engagement strategy to embed sustainability for the long haul?

There is a myth that both people and employees are primarily motivated by pay. The reality is that today's employees are more highly motivated by intrinsic factors such as pride in their work, career ambitions, autonomy, and connection to the company.

This manifests itself when everyone is rowing in the same direction, at the same time, with a clear idea that they can make a difference in the world. This ties directly to sustainability because employees want to feel the following:

- "I'm making a difference."

  There is real meaning in my job.

  My work matters internally and externally.

  My job helps the organization achieve success.

- "My company has my back."

  This is a safe environment, with a culture of trust and respect.

  My strengths are matched to my job description and my day-to-day job.

- "We're in this together."

  I have dependable colleagues and I can count on them!

  There is a balance between "we're all going full-bore" and a more relaxed pace.

  Sane expectations exist.

- "There's trust at work."

  I believe in leadership and in the direction of the company.

  Merit and loyalty are earned, not bought.

  There are no office politics, so my energy is used on my work.

I often pull from Gary Hamel, who was called the world's most influential business thinker by the *Wall Street Journal,* that in today's fast-paced and creative economy, a company's success depends far more on its ability to tap the creativity and passion of its employees than ever before. And I come back to my core belief that you best engage employees when you can engage the head, the heart, and the hands.

This is a pretty hard feat to accomplish, especially for larger organizations where employees might have different ideas of levels of engagement. Therefore, I'm going to hit you over the head with some statistics that will demonstrate how important employee engagement is to productivity and the profitability of your business.

Statistics about Employee Engagement

An engaged employee is a more productive employee, and an unengaged employee is a drag on the company's bottom line.

A Gallup study found that 71% of American workers are "not engaged" or are "actively disengaged" in their work.[2]

That same study evaluated numerous surveys linking employee engagement to key business units and compared businesses in the top quartile of engagement with those in the bottom quartile of engagement and found the following median percentage differences:[3]

- 16% in profitability
- 18% in productivity
- 12% increase in customer loyalty
- 60% increase in quality (fewer defects)
- 49% decrease in safety incidents
- 37% decrease in absenteeism

Moreover, if you are an owner or a shareholder who cares about your return or earnings per share, the following stats will jump out at you:

- There have been 29% above average shareholder returns for companies with high levels of employee engagement versus 1% for companies with moderate levels of engagement.[4]

- These numbers have stayed steady for the past eight years; a study by Melcrum back in 2006 found similar results, but with improvement closer to 27%.[5]

How does sustainability play into all of this? Millennials are expecting sustainability in their jobs and are factoring it into their decision criteria. A 2012 study by Net Impact pointed out:

- 88% of graduate students and young professionals factor an employer's CSR position into their job decision.

- 58% of the student population would take a 15% pay cut to "work for an organization whose values are like my own."[6]

Employees want to bring their values to work, not check them at the door!

And it's not just new employees entering the workforce; with an improving economy, job mobility will increase as individuals will be more willing to leave the safety of their job and check out something that they are more passionate about. Although there was a severe decrease in employee mobility from 2008 to 2012 due to the great recession, people are once again looking to make a change—whether it is to find a more challenging job, more money, a shorter commute, or a company that is better aligned with their values.

Don't forget that the other way an employee can "leave" is when they mentally check out. Let's be honest; we've all had days when we've checked out. Think about how unproductive you were. Almost as big a threat as employees leaving are the ones who stay but are completely checked out. In either case, when employees aren't engaged, this has tremendous financial consequences.

Any business leader or person in HR has learned that employee turnover and retention is a major cost that typically doesn't show up in the profit-and-loss statement. A recent study by the National Environmental Education Fund found that "losing and replacing a good employee costs companies between 70% and 200% of an employee's annual salary."[7]

To put that in perspective, consider that cost of turnover shown in Table 8.1, based on the employee's salary.

Table 8.1   Cost of Turnover

Employee Salary	Cost to Company to Replace
$35,000	$24,500–$70,000
$50,000	$35,000–$100,000
$75,000	$52,500–$150,000
$125,000	$87,500–$250,000
$250,000	$175,000–$500,000

Sustainability and Employee Engagement

I've found that sustainability is one of the absolute best ways to engage employees. Each of the 75-plus companies I've worked with has found that taking action to be more socially or environmentally responsible not only helped reduce their risks and impact in these areas, but also brought employees together around a company-wide and global cause that generated a positive feeling of "we're all in this together."

Bob Stiller, Chairman of the Board of Green Mountain Coffee Roasters, describes this connection between business sustainability and employee engagement: "I've learned that people are motivated and more willing to go the extra mile to make the company successful when there's a higher good associated with it. It's no longer just a job. Work becomes meaningful and this makes us more competitive."[8] Sustainability can be a major factor in creating a more engaged workforce.

Sustainability Also Provides Leadership and Career Development Opportunities

Enabling employees to engage in sustainability in their jobs can also be a valuable way for employees to gain additional skills, demonstrate leadership, and contribute to the company in ways that they normally cannot do in their current role. This is especially true for someone who has a repetitive or mundane job and is looking for other ways to add value and engage their brains a little more at work. Both organizational and professional development can occur when these employees participate in cross-functional innovation and/or green teams.

Train and Make Sustainability Part of the Job

Employees need to be trained in sustainability and understand how it relates to their job. What happens when a customer walks into a store, showroom, or factory floor and asks whether the products they see are fair-trade or sourced sustainably? Do employees have this information at hand? Can they answer questions about the company's labor practices or the carbon emissions associated with its transport? Are they prepared to have a real dialogue with customers or stakeholders? In reality, not frequently enough.

For you to realize the full potential of your employee engagement efforts, you need to tailor your sustainability training to each job function, make it personal for each individual, and deliver the training in multiple mediums to adapt to the different learning styles of your employees.

To begin with, offer a Sustainability 101–type of training so that everyone in the company is on the same page. Tie it back to why your company is doing this, the business case, and your company's North Star, but also be sure to demonstrate how everyone's individual action adds up to a bigger whole.

You might find that for most employees, how they do things just stems from the fact that they've "always done it that way." They might not have thought about how sustainability could be incorporated into their jobs, or they haven't had the time to look beyond what is an immediate priority. So be patient with your training and start with something tangible.

For example, most office employees touch or print paper during the course of the day. So although not a huge behavior-changing item, a first step could be to get employees to switch to e-documents. Explain to them why the company is trying to print less, how it saves money, how it is better for the environment, and the expectation that each person has a role to play. Setting this expectation and following through early on is key. After you've asked them to take a small tangible step, then ask them where else they could take action within their job. Be sure to focus on items that might also make their jobs easier and more efficient because, again, this will increase buy-in.

As Dawn Danby says, "Sometimes you are asking employees questions they have never been asked before. But usually if you give them enough information, data, and the space to figure out the solutions, you'll be amazed at what they'll do!"[9]

ACTIVITY 19: SUSTAINABILITY IN EACH DEPARTMENT

Use the following worksheet to think through how people at your company can incorporate sustainability into their jobs.

Person/ Department	Examples of How Sustainability = Their Job	How to Tie It to Your Job?
Accounting	Track sustainability data in support of measuring company goals and metrics and calculating GHG inventories	
Finance	Attract SRI investment, invest in SRI funds	
Facilities	Energy efficiency, site selection, public transit options, expanding recycling/composting efforts	
Fleets and Logistics	Reduction in fuel purchases, lease more efficient vehicles, and no-idling policies	
Investor Relations	Meet SEC guidelines, CDP reporting, integrated reporting of sustainability and financial documents, responding to shareholder resolutions regarding sustainability	
Office Manager	Purchase recycled content, create sustainable procurement policies	

Person/ Department	Examples of How Sustainability = Their Job	How to Tie It to Your Job?
Travel Coordinator	Analyze trips that could be avoided through video/teleconferencing, develop criteria to minimize business travel costs and emissions, explore price-competitive greener hotel, air, car-rental options	
Tax	Research available rebates, incentives for sustainable actions, facility upgrades	
Legal/Risk Management	Risk prevention and reduction in liability and costs	
PR and Marketing	Communicate to customers/ stakeholders on the company's sustainability plans and efforts, conduct stakeholder engagement, collect feedback and share ideas	
Sales and Business Development	Launch new lines of business, use sustainability to differentiate and sell more of your existing and new products	
Human Resources	Incorporate environmental or wellness benefits, move the department away from paper whenever possible	
Supply Chain	Create a questionnaire on supplier sustainability efforts, ask for their support in what you're doing, open lines of communication, and ask for more sustainable options	
Other Dept. 1:		
Other Dept. 2:		

Proctor & Gamble (P&G) and Patagonia are two examples of how different companies are doing this. P&G is working systematically to help all employees answer the question, "What does sustainability mean to my job?" The company is developing and delivering training in each functional area, providing information about how sustainability is part of every person's job, and helping define specific actions and roles around sustainability for every position.[10]

Patagonia, on the other hand, is doing it slightly differently. Rather than tying it to individual job functions, they incorporate environmental considerations into product design and production processes to build in the idea of "how will sustainability manifest itself through our product?" They call this "Q=E through education, which was meant to be a design challenge with the message that quality and environmental protection had to be one and the same."[11]

Train the Trainers

This might seem like common sense, but this oversight is more widespread than you'd imagine. You need to train the people who are doing the sustainability training! When working with one of our financial institution clients, we found that all company training duties were delegated to their branch managers. This made sense in that the branch managers could reach their own employees on a daily basis, but many of the branch managers lacked any formal education on how to train others. As a result, the quality of the training varied from branch to branch and important information was not being conveyed uniformly or effectively to all employees. So if you are going to ask division or department heads to train their staff, make sure that they themselves have been trained not only in the content, but also in how to deliver the material. Some are natural teachers whereas others are not. Do not skip this step.

Make It Personal

I start this chapter by saying you need to engage your employees' head, heart, and hands.

The most successful employee engagement programs engage employees not only in what they care about at work, but also in what's important to them outside of work. Do they have kids, do they like to travel? Are they hunters, fishermen, or recreationalists? Find out their hobbies and where they most fondly spend their time outside of the office, and you'll also find a personal connection and reason to engage each employee on sustainability.

I think back to a personal example when I was manning an environmental organization's booth at a charitable giving event a few years back. I had been handing out brochures and talking to people about the organization's mission when one particular, burly individual from the Washington State Department of Transportation walked up to me with his chest bulged out, smirked, and said to me, "I plow through wetlands. How does that make you feel?" A normal response could have been "Don't you realize what you are doing, you jerk?"

Instead, I quickly thought through the situation, looked at what this person was wearing, smiled, and asked him, "Hey, do you hunt or fish?" He responded, "Yeah, I hunt elk." And therein was my opening. I said to him, "Really? That's awesome. How is the hunting this season?" He opened up, and started talking fast and furiously about how the herds are so much smaller, and that the available land to hunt on is constantly being threatened by development, blaming all the suburbanites and people with second homes.

I explained to him that plowing and developing of natural areas for cookie-cutter homes was only accelerating the loss of habitat for game such as elk. A light bulb went off inside his brain as he realized the correlation and apparent conflict between his comment and his passion. His whole demeanor changed and he said to me, "I need to go talk to my boss." Then he gave me the thumbs up and walked away.

I hadn't challenged him or attacked him for what he said, but rather I embraced him about what he cared about most personally. I had earned a level of credibility in his eyes that other environmentalists had previously failed to do. Moreover, that one conversation probably had more of a direct effect on protecting the environment than any $25 or $50 contribution I could have gotten out of him.

Another good way to engage the heart is to appeal to people's parental instincts. I've never met a parent anywhere in the world who didn't want the best for their children. And we hear this over and over in the media, about parents making sacrifices for their children—whether it be helping them get a better education, a safer upbringing, or helping them save for the purchase of their first home. Just think about toxins in most of our plastic products. As adults we don't pay as much attention as we probably should, but when lead was being found in children's Christmas toys, parents engaged and started an outcry that eventually led to a ban on those types of toys.

The lesson is that you can always find a way to make a personal connection on sustainability. Each of us is unique in what motivates us, so while attempting to train and engage your employees on sustainability, make it personal.

Have Employees Create Personal Sustainability Plans

When Walmart rolled out its sustainability plan, which included an attempt to sell more than 100 million compact fluorescent light bulbs and to green its stores, it did so without first training its employees. So when customers came in and asked questions, the associates were often ill-prepared to answer their questions, let alone understand how the company's overall sustainability strategy related to their job.

The company realized that it needed to help employees understand what sustainability meant to them personally if they wanted to make it stick. It soon launched its Personal Sustainability Projects (PSP), "whose goal was to help its more than two million associates in 28 countries take everyday steps to live healthier, greener lives."[12]

The program encouraged associates to choose goals most relevant to their own lives and break them down into smaller, everyday actions—whether it's eating a salad every day, pledging to recycle more, quitting smoking, losing a few pounds, biking to work, or getting out more.[13] These goals and commitments are posted by employees' desks at Walmart headquarters in Bentonville for everyone to encourage and congratulate one another. After doing this program, employees had a better grasp of what the company was trying to accomplish because it personalized some aspect of sustainability.

Since the program began, nearly 20,000 associates have quit smoking; together, they have recycled 3 million pounds of plastic; lost more than 184,000 pounds; and walked, biked, or swam more than 1.1 million miles.[14]

We've done a similar thing at my firm, where employees set not only six-month and annual professional goals, but sustainability (health, environmental, and personal) goals as well. They commit to them and we check in on these quarterly when we do performance evaluations. It is a way for all of us to both demonstrate commitment and hold each other accountable to the changes we want to make—whether they be personal, community, or environmental. Moreover, these quarterly check-ins also provide an opportunity to just have a general dialog that often leads to ideas for continuous improvement and new service offerings. So this ends up being a true win-win-win for the business, employees, and sustainability. Here are some examples of SBC staff members' sustainability goals:

- Join a CSA.
- Telecommute once a week.
- Drop 10 pounds by June 1 and 20 pounds by year end.
- Bus every day for one month.
- Start composting at home.
- Eat only unprocessed foods for one month.
- Shop only at farmers markets.
- Practice meatless Mondays.
- Become fluent in sign language.
- Finish an Olympic triathlon.
- Feel as though I've removed stress from my work life.

Remember, the first step in any personal sustainability plan is making your own life more sustainable!

Realize that we all are probably busier and have more stress in our lives than we want. And although I'm not advocating for us all to move to completely different lives with zero stress, I'm trying to be realistic while also imploring people to take a good look at how busy their lives are and what steps they can take to take care of themselves from an emotional, wellness, health, and physical standpoint. It is not just about what you want to do, but about what you need to stop doing as well. I personally have a "stop doing" list on my desk so that I can intentionally flag those things that are life draining and time-consuming and try to instead spend the time on the things that matter to me. As Tauschia Copeland likes to say, "You determine what seeds you want to plant and harvest and what weeds you need to pull."[15]

Implementing sustainability into a company is a long, difficult slog. We are all warriors on this path, so be sure to figure out how to bring more balance, fun, and community to your life because we all need to refresh our minds and bodies more often than we do.

Recognize Different Learning Styles

Although I've spent a lot of words talking about the "what" in terms of sustainability and employee engagement, an important point that is often missed is that you also need to tailor the training to different audiences and various learning styles.

As I've learned through my teaching, how you deliver the content might be sometimes more important than the content itself. It's important to acknowledge and understand that introverts and extroverts process information differently. You need to take this into account when developing your employee training and engagement efforts around sustainability.

The following is according to the Jung theory of personality:[16]

Extroverts:

- Enjoy generating energy and ideas from other people. They prefer socializing and working in groups.

- Learn from teaching others how to solve a problem, appreciate collaborative work, and employ problem-based learning.

- Enjoy working with others in groups and learn best through direct experience.

- Are willing to lead, participate, and offer opinions regardless of experience.

- Jump right in without guidance from others.

Introverts:

- Prefer to solve problems on their own and work alone.

- Enjoy generating energy and ideas from internal sources, such as brainstorming, personal reflection, and theoretical exploration.

- Listen, watch, and reflect. They enjoy quiet, solitary work.

- Like to think about things and choose to observe others before attempting a new skill.

- Prefer to read materials beforehand so that they have time to process and reflect on discussion points.

Understanding these distinctions is especially important if you are the one delivering the training. If it is in-person, and you are the instructor, you're more likely to have a tendency to be more extroverted, and your style will likely resonate better with extroverts. That's why it's important to be aware of your delivery as well as provide alternatives such as online learning or posting PowerPoint online before a class so that those with a different learning style can maximize their ability to process the information in their desired environment.

Every employee engagement program should factor in and include something for each of the five learning styles, shown in Table 8.2, and the different personality types, shown in Table 8.3. The take-away is that just as you need to tailor the message to what people care about in their job function, you should vary your sustainability training across these various learning styles. If you do so, you'll have a greater chance of success of reaching everyone within your firm.

Table 8.2 Learner Types

	Optimal Environment	Ineffective Environment
Auditory Learners	Listening to things being explained Reciting information out loud	Noises might distract, resulting in a need for a quiet place
Visual Learners	Looking at graphics, watching a demonstration, or reading	Listening to an explanation
Hands-on Learners (Touch/Physical)	"Hands-on" experiences Writing and taking notes	Sitting still
Verbal Learners	Using words (writing and in speech) Dialogue (listening, speaking, and repeating)	Working independently Sitting quietly to think things through
Logical Learners (Reasoning)	Asking questions and investigating Solving problems	Being asked to do something without knowing the context or having the ability to ask questions

Table 8.3 Personality Types

Social (Interpersonal)	Solitary (Intrapersonal)
Enjoy learning in groups or with other people	Like to work alone and use self-study
Care about people and their feelings	Are aware of their strengths and weaknesses, moods, and motivations
Approach people with empathy and like to teach others	Are self-motivated but need their own quiet space most of the time
Recognize differences among people and value their points of view	Prefer to study individually
Are sensitive to facial expressions, gestures, and voice	Learn best through observing and listening

Different Leadership Types for Different Trainings

Realize that different trainings and employee engagement strategies are required depending on who is in the room. For example:

- Introverted leaders are more effective than extroverted leaders when dealing with proactive employees.

- Extroverted leaders are more effective when dealing with employees who tend to be passive.

- Introverted leaders are more likely to apply suggestions made by employees, and are less likely to modify these suggestions and make them their own.

- Introverted leaders are more likely to let employees try out new strategies and spend more time listening to those whom they lead.

- Extroverted leaders tend to be better at inspiring otherwise uninspired troops but are more likely to try to put their own mark on whatever work employees come up with.

Empowered Employees

Employees need to feel and be empowered, but if issues of hierarchy exist, this can lead to employees not knowing whether they should take initiative or not. If uncertainty is present, employees are going to be more risk averse and less willing to offer up new, innovative ideas. This is a major barrier to engaging employees around sustainability because your employees need to feel empowered, especially your front-line employees, since they are the ones with the answers.

These three things help to empower employees and avoid issues of hierarchy:

- Employees need to know what is expected of them and why.

- You need to set the framework as to what you are trying to do and also set the constraints. After you do this, they will figure out the best way to get there.

- If employees have ownership, it won't feel like the company's idea; they will make it their own and appreciate the autonomy and freedom they've been given.

All of these are important because you want your front-line employees to be the ones to identify opportunities for sustainability improvements; they live and breathe their area of expertise every day. After they have been trained and empowered to use their "sustainability lens," they will begin to see things differently and offer up ideas about changes to how things are done on a day-to-day basis.

Empower through Expectation

Eli Reich, CEO of Alchemy Goods, says, "I tell employees what I'm looking for and why, and then I try and get out of the way because they usually come up with a better, more creative solution than I could think of. I tell them what the list of guidelines are, whether it is the price, quality, aesthetic, or time, and trust that they'll figure out the process to achieve it with those constraints."[17]

Reich believes in employing what Jim Collins states in his book *Good to Great,* that you want to develop a system with clear constraints, but one that also empowers employees with autonomy, responsibility, and freedom to get the job done within that system.

BUSINESS CASE: WASTE REDUCTION

3M's Pollution Prevention Pays (3P) "rewards employees who have breakthrough ideas for eliminating pollution at its source. Since its inception, nearly 6,000 3P projects have prevented the creation of more than 2.2 billion pounds of pollutants and generated savings of nearly $1 billion, counting only first-year savings from the projects."[18]

Ownership in Their Job

Today's workforce, contrary to the mind-set of their parents' generation, craves autonomy and wants to own the work they are doing. Whether they are a front-line employee, a middle manager, or in the C-Suite, they want to be given the freedom and support to innovate and be responsible for their area of influence, no matter the size. Empowering each employee to exert influence over their specific work area increases the chance that someone will find a process improvement.

For example, at a dairy plant in Argentina, employees "own" their two to five square meters of work space—and are charged with improving processes in their small area of the plant.

Another example is from one of my legal clients. Their office manager, who also led the green team, was said to carry more clout than senior management around sustainability. Because he controlled what happened in the office from a facility and purchasing capacity, he took ownership and just pushed sustainability into everything he did on a day-to-day basis. When he couldn't get more budget for 100% recycled paper, he put all the printers and copiers to default to duplex so that less paper was needed, and used the savings to go ahead and order the 100% recycled content. Because he met his budget, nobody asked any questions. He took ownership of sustainability wherever he could within the firm.

It's important that you recognize that, from time to time, there will be failures. Sometimes the lessons learned from a failure can lead to a brilliant new idea, and other times they won't. Accept this fact. Although you'll obviously want to work to avoid failures, realize that if you fully empower your employees around sustainability with ownership of their tasks, even with a few small setbacks your company will end up way ahead in the long run.

Shared Ownership

This example might seem extreme to some, but a technique used by Terra Anderson when she was at a previous employer was to share the ownership of the ideas. They experimented with an idea where her group of senior managers had to say: "Yes, I will unequivocally accept your recommendation" to their employees. This meant that senior managers and employees were both on the hook for an idea because a recommendation would automatically be accepted.

"This forced everyone to share information more freely, and discuss problems and work out solutions before it got to the recommendation phase. Managers and employees both had to think more systematically and ask each other tougher questions because they both were 100% responsible for any change. This not only led to greater empowerment, but a better understanding of the product, process, and better decisions"[19] because they were forced to get things right the first time around.

Intrapreneurship

Coined in the 1980s by Gifford Pinchot, co-founder and president of Bainbridge Graduate Institute, an "intrapreneur" is an entrepreneur inside of a company. This is someone who "takes direct responsibility for turning an idea or invention into a profitable finished product or service through assertive risk taking and internal innovation."[20]

There are two sides to intrapreneurship: how to get started as an intrapreneur and how to create a work culture that encourages an authentic, proactive pursuit of intrapreneurship around sustainability. The goal is to stimulate the creativity, spirit of innovation, and entrepreneurial value-creation mind-set of employees to further support your engagement efforts.

With intrapreneurship, one or more employees assume the leadership responsibility, financial accountability, risk, and operational challenges of creating business value through the development of an innovative technology, product, or service within a company.[21] Companies need these types of people to address many of the challenges sustainability brings because the most difficult issues have yet to be tackled, so innovative and disruptive thinking is needed.

One reason why intrapreneurship is so important is that big companies are largely averse to ideas from the outside. This means that sometimes the only way to change big business is from within, and that is by using the company as the test lab for intrapreneurship. This will help develop a culture of intrapreneurship, which will be essential to helping your company implement sustainability because it will enable the creativity and innovation of your employees to come forth.

"Contrary to popular belief, the brains of an organization are equally distributed across a company—about one per person."[22]

Starting Out

Intrapreneurs have to trust their instincts and often be trailblazers where there is no road ahead.

At first, as an intrapreneur, you will want the time and space to develop your idea and generate buy-in, because you don't want to unveil your idea until you have run it by a few people, worn off the rough edges, and garnered some support. Be sure to engage people who can benefit from your idea, as well as people who can help you spot land mines along the way. By doing this, the intrapreneur can avoid pitfalls and pick up some valuable wisdom. Moreover, you want to test your idea and iterate it quickly, because you don't want to spend all your time in the planning stage. "Faster learning beats better planning,"[23] so test ideas and iterate, iterate, iterate.

Pinchot has witnessed that after you have tested your idea a few times, you need to start sharing your ideas more broadly. "Holding on to your ideas close to your chest in fear that someone will steal them guarantees that they will not happen. Sharing them with people who can advise you and help you to implement them has a much better chance of success."[24]

The Importance of a Sponsor

Intrapreneurs need sponsors. They can open doors, help give the idea credibility, and provide a bit of protection to the intrapreneur if all the ideas don't pan out exactly as planned. Most important, if they are in a senior enough position, they can also help you navigate the internal politics and budget structure of the organization.

To recruit an intrapreneurship sponsor for your sustainability idea, first seek advice from someone in the company you want to work with, whom you could learn from, and who might have some alignment with what you are attempting to do. Then build your relationship by getting that person to help you. People love giving advice and mentoring whenever they can. Feed that. The relationship will strengthen until the time comes when you are trying to develop the idea more concretely, and the sponsor believes that you are the right person to accomplish what you are setting out to do.

Treat your sponsor like your own internal stakeholder and remember to keep the flow of conversation two ways by giving progress updates and feedback. Tell your sponsor how she helped make your idea better, what changes have been made or improvements have been completed since the last time you talked, and where you are headed next. Be sure to be transparent and share both the good and the bad news because the sponsor should hear that news from you directly and might have suggestions for other ways to tackle the issue. All of this is essential because if you can get commitment from a sponsor or team of sponsors, especially at the management level, they'll be more bought in and less likely to let you or your idea fail.

Nurturing an Intrapreneurship Environment

There are several key elements to creating an environment for intrapreneurship, including these:

1. Realize that ideas change and evolve. Things don't always turn out according to plan. The more innovative/disruptive the idea, the more learning that will need to take place, and the idea might change, grow, or pivot accordingly.

2. Ideas without intrapreneurs are just that. They add little value. You need people who will own and operationalize the idea.

3. Most of the success has to do with the person and the team involved with the project versus the quality of the idea.

4. All managers have the ability to support intrapreneuring around sustainability. They just might need to couch it under different wording—continuous improvement, innovation, efficiency, risk management, and so on.

5. The quality of the relationships of the people *within* an intrapreneurial team is equal to or more important than the quality and titles of the people *on* the team. Too often people focus on the titles and skip over the fact that if a team gets along, they are more likely to be able to overcome the obstacles and innovate around them. And if they don't get along, the opposite is true.

6. Things will take twice as long as you think, and the more innovative the idea, the more flexible people will have to be with their budgets.

As mentioned previously, there are going to be naysayers and obstacles along the way, but knowing all of these facets ahead of time will help you create a successful atmosphere within your firm for intrapreneurship around social and environmental issues. Or, as I like to call it, sustainapreneurship.

Employees are the least engaged that they've been in the past 20 years, and the best way to authentically engage your employees' heads, hearts, and hands is through sustainability. The business benefits are clear: An engaged workforce is more productive, is more profitable, performs higher quality work, and the employees themselves tend to garner higher satisfaction.

Lessons Learned

The following are key takeaways from the "Engaging Employees Around Sustainability" chapter:

- When training employees, recognize the different learning styles and realize how best to communicate with and engage both introverts and extroverts.

- Tie sustainability to people's jobs and don't forget to connect with employees on a personal/human level.

- Empower your employees. Tell them what you are trying to do and why, tie it back to the business case, and then get out of their way.

- Cultivate a culture of intrapreneurship, because many of today's greatest social and environmental challenges will need the creativity and innovation of an engaged workforce.

9

Systems, Decision Making, and Internal Alignment

A fter you have the employees engaged and trained, you need to prioritize your actions, build your systems, and develop your decision-making processes and policies to sustain momentum for the long term.

Prioritize Your Actions

Develop an implementation plan that targets those areas that have the greatest sustainability impact and prioritize by opportunity for improvement and business benefit.

If we all arranged and clarified our work around this principle, and cut out everything else, companies could see vastly improved social, environmental, and financial performance.

Then after you have prioritized those focus areas, put people in charge who are highly motivated with the skills to get the job done. There is nothing more frustrating than spending the time and money on a sustainability baseline, prioritizing actions, and then handing it off to a highly passionate person who lacks the skills to get the job done.

As Ben Packard says, "Put smart, trusted people on the case or buy talent and make it happen. Go after it because you'll either win fast or fail fast."[1]

Incorporate into Decision Making

The most effective way to implement sustainability is to incorporate sustainability into your corporate decision making. Although this might seem radical to some, it's actually quite simple in execution.

The company needs to arm its management with the policies, processes, procedures, and decision-making criteria to make sure that things stick, because implementation won't just happen on its own.

As the author, speaker, and sustainability champion Bob Willard states, "Management must tie sustainability back to business case and vision, and put in place the policies to ensure that social and environmental impacts are factored into corporate decision making,"[2] whether that is through a balanced scorecard or some other method your company uses to make decisions. You don't have to start out by making social and environmental criteria weighted equally with financial, operational, or brand considerations, but just by giving some points to these criteria, you will change the discussion and mind-set of those making the decisions.

For example, corporate America didn't just ask its employees to be "more aware" of sexual harassment or to try to hire "more diverse" employees. They had to create policies and procedures to stamp out sexual harassment. They also had to change their decision-making criteria to support positive change by putting into place policies that would lead to a more diverse workplace.

The same is true with sustainability. But be forewarned: You can expect some pushback because people are worried that you are asking them to put social and environmental factors above the overall health of the business. For example, I often hear the following comment when we first broach the discussion around sustainability: "We aren't going to change our entire business model just to be more green!" This attitude is common, whether it is a travel company whose employees are concerned that after they begin to think about carbon emissions they'll be asked to stop all air travel, or an apparel provider whose employees worry that if they incorporate sustainability into their designs, they'll be forced to create a green shoe that nobody will buy.

This is the type of misunderstanding that is out there, and you can be sure that somewhere on the management team or board, somebody has this concern.

For example, I remember sitting in a citizens' advisory meeting in 2012 when we were discussing how a local municipal airport could improve its sustainability performance. The airport had huge costs and impacts associated with its storm-water management. However, when we began the conversation about sustainability and ways to reduce storm-water discharge, a member of the advisory committee blared out, "We have to be careful. We can't just go about becoming some green airport that will be too cost-prohibitive that no pilot can land here!" This is the type of mind-set that you'll be up against. This individual totally missed the fact that when the expenses associated with this storm-water runoff were reduced, the savings would actually be passed on to the pilots in the form of lower landing fees and slightly reduced leases for their hangars, while simultaneously lowering the environmental impact of the airport.

HSBC (The Hong Kong and Shanghai Banking Corporation) has successfully integrated sustainability into their decision making by explicitly adding "sustainability aspects to their balanced scorecard's strategic management system, ensuring all senior managers worldwide monitor energy management, carbon emissions, water use, and waste reduction."[3]

Figure 9.1 shows an example of a tool that my firm uses to incorporate both social and environmental criteria into decision making with clients. This is a variation on the balanced scorecard because it uses five categories instead of four. This example breaks down decisions quantitatively by objectives and targets so that you get actual measurable numbers. It also provides a space to qualitatively demonstrate the measures and initiatives you will put in place to achieve them. Feel free to copy it or make it your own.

Financial: Revenue, Expense, Cost Savings, Payback

Objective	Measure	Target	Initiative
Increase revenue from new products & services	% revenue from new products and services	15% by 2015	Marketing to new target markets
Achieve cost savings in internal processes	% reduction in costs of goods sold	10% reduction by 2015	Identify cost-saving measures in internal process across all lines of business
Implement sustainability initiatives for $ benefit	ROI of each initiative; # of new initiatives	Payback of 3 years or less; 5 new initiatives by 2013	Allow a longer payback for sustainability initiatives

Brand: Customers, Investor, Reputation, Supplier/Vendor

Objective	Measure	Target	Initiative
Gain new customers	% new customers from year-to-year sales	5% by 2013; 10% by 2015	Target nontraditional corporate customers
Increase market value	Annual market cap	15% increase in market cap by 2015	Share company best practices with investors & financial analysts
Attract SRI investors	% investors affiliated with SRI	5% by 2015	Market to SRI investors & stakeholders
Enhance reputation with suppliers	% supplier screens passed (incl. sustainability)	100% by 2013	Engage with suppliers on new sustainability-related supply chain requirements

Figure 9.1 Goals and objectives (continues on next page).

⚙ Operational: Process/Procedures, Training, Human & Physical Resources

Objective	Measure	Target	Initiative
Funding for key capital process improvements	% budget allocated	3% of R&D and Operation budget	Identify and prioritize key capital process improvements
Train all employees in sustainability and cost-saving opportunities	% employees trained in sustainability	100% by 2013	Sustainability training for current employees and embedding sustainability in new-hire training

👥 Social: Employees, Community

Objective	Measure	Target	Initiative
Be a recognized best place to work	Placement in the Fortune 100 Best Places to Work	Top 50 by 2014	Identify new opportunities for workplace productivity and work/life balance
Be an active contributor to the surrounding community	Community donations	Donations in every community we operate	All employees take advantage of existing contribution opportunities
	Recognitions	3 awards in next 3 years	Apply for relevant awards
	Volunteer hours	Volunteering in every community we operate	All employees take advantage of existing volunteer opportunities

🌲 Environmental: Resource Use, Pollution/Waste

Objective	Measure	Target	Initiative
Reduce GHG emissions	Per employee GHG emissions	10% reduction by 2015	Launch alternative commuting program
Increase use of renewable energy	% energy from renewables	15% by 2015	Purchase RECs

Incorporate into Systems

After you've integrated sustainability into your decision-making process, you next need systems and processes to support those efforts.

Systems and policies ensure that actions are embedded in how people do their day-to-day jobs, and they move the organization to the next level so that a company isn't reliant on a single person or leader to inspire people. Systems enable sustainability to become a norm in how the company operates.

There are various systems that companies are using to embed sustainability and I've listed a few different ways in the following subsections. The three most common are Kaizen, LEAN, and SMS (Sustainability Management Systems).

Kaizen

Kaizen is a Japanese concept that refers to a philosophy and process based on *continuous improvement*.[4] W. Edward Deming, among others, started the quality movement in the United States called Total Quality Management (TQM), which is the same concept as Japanese Kaizen. It has traditionally been used in manufacturing, engineering, and business management, but the model has expanded into community engagement, governance, and anything where a critical eye, awareness, and openness to change result in efficiency and progress. Sustainability is all about continuous improvement because it is a journey with no end, so a Kaizen approach is applicable and attractive to many companies.

In the Kaizen system, if something isn't performing, it is up to the entire team to get each member a piece to reach optimal performance. Teams are meant to stop and look at issues together, and solve problems holistically, from shop employees to executives alike. This is important because many sustainability issues require holistic, systems thinking so that a fix or solution on, say, carbon emissions, doesn't lead to a solution that causes burdensome extra hours to staff or increases water usage.

What are the business results of Kaizen? Toyota is one of the most successful companies in history, and Kaizen has been a major component of its success. For example, while most car manufacturers would keep their lines moving during the manufacturing process to produce as many vehicles as possible, when Toyota recognizes a problem, it stops the entire line to fix the issue, even if it can cost thousands of dollars a minute. The result is that it makes fewer vehicles with defects, and the company avoids many other costs and environmental impacts associated with fixing the issues after the fact. And as I write this, know that I'm well aware that like any car company, Toyota has faults that have led to recalls, but it's their use of the Kaizen process I want you to remember.

Sam Walton, the founder of Walmart, is also known for Kaizen. Everywhere he went, he would ask employees on the spot, "What can we do better for our customers?" He was committed to continuous improvement, and he showed that employee opinions were valued by making sure that direct action was taken to meet recommendations. Kaizen is not a new idea; it can be a valuable system and mind-set to employees when they are implementing sustainability.

LEAN

LEAN is another system that practices minimizing waste while maximizing customer value. Anytime you are reducing waste, cutting down on pollution, and improving process efficiency, you are acting in a more sustainable manner. These are the seven traditional types of waste that LEAN focuses on:[5]

1. Defects

2. Overproduction

3. Inventories

4. Overprocessing

5. Unnecessary motion of employees

6. Unnecessary transport and handling of goods

7. Waiting

Each company can find their own list of waste within and around their business processes and look to reduce it whenever possible. When you do this, teach your employees to look for things that do not add value to the end consumer,[6] and anything you find that removes waste is positive.

LEAN is typically thought of in manufacturing, but it is also used in service-oriented businesses, when evaluating Purpose, Processes, and People. Reducing waste and waste of time in each of these areas speaks to efficiency, as well as customer and employee satisfaction, so put in place systems to enforce this ethic because by doing so you'll likely be improving your social, environmental, and financial performance at the same time.

Sustainability Management Systems (SMS)

A Sustainability Management System is another set of processes and procedures. More comprehensive than a traditional Environmental Management System (EMS), an SMS has a broader focus on social, financial, and environmental performance. Traditionally, an SMS follows the recognized Plan, Do, Check, Act system for continuous improvement:[7]

> **PLAN:** Establish the objectives and processes necessary to deliver results to meet goals/targets.
>
> **DO:** Implement the plan, execute the process, make the product.
>
> **CHECK:** Check and record progress.
>
> **ACT:** Take preventive and corrective action, make changes to the SMS as needed.

3M uses an SMS that integrates sustainability into the design of new products all the way through the products' entire lifecycle. The company's Life Cycle Management process "reviews every new product for all environmental, health, safety, and energy impacts from raw material acquisition through manufacturing to customer use/disposal."[8]

IBM uses a similar system. It calls it an EMS, but the implementation, goal, and desired results are the same. According to Wayne Balta, head of Corporate Environmental Affairs at IBM, "the company uses its environmental management system as the foundation for policy deployment, practice management, goal setting, decision making, and data capture. IBM uses the technology to embed environmental strategies into all areas of the business, from R & D to operations to end-of-life product disposal."[9]

Sustainability Reporting

There is also a movement toward integrated reporting, which is the idea of companies creating one report for shareholders and stakeholders that combines a company's financial, social, and environmental data in one place. This can become a valuable management tool and process for executives and the board by providing both quarterly and annual milestones to truly access sustainability and financial performance at the same time.

Currently there are more than 90 companies and organizations testing out the new integrated reporting standards from the IIRC as part of its business network, which is following the leadership of Novo Nordisk, one of the first companies to create an integrated report a few years back. SASB is also in the development process for industry-specific integrated reporting that includes SEC guidelines.

Additionally, PUMA recently created an environmental profit and loss (P & L) statement and became the first global company in the world to put an economic value on the GHG and water impacts of its supply chain through the production of its sports shoes and apparel products.[10] For example, "the economic valuation of its environmental impact revealed that PUMA would have to pay 8 million Euros to nature for services rendered to its core operations such as offices, warehouses and stores, alone."[11] This helped demonstrate the potentially negative impact the business activity had on natural services. It did this to give management a tool for better understanding these impacts both financially and environmentally, and PUMA is looking to expand this to include social aspects and create a social P & L account in the near future. Both of these are other systems that companies can incorporate to better track and manage their sustainability performance over time.

Other Models and Tools

There are also software solutions that help companies understand the sustainability impacts of their product decisions while still in the design stage. Most are for the built environment, including Autodesk's building information modeling (BIM) and Kieran Timberlake's Real Time Environmental Impact Tool (RTEI),[12] that evaluate the embodied energy, carbon, water, and other environmental impacts of the materials and products being considered.

Other Sustainability-Related Systems

Following are some other examples of companies that have developed innovative internal systems to support their companies' overall sustainability objectives toward carbon, water, and energy reductions.

- Microsoft's internal carbon trading program tracks data on energy use and air travel for its 90,000 employees in 100-plus global offices and data centers and charges a fee for every ton of carbon it produces. The price is set to reflect not only the price for the consumption but also the additional cost of offsetting the carbon emissions associated with the activity. This money, traded internally, is used to fund renewable energy and offset projects.

- The company WSP has a Personal Allowance Carbon Trading (PACT) incentive scheme.[13] Designed to help employees manage their personal carbon impacts outside of the office, it gives participants a yearly personal carbon allowance and access to an online portal to track their home energy usage and travel activities. Bonuses are then given at the end of the year if emissions fall below the overall threshold set by WSP.

A few other systems to consider at later stages of your sustainability adoption curve are listed here:

- The concept of Design for Environment (DfE) encourages companies to select safer chemicals and technologies in producing products so that they can be redesigned to be broken apart and reused or to naturally break down and not negatively impact the environment.

- Biomimicry uses the lessons of nature to solve human and technical problems. The idea is to mimic how nature would work and use a natural solution for a chemical, mechanical, operational, or technical issue. For example, Michael Phelps made famous a swimsuit that is made up of miniature scales that mimics shark skin, and the most common example is of course Velcro, which mimics burrs. The idea is to use natural solutions to reduce your company's environmental and social impact.[14]

- Cradle-to-cradle is a design process in which products are developed in a way that allows them to return to their original state, or as close to it as possible, at the end of their usable life. Most products are currently designed from cradle to grave (i.e., landfill), and what cradle-to-cradle is espousing is an infinite loop in which the product can be put back into use as a raw material for the same product over and over. An example of this is Interface carpet tiles, which have been designed to be ground up and reused as raw material for future carpet tiles.

After considering these different methods and examples, take a moment with this systems thinking activity to consider your own company systems and how they incorporate sustainability.

ACTIVITY 20: QUESTIONS TO PROMOTE SYSTEMS THINKING

The following questions will prompt your thinking into a systems approach:

- In what ways could your company better incorporate sustainability into its existing systems?

- Which of the systems elements outlined earlier could work well within either your company or a particular department? Specify where.

- How could you use biomimicry or cradle-to-cradle thinking in your product/service design?

- Where have you already tried to tackle waste within your company (materials, process, time) that could be replicated elsewhere?

- Many companies claim to have a culture of continuous improvement but don't actually educate employees in Kaizen or incorporate this into new employee orientation. Is this the case with your firm?

Investment and Procurement Policies

Making a blanket statement that all procurement and investment decisions should incorporate sustainability sounds like an easy and attractive thing to do. The reality is that incorporating sustainability into every policy and procedure is actually a difficult task that requires intentionality. This section maps out how that can be done.

Sustainable Investment Policies

Putting your money where your mouth is often is harder than it should be. When it comes to investing your cash and short-term investments into anything other than what the company has traditionally done, a lot of convincing needs to take place. That's why I went to such lengths in Chapter 1, "The Business Case," to describe the returns that SRI investments have been receiving.

This is where you'll want to be eventually, but for many companies, this requires approval by the Board's Financial and Audit Committees. There will be great hesitation at first and people will be worried that they'll be sacrificing a financial return or violating their fiduciary responsibility if you shift investments and deposits into an SRI fund or more sustainable bank. Therefore, try a phased approach and just move a small portion of the company's total investments into SRI funds in the first year, say, between 1% and 5%. Then work over a three-, five-, or seven-year plan to shift to 100%. After skeptics see that the returns meet their objectives, their resistance will fade and you can shift to 100% sustainable deposits and investments. Or if you want to divest from fossil fuels, realize you aren't talking about divesting from everywhere, but actually closer to just 40 companies worldwide. Although it seems daunting, it's not as tough as it seems.

Sustainable Procurement Policies

"Making change around sustainability starts with your pocketbook and where you spend your money."

Another way to put your money where your mouth is, is through your procurement policies. Embedding sustainability into all of your purchasing decisions is a way to push sustainability further through your value chain and ensure that the dollars you spend are in alignment with your vision and goals. It also begins to encourage the type of behavior in your suppliers that you are seeking to accomplish. Moreover, it will ensure that you start with the right product with the lowest environmental and societal footprint at the beginning, rather than trying to weed it out in your own processes. This does not mean paying 20% more for a product just to be green. What it does mean is adding sustainability to your selection criteria, and maybe being willing to pay a slightly higher premium to support the environment or local community providers, but, most important, informing them of your intentions so that they can partner with you to provide a product or service option that meets your financial, quality, and sustainability needs all at once. I go into great detail at the end of this chapter with an activity to help you create your own policy, but you want to set clear expectations and detail how the policy will be monitored and enforced.

Policies/Systems Provide Protection If Sponsor Leaves

One reason I spent so much time on this chapter about systems and policies is to ensure that your programs will continue if/when a key leader or supporter leaves the organization. You want executive sponsorship, but there is always the question of what to do if they leave. That is exactly why you need to work diligently to embed sustainability into not only the culture and ethic of your employees, but also the systems that support it.

I've witnessed firsthand a few examples where a company had relied too heavily on specific individuals, and when the executives who most supported sustainability left, the programs stalled, lost momentum, or completely stopped. In each of these cases, they had not gotten to the point where they had fully implemented systems and policies throughout the company on sustainability.

Molly Ray, former global responsibility manager at Pan Pacific Hotels, says she found that "sustainability needs stability. It needs process."[15] To add, Terra Anderson has found that "leaders will move on, so without process, skeptics and naysayers can always try and wait them out."[16]

Therefore, while working to support the individuals leading the charge, be sure to focus on supporting the process and systems that are necessary to make sustainability stick for the long term. Activity 21 is a sustainable procurement activity as an example of one of the policies and systems you'll want to put in place.

ACTIVITY 21: SUSTAINABLE PROCUREMENT GUIDELINES

RFPs or Supplier Questionnaires Statement

Following is a sample statement to include in all your RFPs and supplier questionnaires that explains the reason behind these new questions on sustainability and why it's important to your organization.

We are committed to sustainability and prefer to work with customers that are demonstrating their commitment to the environment and society. Please detail all the ways your company is incorporating sustainability into your products and day-to-day business operations.

Procurement Policies and Supplier Focus Areas

You obviously will want to craft these to your company and industry, but I've detailed ten focus areas that are common to most industries with specific questions you can use or build off of. Tailor them to your company and think through how they can support your own business case, in addition to your social and environmental performance.

Environmental	1. Resource efficiency (energy, water, renewable)
	2. Waste reduction and minimized packaging
	3. Product take-back and reuse
	4. Greenhouse gas emissions
	5. Recycled content
	6. Toxicity and product safety
Social/Community	7. Diversity and inclusion
	8. Sourcing (fair trade, shipping miles, etc.)
	9. Fair labor practices
	10. Community involvement

Sample Sustainability Procurement Policies and Supplier Questions

Following are a few examples and questions to include in your supplier questionnaires. Utilize the top-ten focus areas described previously as a guide to creating your own sustainability procurement policies and supplier questionnaires.

General

- Does your company have a sustainability or CSR policy?

- Have you performed a sustainability audit? If yes, please provide a copy.

- Has your company formally conducted an assessment of the risks and opportunities from social and environmental issues?

- Has your company formally set and documented its sustainability goals and targets? If so, how does your company report or track progress?

Waste Reduction and Minimized Packaging

Policy: All vendors should demonstrate a commitment to minimizing packaging and reducing waste.

- Has your company performed a waste or packaging audit?

- What steps have been taken to reduce waste and packaging?

- Are there more environmentally friendly packaging alternatives to what is currently used?

- Can the packaging be reused or sent back to the supplier?

- How has packaging been optimized (lower ratio of packaging to product weight, bulk, combined shipments, refillable/reusable packaging, etc.)?

Toxicity and Product Safety

Policy: Choose products that do not contain harmful toxins (carcinogens, hormone disruptors, phosphates, etc.).

- Is the product free from toxic/hazardous ingredients that would require special disposal (e.g., mercury)?

- Does the product meet Restriction on Hazardous Substances (RoHS) guidelines?

- Is the product less polluting during use compared to competing products (e.g., nontoxic, organic, biodegradable cleaners)?

- Would you allow your own children to be exposed to your products directly?

- Could a nontoxic product potentially lower workers' compensation costs and reduce the number of sick days for your employees?

Sourcing (Fair Trade, Shipping Miles, Etc.)

Policy: Source ethically, fair trade, and do no harm to fragile ecosystems.

- Are your products ethically and environmentally sourced (FSC, fair trade, etc.)

- Are any biodiversity hot spots or cultural heritage sites negatively affected by your sourcing choices?

- In what ways are you working to limit shipping emissions of your products (biofuels, local sourcing, etc.)?

- What certificates or verifications can you provide to guarantee the source/origin of your materials?

Take these examples and build out sustainable procurement systems and policies for your own company.

Some Lessons Learned from Implementing Sustainable Procurement Policies

Often, to get suppliers and managers to participate in sustainable procurement practices, all you have to do is ask. You'd be surprised at what you might find. Your supplier or vendor might already have a more sustainable product but just might have never been asked about it. The following is a list of examples to get an idea of what each group might already be doing:

1. You might have an internal ally at the vendor. Usually there is someone who has been arguing or trying to get the company to improve the sustainability performance of their products, but without customers' demand, the vendor hasn't been able to make that case to management. Just asking for the change might get the vendor on board.

2. If the vendor cannot meet your requirements, they might ask for some time (up to a year) to meet the requirements. If you have to, give that to them, but hold them to this timeline.

3. They might say they can do it for the same price, but they just might need a longer commitment. One of our financial clients asked their paper supplier if they could provide 100% recycled paper at the same cost as their current virgin paper. They said that they could, but only if our client would commit to a two-year contract instead of an annual one.

4. If they say no, unless you are in a very specialized industry where there is only one supplier or vendor in the entire industry, there will be alternatives or someone else will step up pretty quickly.

If You Still Hear No

Combining forces with others in your industry or other companies that use the same vendor is another approach that has seen success. We've done this for our clients; when we've noticed that two or more of our clients were running into resistance from the same vendor, we've introduced them to one another, and with their combined pressure on the vendor, the ball has gotten rolling.

Align Philanthropy and Community with Sustainability

Companies tend to miss out on a major opportunity to leverage all of their various sustainability efforts by failing to combine their sustainability program with their philanthropy, community volunteerism, and other outreach efforts. This is typically because these programs are run by different departments, with different people, with different priorities and responsibilities. Table 9.1 shows where these efforts typically get stove piped.

Table 9.1 Where Sustainability Fits in Each Department

Topic Area	Department
Community relations with supplier	Supply chain/merchandising
Philanthropy and community donations	Foundation or community affairs
Employee volunteerism and pro bono work	HR
Sustainability/CSR	CSR department or green team
Green product benefits	Design and R & D
Actions the company has taken internally	PR
Marketing to green consumers	Marketing and sales

Companies are wasting thousands of dollars in fragmented efforts around sustainability, whereas if they were properly aligned, they could leverage the full assets of the company and more easily measure the impact.

The Move to Strategic Philanthropy

"Most corporate philanthropy professionals say they are under increasing pressure to align corporate philanthropy and giving with business objectives,"[17] says the Council on Foundations.

Back in the 1980s and 1990s, most companies thought of sustainability as simply philanthropy and community volunteerism. Being a "good corporate citizen" meant giving money to the communities to which they belonged or using it to diffuse NGO concerns over their social and environmental practices. That has all changed due to increased pressure to align philanthropy with business objectives, a reduction in giving from the economic recession, and changing stakeholder needs. They understand the business case for sustainability and thus are switching from the mind-set of "giving away" money to community organizations to the idea of "investing" to meet the company's social, environmental, and business goals.

Companies that strategically line up their giving efforts with the sustainability and business goals of the company are gaining benefits such as these:

- Increased brand value and recognition

- Higher employee engagement, attraction, and performance

- Stronger supply chain and business with other companies

- Improved community and stakeholder relations

Additionally, by doing so, the company is providing the following:

- A clear, mutually reinforcing message to stakeholders

- A better understanding as to how all the various activities add up

- A transparent way for stakeholders to see that the company is putting its money where its mouth is—that it is walking the talk

Seven key trends have emerged:

1. **Focused Giving:** Aligning philanthropic efforts with business objectives, sustainability actions, and the mission of the company.

2. **Workplace Giving:** Connecting employee giving with company sustainability goals.

3. **Customers as Co-Creators:** Partnering with customers to select organizations to give to.

4. **Involving Supply Chain:** Investing in the communities of the suppliers to enhance their quality of life and to gain better market intelligence of the markets they are operating in.

5. **Issue Targeting:** Concentrating dollars and pro bono work toward one specific issue.

6. **Aligning with Volunteer Efforts:** Supporting the places where employees are volunteering with corporate donations.

7. **Impact Giving:** Rather than spreading donations around to a number of organizations, they are targeting funding toward fewer organizations, with larger grants that can have an impact.

Listed here are a few examples of the strategic philanthropic trends around sustainability.

Focused Giving

Pearson, one of the largest publishers in the world, including the Financial Times, Penguin, and Random House, realized that paper is its largest environmental impact area. Therefore, the company has focused its corporate giving, along with its purchase of carbon offsets, toward organizations working to prevent deforestation such as the Children's Tropical Forests in the U.K., the Nature Conservancy in the U.S., and the World Wildlife Fund's Forest and Trade Network globally. This offsets their impact and ensures a sustainable paper supply.

Involving Suppliers

Green Mountain Coffee is utilizing its philanthropic efforts to help build a more resilient supply chain. It supports nonprofit organizations working to help suppliers receive a fair price for their product, make business decisions that support their families, and build healthy, environmentally sound communities. According to Green Mountain, they do this because they are focusing on the biggest challenges in their coffee-farming communities, such as food security, access to water, education, and healthcare.[18]

Their belief is that while they are doing this, it is also helping to build brand awareness and equity, strengthen customer loyalty, and increase sales in key regions, all while ensuring their coffee supply.[19]

Customers as Co-Creators

Nau, a retailer focused on integrating economic, environmental, and social factors into their business model, has committed to giving 2% of every sale to humanitarian and environmental organizations. Customers get to choose where that money goes and they are encouraged to select from five organizations.

Crossroads Trading, a Seattle thrift shop, gives customers a token when they do not use a bag for their purchase. There are up to ten slots at the register for different charities, and the customer gets to choose where Crossroads Trading gives a dollar. This encourages people to come back in and to remember their shopping bags.

Impact Giving

I once served on a Foundation Board responsible for the corporate giving for the chemical and real estate company Reilly Industries. When I first got on the Board, the company was giving to a large number of organizations across four main issue areas.

However, the company and its employees realized that in order to make more of a difference, the philosophy needed to change; instead of giving small grants to dozens of organizations, they would give $20,000 grants to fewer, larger charities that would be more impactful to the organizations themselves. This strategy also strengthened the relationships among donors, grantees, and employees because the company's attention was more focused and it could concentrate its time and energy on fewer organizations.

Workplace Giving

Workplace giving is where employees can choose from a long list of organizations to have donations taken directly from their paychecks.

Every company will have a different philosophy, because some don't want to play big brother and tell their employees where they can give. But if you are a matching organization, you might want to align your workplace giving programs with your larger sustainability goals of the company so that you can magnify your collective efforts.

For example, if you are trying to leverage your environmental issues, enabling your employees to give to EarthShare makes sense, or if you are focused on food-scarcity issues, providing the Food Resource Network Federation as a potential donor federation makes sense.

Making this type of shift is probably the most controversial element of philanthropy and will definitely anger some people. One approach I've taken is to tell companies that maybe they could still match all donations, but maybe match up to a higher amount for the sustainability issue the company is most engaged in.

Operationalizing Your Green Team

Most companies start by forming a green team, and then as they get more sophisticated they might have multiple teams across the company and across the world.

For example, Deloitte established a Green Leadership Council (GLC) composed of senior representatives from each global region and from their Talent, Community Involvement, Field Operations, IT, and Enterprise Sustainability groups. The GLC maintains regular dialogue between national leadership and people on the ground.

We realize that many companies are beyond this initial step, but if your company is just getting started on sustainability, following are some tips that I've compiled from the leaders and from my consulting experience that are helpful to effectively running your green team in the first few years.

GREEN TEAM TIP SHEET

1. **Hold regular meetings:** It is important to have regular meetings that people can schedule and put on the calendar; otherwise, these will have a tendency to slip. At first you might want to have monthly meetings to keep momentum going. After a while, you might decide to switch to every six weeks or bimonthly. But these meetings need to be regular and scheduled in advance.

2. **Have someone in charge:** Although you might not want to have a committee chair, it is important to have a person in charge. That person will serve as a representative within the firm and can be counted on to make sure that agendas are created.

3. **Divide up assignments:** To ensure the chair isn't overwhelmed with the admin side of running the green team, the team should appoint an admin person to take notes and distribute them after meetings, order the food for meetings, do the meeting scheduling, and so on.

4. **Create a leadership/executive committee:** Too often green teams can become unwieldy in their size and decision making, so it is important for the larger green team to appoint a leadership/exec

committee of three to five individuals for when decisions need to happen fast. This committee can also report on the major issues between the larger green team meetings.

5. **Establish subcommittees/task forces:** Develop small task force groups to tackle specific issues that people are passionate about. Involve subject matter experts (SMEs) from around the company in these task forces to get the best ideas and input, and make sure that the green team isn't duplicating efforts.

6. **Publicize, promote, and share your successes:** One of the best ways to generate visibility and support within your company is to be sure to "shout from the rafters" any time you do something that benefits the company. Too often the green team wants to wait and unveil something big. Don't wait—when you have small successes that address a company need and either save money or green the company, share them! People need to know. And highlight the people responsible, whether or not they are on the green team. Making people look good, and making sure that their bosses know what they are doing, will encourage people to do more.

7. **Document your progress:** Realize that around Earth Day, or at any point when your company is going for an RFP, someone will likely come to you and ask, "What are we doing/what have we done?" Keep track of things and place these on an internal website so that you can be the knowledge source and you can quickly and efficiently share what you have done around sustainability. Always document cost savings or new revenues!

8. **Develop agreements:** Make sure that there is responsibility for being part of the green team. Come up with agreements as to what you are trying to do as a group, and make sure that if people are using their discretionary time and energy, you have an agreement on structure and accountability. Agreements provide the foundation for a learning conversation when we don't live up to them. Without them it is hard to have a conversation that is not based on either fight or flight.[20]

9. **Realize that different people are needed at different times:** At first, you need passionate individuals (doesn't matter their position) who will cheer, lead, and talk up their efforts, as well as senior management. But as you mature, you really need decision makers and people who can effect change and be advocates.[21]

Lessons Learned

The following are key takeaways from the "Systems, Decision Making, and Internal Alignment" chapter:

- Prioritize. Focus on what matters.

- Embed sustainability into decision-making processes. Realize that this will take time to get fully adopted, but make sure that it at least is being brought up at first. Then move toward weighting the decisions equally.

- Remember the old African proverb "If you want to go fast, go alone. If you want to go far, go together." You need the systems and policies to bring other people along. But be sure to pick a sustainability process and system that work best for your company and culture.

- When you introduce a sustainable investment policy, don't try to get 100% in the first year; start slow with a low percentage and let the returns speak for themselves. If people push back on the sustainable investing or deposits, just ask for 5% to be switched, or a small dollar amount for a period of time, so that you can prove out that the risk and fear are unsubstantiated.

- Educate your suppliers as to what you are trying to do, and just ask them how they can help. You'll find that they've probably been thinking down the same lines, but have just needed a customer to ask.

- If policies or systems failed to take root, go back and find out why. Was it the policy or lack of enforcement? Is it a technological or process fix or a cultural fix? You can't fix what's broken unless you know why it's broken.

- Leverage all of your sustainability efforts across departments and align with your philanthropy. Seek ways to collaborate, combine messages, and save money.

- If you run into resistance for implementing a new system, ask the cost of *not* implementing the system. Show all the inefficiencies that won't be fixed or addressed. Put dollar figures on them.

10

Institutionalizing Sustainability

T o make sustainability stick, you must embed it into the fabric of your company. This means that it must be institutionalized into your recognition and rewards system, into job descriptions, evaluation procedures, compensation, and benefit packages. This takes time and commitment, and it is often the most difficult aspect of sustainability implementation, which is why so few companies have actually been successful. These are essential requirements, however, because you need to provide the carrot, stick, and processes for institutionalizing sustainability for the long term.

Job Descriptions and Onboarding

If you want to make sustainability part of the culture, the first step is to include it in people's job descriptions. This step is simple and it can be done for both existing and new employees. In fact, for new hires, this offers the chance to incorporate sustainability at the very beginning of the process before you even start receiving resumes. It's pre-emptive. By asking the appropriate questions regarding social and environmental issues during the interview and screening process, this will save the company time and money in not having to try and get a skeptic to care about sustainability. Go out and recruit the best person for the job, and make sure that this individual is onboard from the very beginning.

Canada's Mountain Equipment Company (MEC) is attempting to do just that. According to Esther Speck, the company's director of sustainability, MEC has "made a decision that rather than adding a generic statement about sustainability, they would specifically clarify how sustainability was a part of each person's job."[1] This chapter will show you how to do that.

Start now and you can actually also take advantage of employee turnover. If, let's say, the average turnover for your company is 4.6 years, which is the U.S. national average, then by adding sustainability to your job descriptions and onboarding, you'll realize that about 80% to 90% of your company will have been trained within 5 years. This allows you to turn what's normally a negative into a positive.

Sustainability and the Interview Process

Now, of course we all understand that the first priority is hiring the most qualified candidate with the right skills and experience, but don't overlook asking sustainability-related questions during the interview. You will be surprised at what you'll find. You might discover the perfect supply-chain expert, who is also secretly very passionate about the environment and is looking for a way to use that knowledge. You might also uncover that a qualified candidate on paper is a complete climate skeptic or someone who is completely indifferent.

If your questions about sustainability end up turning away a few people, that's okay because this will mitigate any potential unnecessary battles around implementation later on. Realize that if people are excited about sustainability, they'll likely come to the job with some new ideas and added value. Plus, as Ben Packard states, "This will help build the 'CSR muscle of the company' outside of that department."[2]

For example, Toyota asks Kaizen questions during its factory job interviews, which include a visit to the shop floor, where candidates are asked, "What do you think we could do to be more efficient?" If the candidate doesn't see anything or isn't willing to say anything, this means they might not be right for the Toyota culture of continuous improvement. This doesn't necessarily work for all offices and interviews, but it is one technique that Toyota has found effective. It's easy enough to do around sustainability as well.

Make It Part of the Orientation

When onboarding or training new employees, be sure to share the company's vision, goals, and philosophy around sustainability. Set the right tone and expectations for new employees right from the start, the same way you would with quality, safety, and company culture. This will empower and inspire new employees to think and work with a sustainable lens from the outset.

What About Existing Employees?

Dealing with existing employees is a little more difficult, because people tend to be averse to change. Sometimes, the longer the people have been with the company and at their current job, the more resistant they will be to change, even if it's just the wording in their job description.

There are three ways to handle this situation. The first method is to have management dictate a "thou shalt do as we say" mandate to all employees and just write it into their job function. This can work if you have a command-and-control type culture, but it's going to be less effective for the long term, and it definitely will not work in a more collaborative or cooperative culture.

The second way is to utilize an engagement strategy to seek out workers' ideas and input, as well as those of the co-workers in their department; identify what activities they have control over that they could do in a more sustainable manner and collaboratively write the job description changes. This is an empowering approach because employees can now help design the changes. Just make sure that there is someone to do a final review to ensure that the requirements aren't too outlandish and that nobody is trying to game the system.

Lastly, what I call the review approach is to wait until the annual performance review or a time when someone is up for a promotion. This provides an excellent opportunity to talk with the employee one-on-one about the part that she can play in the company's sustainability success and to update the job description as well.

Leadership and the Board Need It as Well

Trends are pointing to the importance of senior executives and the Board having both an understanding of and an influence over sustainability issues within an organization. More and more organizations such as the CDP, GRI, and investors are asking questions on Board-level oversight, expertise, and training on sustainability issues, including whether or not these are included in job descriptions and the process to select a CEO or elect new members to the Board.

The reason external groups and investors want leadership and the Board to have these things in their job descriptions is that they expect these individuals to have a firm grasp on the risks and potential opportunities that social and environmental issues pose to the organization. They are beginning to expect it as part of Board members' fiduciary responsibility.

Evaluations and Aligning Benefits

One of the most important and most overlooked aspects of trying to get sustainability to stick within an organization is tying performance to individuals' evaluations and their benefit packages. I like to think of this as a carrot-and-stick approach where you align benefits with the behavior you want to see and use the evaluation (as the stick) to make sure it happens.

Evaluations

Too often, companies do not set clear expectations for employees around social and environmental criteria; hence, employees don't know what they're being evaluated on and subsequently won't take these issues as seriously or be as effective as they could. The behavior that gets evaluated gets changed.

Dow, for example, has "incorporated sustainability objectives into compensation models, reviews, and other management processes, including a requirement that all newly promoted business unit managers review their units' sustainability plans with senior management within 90 days."[3]

There are three other considerations that are essential when you are incorporating sustainability into evaluations:

1. First and foremost, it has to have meaning.

    Sustainability cannot be 1 of 20 things that someone is evaluated on. Each person and role will be evaluated differently, but sustainability has to be within the top eight criteria for someone to take it seriously. It needs to be real and they need to be held accountable. As always, there have to be rewards for success and consequences for failure. If it is one out of twenty criteria, then it really isn't that important in the grand scheme of things.

2. Match the evaluation criteria with areas they have control over.

There is nothing more demotivating than to be evaluated on something that you don't have direct control over. So if someone is being evaluated on something that is beyond her control, such as the company's overall GHG performance, and she is in a department with very little impact, this will end up being disheartening and demotivating.

3. Don't draw evaluation criteria too narrowly.

You want people to think systemically about sustainability and not focus on something very small that just happens to be right in front of them. What can happen is that employees might not be able to "see the forest for the trees." So don't draw criteria so narrowly that they focus entirely on one small thing and miss the bigger opportunities for impact by collaborating with other departments and individuals. You don't want a situation where an employee meets her goals but ends up negatively impacting the company overall.

Benefits

Aligning benefits with sustainability simply means matching your non-financial compensation methods with the social and environmental goals you are trying to achieve.

When I've described how I use benefits in this regard to fellow business owners and CEOs, I'm often astounded by the response that I receive, especially with those in the baby boomer generation. Their response is typically something along the lines of, "Well, when you get to my age, you'll realize you cannot afford all this." Those comments do nothing but anger me because I've seen firsthand, with both my company and others, how the data to support my argument holds up. Although it can be challenging at times with limited resources, that only means that you have to be a little more creative to find ways in which your benefits package can help your company reach its sustainability goals.

Clif Bar, for example, has sustainability embedded in employees' benefits package, including incentives for such actions as purchasing a fuel-efficient car and making eco-friendly home improvements. Momentum is ensured at weekly staff meetings, where employees share practical tips for living greener, and at yearly award ceremonies, where individuals are recognized for excellence according to the company's values.[4]

My company follows that of Clif Bar, in that my philosophy has always been to try to create a great place to work, one that if my best friends or I were looking for a job, we would want to work here. So I've aligned our benefits with our sustainability and business goals in attempt to do just that.

At SBC, this is part of our philosophy that we call life-work balance, not the other way around. We offer great benefits and try to have fun in our workplace while we work with our clients and partners.

We focus on a highly efficient 35-hour workweek with the goal of allowing our employees time outside the office to pursue their professional goals, contribute to their community, and enjoy those activities that nurture their lives. As I've reviewed my employees over the past five years, I've found that these reduced work hours in the office means they are heads-down on their work when they are in the office and typically are more productive. And it ties to our sustainability goal of being a great place to work as well.

In addition to the traditional benefits of healthcare, dental, life insurance, vision, 401k/IRA, there are a number of ideas in Table 10.1 that can further your own company's sustainability performance, while simultaneously working to improve the wellness, satisfaction, and health of your employees. These are taken from my company and you can obviously tailor these to your company. For a complete list of benefits at Sustainable Business Consulting, go to www.sustainablebizconsulting.com.

Table 10.1 Social and Environmental Goals

Community	Environment	Wellness and Health
24 hours of paid time for volunteer work in the community each year.	Personal e-waste recycling for employees where they can bring their own e-waste from home and the company will dispose of it.	Money toward a fitness/health and wellness membership.
"Boss Does Your Chores" perk. When staff reaches a certain sales goal or other benchmark, the management team is responsible for performing the more menial duties of its staff members.	Guaranteed "Get Home" policy stating that if an employee is stuck at work without a car because they carpooled, walked, or bussed that the company will pay for public transportation or a taxi if necessary.	Free flu shots.
Election Day (presidential years) is a paid half-day holiday, and employees are encouraged to participate in this important civic exercise by canvassing and/or getting people to the polls.	To encourage alternative commuting, staff shall receive one company dollar for each day they commute in an alternative fashion, redeemable in the company store. Other companies pay employees $6/day for commuting by walking, biking, bus, or car pool because this is cheaper than downtown parking.	Paid five-week sabbatical every three years from start date of full-time employment.
Match "dollars for donations" up to $150 per employee annually.	$250 reimbursement per year toward making home more sustainable.	Offer free or discounted yoga classes to relieve stress.

Community	Environment	Wellness and Health
Monthly Hero award programs in which employees are given a $50 monthly allowance to award as a bonus to a colleague for leadership on sustainability. The chosen hero gets a covered parking spot for a month, a $150 gift card, and a cape.	Host a CSA box at the office so employees can share fresh fruits and vegetables and not have to purchase a whole box at home.	Two mental health days per year. Kayak/powder day can be used during the summer/winter on those amazing days when one needs to be out of the office and in the sun or on the slopes.
Company co-op garden and internal site for gardening tips and recipes.	Company subsidy for a hybrid or electric car.	Free vacation day on their birthday or an anniversary.
Quarterly community volunteer events chosen by employees.	Personal carbon offsets paid for by the company.	Sponsorship for up to two or more races/charitable events each year.

Rewards, Recognition, and Compensation

After you've set up the evaluation criteria and benefits to align with sustainability, it's important that you develop the appropriate recognition, reward, and compensation structures. The latter is one of the most difficult and controversial aspects around institutionalizing sustainability because whether it is necessary truly depends on the culture of your company. My answer to this question is, "It depends." I know, not too helpful, right? So in this section I'm going to share the pros and cons of tying compensation to sustainability performance while also highlighting the importance of rewards and recognition. Remember the Chess star from Chapter 7, "Understanding Change Management to Guide Implementation"? This is where the actions lie. That way you can apply the solution that is best for your company. In fact, recent studies have proven that nonfinancial rewards are just as effective as, if not more effective than, traditional financial incentives in encouraging the type of behavior you want to see.

Compensation

Linking compensation with sustainability performance is a little more difficult than tying it to evaluations, which is why even the most progressive companies have resisted this method. Even though they have other monetary reward systems, the success of trying to do this will vary by company, type of job, and the individual because for some a financial incentive to be more sustainable will be extremely motivating, whereas for others, not so much.

Many companies are wrestling with these questions:

- Should we do this?

- If so, how?

- How can we make sure that the criteria are specific, measurable, and clearly communicated?

- Will this end up being motivating to our employees?

There is also the added risk of employees beginning to act out of fear that their pay will be docked if these goals are not met, which might end up being demotivating. Therefore, due to the variability associated with incentivizing employees around sustainability, there are four trains of thought on this issue:

1. If you incentivize people financially for the behavior you are trying to effect, eventually people will come around. When people start seeing others profit and earn bonuses, even the most skeptical people around sustainability will jump onboard quickly.

2. The second train of thought is that competitions and financial incentive work best together when tied to the specific behavior you are trying to encourage. For example, providing an incentive that encourages behavior change to reduce energy usage by

10% at a facility is great, but since the anticipation of financial incentive can actually be more motivating than the actual cash payment, competition is great way of fostering that anticipation.

3. The third way is to tie everyone into a bonuses pool that is paid out if and when the company achieves its sustainability goals. For example, Intel calculates each employee's (including CEO and top executives) annual bonus according to sustainability results. It does this by "challenging all departments to improve their processes and products with sustainability in mind with a focus on three areas: energy efficiency, GHG reduction and improvements in its environmental reputation." The results have been successful in that in the first four years of the program, the company has reduced "GHG emissions by 23% and energy use by 8%."[5]

4. It depends on the work itself. There is a big difference between "routine" and "nonroutine" work. If the task itself is mundane or routine, a financial incentive toward faster or more efficient work might succeed. However, if the work involves creativity, writing, or innovation (as many sustainability solutions do), then throwing more money at the situation isn't going to accomplish what you hope it will. I know that, for me, when I'm trying to write, someone offering me money to write this book differently or faster would not have been a motivator because I would still have needed time and space to think about the issues, put them on paper, noodle them over in my head, and then type them up.

So if your company is considering tying people's compensation to their sustainability efforts, make sure you know that it works with the culture of the company and the individual, because your employee could fall into any of these trains of thought, and you want to make sure you implement the right one accordingly.

Examples of How Companies Are Tying Compensation to Sustainability

Several models have been successful in tying compensation to sustainability; the following list provides a few examples.

Xcel Energy

- **CEO:** One-third of the CEO's annual bonus is tied to environmental performance, as measured by renewable energy, emission reduction, energy efficiency, and clean technology.

- **Long-term incentive awards:** 25% of restricted stock units that are granted have a performance-based vesting schedule related to Xcel's position as a leader in environmental conservation.[6]

- **Other executives:** Annual incentive awards are tied to sustainability performance metrics, including environmental metrics (GHG goals) and social metrics (employee safety), increasing the amount of renewable energy available for commercial operation, improving energy efficiency, and integrating new technologies.[7,8]

Alcoa, Inc.

- **Executives:** Long-term sustainability goals are incorporated into the annual bonus plan. 80% is still tied to traditional financial metrics, but 20% is reserved for nonfinancial goals including safety, diversity, and environmental health.[9]

- **Employees:** A variable compensation plan called the Employee Bonus plan is a profit-sharing plan for employees. It has three main components: absolute financial performance, relative financial performance, and operational goals. Sustainability metrics are integrated into the operational goals component.[10]

Rewards and Recognition

Although financial incentives are trendy, the reality is that for most employees, traditional rewards and recognition such as praise from immediate supervisors, opportunities to lead projects, and recognition from company leadership are as motivational as, or no less motivational than, traditional financial incentives such as bonuses, stock options, and pay raises.

A *McKinsey Quarterly* survey[11] found that, in general, people want to do a good job, have their work recognized, and have the autonomy and ability to do their jobs. In today's fast-paced work environment, where many benefits have been curtailed since the financial recession, some of them permanently, offering praise and recognition is a very low-cost way of maintaining employee satisfaction and retention. This type of reward is basically free to the employer, and it can mean a lot to the employee.

Why do so many organizations and managers fall down in this regard? In most cases, the nonfinancial ways of rewarding and recognizing people are more difficult because they take more time, energy, and commitment from managers. Additionally, bosses tend to be more removed from the day-to-day work and don't necessarily know what drives their employees personally, so they offer compensation as a reward because it's just easier and simpler to do.

As Daniel Pink points out in *Drive,* some of our most poignant experiences in life are when we're doing something that is bigger than ourselves. Realizing the satisfaction of a job well done on something that is important and can make a difference can drive people to do even more.[12] Sustainability is just that.

Social Feedback Loops Are Reinforcing

Positive recognition and rewards go a long way in today's workforce, where people are working longer and harder than they have in a generation.

In many companies, a culture of LEAN or Kaizen (continuous improvement) can force employees to focus on what's not working and how they can fix the problem. Because sustainability is a journey that will never be finished, it's important to recognize positive behavior and to take time out every once in a while and celebrate successes as well.

Making change around sustainability can be uncomfortable for people; therefore, positive recognition and rewards are important. An absence of positive feedback can give employees the false impression that their efforts weren't appreciated, acknowledged, or useful. According to Christine Manning, visiting assistant professor of environmental studies at Macalester College, "There needs to be a social feedback loop that says, 'I'm glad you did that,' so be sure to balance your feedback loops with both positive aspects and opportunities for improvement."[13]

At my office, where we constantly focus on continuous improvement, we also make sure to take a moment to celebrate every new contract, no matter the size. This small gesture is a way of involving the whole office in the success of the team that brought in the project, and it provides a short pause for people to look up from their screens and share in the excitement.

One caution on rewards and recognition, though, is to make sure it is authentic. For example, I once consulted with a small business where the sales and service people met their quarterly goals, so the CEO thought it would be great to order pizza to celebrate. However, he then thought he was done, and when the pizzas arrived he didn't even acknowledge or celebrate with the team. What made this worse was that most of the employees had recently gone on diets and didn't want to be eating pizza. What type of message do you think was sent? Some of the employees commented to me a few months later, "So what? If we miss our goals, we miss out on a pizza party that we don't want and leadership won't attend anyway!" So if you are going to recognize and reward people, be sure to take the extra time and effort and tailor the reward to your employees and be authentic.

Gamification

Gamification is the process of using game mechanics to engage individuals and solve problems. It is increasingly being used by companies to engage employees around sustainability. Games in the workplace have become more common today than ever, especially with the emergence of social media. Games and competition have a way of making things that otherwise might seem tedious become fun, and they sometimes lead to a higher level of learning, understanding, and adoption. Gamification around sustainability will enable your company to do the following:

- Empower your employees to take initiative and generate ideas

- Get trained faster and more effectively

- Create shared project landscapes and compelling narrative

- Solve problems

- Engage and educate employees about sustainability in a fun, nontraditional manner

- Encourage performance and participation

- Generate feedback loops more quickly

Claudia Capitini says, "Be sure to couch things in levity and ridiculousness. Games are real time education and mentoring,"[14] and people tend to absorb and remember things that they were a part of that they enjoyed.

The idea is not necessarily creating a mobile application but rather using the elements and mechanics of gaming to accomplish a business goal.

A University of Colorado–Denver Business School study found that those trained on games do their jobs better, have higher skills, and retain information longer than workers learning in less interactive, more passive environments. This report examined 65 studies and data from 6,476 trainees and discovered that those using games (in this instance video games) had the following benefits:

- An 11% higher factual knowledge level

- A 14% higher skill-based knowledge level

- A 9% higher retention rate than other trainees[15]

Gamification, Innovation, and Engagement

The technology consultancy Gartner has projected that 50% of corporate innovation will be "gamified" by 2015[16] and Deloitte cited gamification in the business place as one of its *Top 10 Technology Trends*.[17] This is because games and competitions are a way to try to get people to think and act outside of their traditional roles, especially in a corporate setting. They can also offer people a safe environment in which to innovate, experiment, and try to tackle things that otherwise might seem too daunting.

Use Games to Engage the Alphas

This is a nontechnology example of how I used gaming and its competitive elements to accelerate sustainability learning. A few years ago,

SBC was hired by a change-management firm to help them get a better understanding of corporate social responsibility so that they could be better informed when dealing with their clients. This was where I personally stumbled upon the power and effectiveness of games and competitions in the sustainability space.

While I was running the client through a CSR training that was focused on meeting GRI reporting criteria, it became quickly apparent that although there were only 15 people in the room, there were 3 alpha males in the room, all of whom were competing for air time. I broke them into three separate groups with an alpha in each.

Usually I'd give them about three hours to work through this process, but sensing the machismo in the room, I decided to add a competitive element to the exercise and instead gave them only one hour to try to complete a C-Level CSR template about their company.

At first, each team was all over the place trying to figure out how to get started. Sensing this and because I wanted people to get going, I went to the first team and simply said, "Come on, guys, you need to pick it up and start filling in the template because team 2 is already beating you!"

Of course there was no real competition, but this prompting instantly changed the attitude of team 1. Their energy level picked up and they stopped talking about the process and just started working. So next, I walked over to team 3, which actually was doing very well, and told them, "Keep it up—you guys are killing team 1, but team 2 is about to catch up!" This didn't sit well with team 3's alpha, so he decided to break the team into small subgroups, each with their own sections of the report, and gave them 20 minutes to complete their sections. The team members quickly got on their cellphones and called the office to delegate research tasks, and within 10 minutes information started to fly in. I kept pushing people during the final 30 minutes, bugging them every once in a while by just pointing to another team and saying, "They're ahead of you."

The result was astounding. In that one hour all three teams came back having adequately filled a C-Level GRI CSR report, something that can take some companies weeks. By giving them time pressure and the impression that they were trying to beat the other teams, their competitive nature took over. More important, they were laughing, smiling, more confident, and no longer intimidated by the CSR process. Plus, they had a better understanding and were further along than any of them ever thought they could be after such a short time.

Although this technique is effective, remember that not everyone who has influence is an alpha. Be sure to also engage the "cool kids" within your company. In many ways, it's just like high school. We all followed what the cool kids did and the same is true within organizations. These are respected individuals and the trendsetters within a company, who most likely are not in the "C-Suite." Find out who those people are and ask them to help you in the implementation, because employees will follow their fellow peers in a way that they might not follow leadership. Try to take advantage of these individuals' popularity and enlist them in helping you share the sustainability message.

Examples of Companies Using Gamification

One example comes from a utility company. The company utilized an online system in which employees could log in and document a situation they recognized as an opportunity to bring about a change in the workplace by their co-workers. An example would be carpooling with a colleague rather than driving alone. The system would calculate both the cost savings and the carbon savings. At the end, a proportion of the monetary savings was shared with community causes chosen by staff. In the end, the pilot program saved $32,000 in costs and 66 tons of CO_2, and nearly 5,000 actions were undertaken.[18]

SAP created a "sustainability quiz" that taught employees about sustainability initiatives through a virtual Monopoly game in which users were pitted against Betty Sustainability. Question topics included energy efficiency, recycling, and sustainable behavior. Players continued to play the game over and over again to discover new sets of questions—and to try to win an iPad 2.[19]

Match the Game with Your Culture

What type of game best fits your company culture?

- **Killer:** Employees engaged by direct peer-to-peer competition.
- **Achiever:** Employees engaged by earning badges or other rewards with each accomplishment.

- **Socialite:** Employees engaged by leader boards that show who is winning.

- **Explorer:** Employees engaged by new experiences and choices.

Here are some examples of sustainability-related games you could try within your company:

- **Paper-LESS:** Have a competition to reduce or eliminate paper among departments.

- **Talking Trash:** Launch a recycling/composting campaign to reduce waste per facility.

- **Kilowatt Krackdown:** Have a competition on energy usage by division or facility.

- **Commuter Challenges:** Encourage employees to use human-powered or public transportation to get to work. These are common around bike-to-work month.

A fun game that one of our past clients conducted was a Fun Mug Contest. Typically, when companies want to move away from disposable or Styrofoam cups, they make the commitment and go out and buy a bunch of company-branded mugs. Although this is great, and okay for the meeting room, we discourage our clients from doing this because it is an unnecessary expense. Everyone has an extra coffee mug at home. So what this client did was have a Fun Mug Contest and had people bring in their funniest mug or even one that they decorated themselves. Some employees made them fun, others made them obnoxious, and some of the men of course showed no creativity at all. The company then brought all the employee participants together and gave out $100 for the person with the funniest mug. This competition gave the company another opportunity to tie the contest back to the business case and why they were doing this: to save money and, at the same time, lower their environmental impact.

No matter what competitions or games you decide to use within your firm, make sure that they are fun and that all employees can participate, and as Derek Eisel, the former global environment program manager at Expeditors, says, "Make sure the competition is real. If you are going to have a 'Branch or Department of the Month' around sustainability, then you have to have the data platform in place for them to actually compete using hard data on energy, paper, waste, or whatever you are competing on. It can't just be qualitative; it has to be backed up with numbers and people really need to win it!"[20]

Lessons Learned

The following are key takeaways from the "Institutionalizing Sustainability" chapter:

- Incorporate sustainability into job descriptions. It sets the tone and expectation not only in current employees but in all new hires. Use turnover to your advantage and make sure that all your new hires get sustainability training and have it embedded in their job descriptions from day one.

- Sustainability must be part of employees' evaluations. It cannot be 1 of 20 criteria; it has to have meaning.

- Align benefits and compensation to encourage the sustainable behavior you want to see.

- Leadership needs to be evaluated and compensated around sustainability as well. When this occurs, they are more likely to care and ask questions throughout the rest of the organization.

- People are competitive. Use games to get them to break habits and think differently. They push themselves to try to do things that might be new, different, or even surprising.

- Engage the alphas and the cool kids. Use their personalities and competitive nature to bring sustainability to the forefront.

11

Communicating Sustainability Internally

Many organizations are falling short in communicating their strategies, goals, and actions around sustainability, especially internally. Typically there is a big push in the first year of a program and a flurry of communications around Earth Day and reporting season, but for most companies these efforts eventually fade away.

For sustainability to be in people's minds on a daily basis, there needs to be a consistent communication that is authentic, purposeful, and across various mediums. Companies need to tell their sustainability story in a way that resonates with people, internally and externally; is aligned; and reinforces what the company is trying to accomplish.

One could write an entire book about marketing and communicating your message externally, so the focus of this chapter is primarily on internal communications.

Continuous Communication Reinforces Your Message

"Say things over and over again, until people get it!"[1]

Building off what was stated earlier, after you know your North Star and know how sustainability relates to your company and employees, you need to continually reinforce this message. The goal should be that everybody within your company understands it, can effectively communicate it, and can use it to influence their decisions throughout the day. This requires a commitment not only from the PR and HR departments, but from all departments, and especially middle management because that is where the breakdown in the communication chain usually occurs.

A significant opportunity exists for organizations to improve the frequency, effectiveness, and relevance of their communications to employees, especially considering that most employees I come into contact with say they want more information, education, and opportunity to contribute around sustainability, not less.

To do this effectively, you'll have to piggyback and tag sustainability onto other communication methods however you can, whether they are e-mails from HR, part of a monthly newsletter, e-mail blasts to employees, social media, or something similar. Realize that to get your message heard with all the other "noise," you are going to have to be persistent and a bit creative at times.

So find partners within your firm and work with your communications department to set up your communication structure in way that, as John Koriath encourages, "will not only push messages out, but that will also continually gather stories so that it becomes a self-reinforcing cycle of gathering and communicating sustainability messages."[2]

Share across platforms. If you have a message, tip, or story, it can and should show up in as many places as possible and be communicated using the strategies outlined in Figure 11.1. Platforms can include, but are not limited to, the company blog, Web pages, newsletters, social media, online forums, Internet sites, press releases, or spinoff pieces from sustainability reports, events, brochures, and packaging.

Use the Calendar to Help Reinforce Your Message

Be sure to take advantage of the calendar to put sustainability into people's mind about things they are already thinking about, both inside and outside of work. For example, combine messages around back-to-school timing, holidays, Earth Day, quarterly and annual reporting, seasonal changes, and so on. Employees are already thinking about these things, and you'll be more successful if you can tie sustainability into your communications around these time periods.

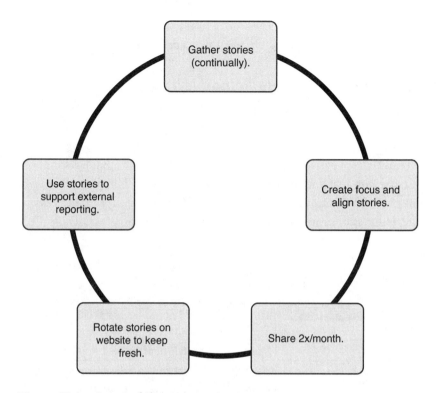

Figure 11.1 Sustainability communication.

This approach extends to competitions as well. For example, a workplace energy-reduction contest makes more sense in the winter, and a water-conservation contest makes more sense during the summer. Also, because utilities often are also thinking about conservation seasonally, keep an eye out for opportunities to use free resources and collateral provided by local utility companies around their programs to leverage and support your communications during seasonal times.

Share Both the Good and the Bad

Consumers are increasingly skeptical of companies' "green claims," making it paramount that companies communicate their entire story, both the good and the bad of their sustainability efforts. Authentically disclosing your successes, as well as the areas in which you still need to improve, will increase stakeholders' confidence that your communications are accurate and will help minimize accusations of greenwashing.

Put Sustainability into Relatable Terms

Be sure to put sustainability actions into terms people can understand and relate to. Make it real. For example, when someone talks about climate action in terms of metric tons of CO_2 equivalents, people's eyes glaze over. Not many people will know what to do with that information because they just don't know what a ton of CO_2e is. Therefore, whenever you can, put things into terms people are familiar with. Provide visuals and tailor the terms to your company whenever possible. Table 11.1 provides a few examples:

Table 11.1 Communicating Impact

Category	This Equates To
Energy use	The number of homes it would heat or light
Fuel use	The number cars taken off the road
Paper use	The height of a stack of paper sheets compared against the height of your corporate HQ
Business travel	The number of trips around the world or across the country
Commuting	The number of trips across the U.S. or home state
Waste	The number of garbage trucks or bags of trash per person
Cost of benefits	Sales; for example, paying one employee's benefits is the number equivalent to selling 40 pairs of running shoes or 1,850 cups of coffee
Jobs created	The number of employees this equals, for example, 10 full-time employees at $50K salary
Food	The number of families this would feed
Stakeholder engagement	The number of individuals who were touched
Diverse workforce	A percentage increase in employee diversity

Lastly, after you have the best terms and practices in place, it's important to put the information in as many languages as possible. This not only means the different corporatespeak around the company (facilities, finance, engineers, etc.) but also the languages of your employees. For example, we were working with a restaurant that communicated its sustainability efforts in English, but the majority of its cooking and wait staff spoke and read Spanish as their primary language. Not surprisingly, even though they had done major outreach in English, the company didn't begin to experience any change in behavior until they translated sustainability into Spanish and into terms the wait staff could relate to.

Storytelling Is Key

Storytelling is the best way to make sustainability relatable to most people because people remember stories and myths. Too often people have tried to communicate with data and metrics alone. Although this might initially persuade your audience, it's not what they will remember over time. People remember stories. Similar to the way we learned lessons as kids, we connect with a story or myth, whether it is "The Boy Who Cried Wolf" or whatever comes to your mind. The power of a story can really help anchor the sustainability message into people's minds.

Storytelling is also a good way to see whether what you are sharing is relevant to what people care about. Data is cool for the geeks, but not everyone remembers data points. If nobody cares, listens, or comments about your story, you either are telling it wrong or, more likely, you are telling the wrong story.

So remember that, although we've been taught to always make the business case, if you want something to stick, connect with people's heads, their hearts, and their hands so that they are thinking, *Hey, I can do that too!* Use a story to help them relate, remember, and be compelled to act.

As Dawn Danby states, "It's often surprising that when you talk to an executive, you think you need to be totally focused on the bottom line, but the magic occurs when you can tell a great story about sustainability that involves the business case. Often they'll respond by saying, 'Get more stories like that!'"[3]

Align Your Communications Efforts

The benefit of an aligned strategy is a clear, consistent message that all stakeholders understand and can repeat. Moreover, when departments work together and support each other's communications efforts, they can save money, resources, and employees' time.

Similar to what I mentioned about the importance of breaking down silos between departments on the operational front, companies need to align their communications strategy around sustainability. You want to have one message so that different stories and actions support that message. You don't want to have divergent messages all saying multiple things, such as these efforts support our goal of carbon-neutrality, being a better corporate citizen, or being the best place to work. These all have different meaning. You want your communications aligned with one message that is consistent so that every action taken leverages the efforts of others and reinforces your North Star.

Nonaligned communications occur when the PR, marketing, HR, supply chain, sales, CSR, philanthropy/community, and design departments are all sharing different messages with different stakeholders independently of one another. They are not sharing resources or budget and aren't working to mutually reinforce and support one another. Figure 11.2 displays many of the places where you should think to align sustainability messaging.

"When your company and its employees speak with one voice about sustainability, magic happens."[4]

For example, you might have a policy that supports alternative commuting, but people aren't engaging and taking advantage of it. Table 11.2 shows a way one client used continual and reinforcing messaging to increase employee engagement and participation.

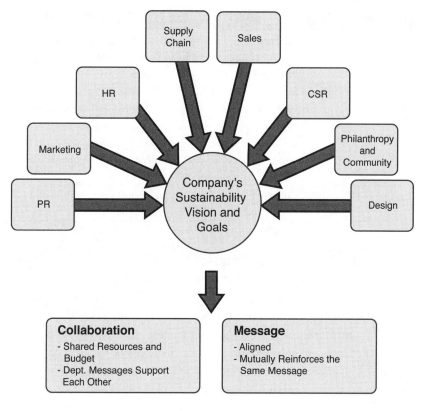

Figure 11.2 An aligned communication strategy.

Table 11.2 Example of Mutually Reinforced Messaging: Alternative Commuting

Department	Action
Communications	Sends alternative commuting tips to employees via e-mail, newsletter, and internal social media site.
CSR	Sets up an alternative commuting challenge: department versus department.
Marketing	Partners with a sponsor for Bike to Work Month to encourage employees and community members alike to participate.
Community Relations	Sends out alternative commuting tips from a local bike group such as the Cascade Bicycle Club.

Department	Action
HR	Explains company's alternative commuting benefit options at annual health fair (cash incentives for biking, bus passes, wellness stipends, etc.). Invites local metro bus representative to explain bus and car pool options to employees at lunch-and-learn events.
IT	Shows employees how to utilize Work From Home options and how to set up systems at home. Provides online tutorials for virtual meetings using WebEx, Skype, Google Hangout, or FaceTime.
Facilities	Communicates where bike racks and cages are located. Installs lockers for bike commuters.

The goal of an aligned communications strategy is for your company to get the most "bang for its buck" and be able to use messages in multiple ways. For example, something that was created by the CSR (Corporate Social Responsibility) department could be written in a way that can be reused for multiple audiences, for sales to help differentiate itself with potential customers, or as information for investors or for local community outreach efforts. Such integration saves time, resources, and money, and delivers a more coherent message.

If you have 24 short stories or case studies that typically make up your CSR or Sustainability report, you could slice and dice them into distinct categories (energy, waste, volunteerism, water, etc.), and use these categories as "the issue of the quarter" that your company could work on. Then you could communicate 2 to 4 of these stories per month (6 per quarter) to provide a mutually reinforced and aligned message.

ACTIVITY 22: SUSTAINABILITY COMMUNICATIONS ALIGNMENT

How aligned are your sustainability communications?

- List all the ways you currently communicate your sustainability efforts, internally and externally.

- Where do your efforts best align?

- Which department's efforts are currently not aligned?

- How could they better collaborate this year? For example:

  How are marketing, sales, and PR working together to reinforce each other's message?

  How are sales and marketing working with design, R & D, and new product development?

  In what ways could community affairs, CSR, and philanthropy better support other departments' communication efforts around sustainability?

- What is each department's estimated spending ($ only) on communicating sustainability?

- Which departments are doing the best job of communicating the company's sustainability vision and goals when interacting with stakeholders? How can we replicate this across the company?

Share Best Practices

Sharing best practices internally is one of the easiest and most cost-effective ways to align and improve the effectiveness of your company's sustainability program. This seems like a no-brainer, but I've been amazed at how few companies excel at doing this. A company typically has a few rock-star offices that are further along the continuum because they've already figured it out and have been doing it, but this info fails to get disseminated throughout the company because there is a lack of information sharing among departments and facilities.

The reality is that what can be accomplished at one office, facility, or plant can be mirrored in another of similar size.

Therefore, every company needs management to empower individuals, facilities, and departments to create an open dialogue for information sharing. Living, breathing documents around sustainability need to be created that are accessible, easy, open source, and updatable. This could be through an internal blog, an intranet site, or social media. This needs to be done; otherwise, you'll still run into issues of people being in their own silos and missing out on readily available best practices.

Use Social Media Internally

Over the past few years social media has become the most effective medium in communicating sustainability messages to both Gen X and Y stakeholders because of the ability to share information and ideas within a virtual community almost instantaneously. Many of these qualities, such as reach, frequency, usability, and immediacy, offer many different opportunities for companies to engage employees and stakeholders across many platforms.

I'm going to focus on how companies can use social media internally because of its effectiveness at internal sustainability communications. Companies are turning to social media forums from their own Web portals, wikis, blogs, Twitter, Instagram, and corporate Facebook pages because social media creates an online community, support network, and solutions for overcoming barriers within the organizational culture. Additionally, it provides the opportunity to do the following:

- Share ideas, insights, and best practices
- Engage in dialogue on numerous issues with different perspectives in real time
- Educate and provide asynchronous learning for employees
- Provide a venue for fun and social connections, as well as a way to manage internal competitions
- Put a human touch on actions by sharing stories, photos, and videos
- Allow employees to self-select and follow groups/areas of interest
- Crowd-source and recruit employees for projects, whether they be work-related innovations, philanthropic, or volunteer efforts
- Reinforce the corporate strategy and track progress on goals, initiatives, and sustainability actions

Moreover, social media enables employees who tend to be humble with an opportunity to engage, to share their, passions, successes, fears, and even stumbling blocks in a safe community environment.

Don't forget though, for internal social media to be useful, someone needs respond to the input that garners reaction. There needs to be someone managing the content, and if you can get a person of influence (manager, department head, or executive) to respond, people will notice that they are being listened to and that their ideas are being noticed, and they will be more engaged to participate.

Examples of How Companies Are Using Social Media Internally

There are many examples of successful social media campaigns; here are a few examples of social media promoting sustainability.

1. Timberland established their Voices of Challenge online platform for dialogue on key sustainability issues ranging from labor practices in their supply chain to climate-change policy. The website's purpose is "to put thought leaders, issue experts, practitioners and everyday consumers at the heart of an online dialogue designed to present ideas for future innovation—for Timberland, for their industry, and for others in the social and environmental arenas."[5]

2. Intel created a green.intel portal for raising awareness, communicating information about company initiatives, sharing best practices, and providing support, videos, updates, blogs, and open discussion forums for all employees.[6]

3. IBM's On Demand Community (ODC) program features a Web-based portal that helps IBM manage its global volunteering efforts. IBM held a three-day participatory online ValuesJam on the Web to craft the values that now guide decisions.

Before Launching Internally

Companies can miss the boat if they launch into their internal social media strategy before assessing their company's cultural readiness. As mentioned in Chapter 7, "Understanding Change Management to Guide Implementation," you have to assess how your company and employees manage change because although social media might be easy and preferred for younger employees, you might run into resistance from older employees.

Also, if you have a command-and-control type of organization, realize that social media tools are organic and democratic, so after you unveil them, management will have given up control. The users will decide which functions and forums they want to use and how to use them. So go in with eyes open to that reality, but don't hesitate at the beginning to set expectations about the culture you want to promote online.

External Reporting

If you are being asked by your investors or your customers to complete an external report such as the Carbon Disclosure Project or a supplier questionnaire, it's required. However, we get asked by clients and prospective clients all the time about where and how they should report voluntarily, and our answer is almost always the same: to the organization and in the format that makes the most sense for your company while meeting the expectations of your stakeholders.

This might depend on a number of factors, including these:

- Your position in your industry

- What stage your company is in on the Hagen-Wilhelm matrix

- The expectations of your stakeholders (investors, suppliers, and customers)

Determining the reporting system that works for your company and your goals can seem like a big decision, but the good news is that there's no wrong answer. All roads lead to a more sustainable company, but some reports might be better suited for your company than others. Moreover, reporting guidelines are constantly being updated, so here are a few ways to choose among external reports:

1. Determine which report would provide the most value to your primary stakeholders.

2. Decide which report you feel is the most applicable to your company. CDP focuses mainly on materiality and emissions, as opposed to the GRI, which focuses on the company's disclosure

management approaches and responses to six indicator categories (economics, environmental, societal, human rights, product responsibility, and workplace).

3. Determine the companies you would like to be benchmarked against and find out which report those companies are using. Companies that use the equator principles, for example, are typically multinational companies working in developing countries in energy/mineral extraction.

4. Figure out the type of results you want the report to show. Bloomberg has GHG reporting that shows emission per dollar, whereas GRI shows year-to-year GHG emissions performance against a company's baseline.

Some companies even ask the stakeholders (clients and employees) whether they have a preference.

If you want to quickly assess some of the types of questions and categories being asked by these reporting agencies, see the TKR metrics stated earlier in Chapter 5, "Goals/Vision and Your Sustainability North Star."

Benefits of Reporting—Sustainability Rankings

One of the benefits of reporting externally is the opportunity to be ranked and compared against your peers on your sustainability performance. And although various methodologies are being used by different agencies such as Newsweek, Corporate Knights, Climate Counts, Fortune, and many others, one thing is clear: A high score across multiple rankings can communicate how well your company is doing on sustainability to interested stakeholders, while requiring no additional effort on your end.

I actually have written about this topic multiple times under the heading of "Sustainability Rankings Craziness" because of the variance of companies' scores on whether they are being judged on sustainability, on "green," which just means environmental criteria, or for their community citizenship and how they treat their employees. For those that score well across all these categories, these rankings can supplement the company's communications, provide free PR, and enhance the brand value not only with employees, but with customers, suppliers, and investors.

For a comparison of how companies are doing, check out this article at www.sustainablebizconsulting.com/articles/sustainabilityrankings2013.

I've found that no matter the extent to which a company decides to report externally, going through the reporting process provides business value by uncovering blind spots and revealing previously unknown gaps.

Awards

Awards provide similar benefit. Nothing can give you credibility and reinvigorate a program like winning an award. If you win, as Molly Ray says from experience, "for some reason it makes it more real to employees and it gets management jazzed."[7]

Transparency Builds Trust

One of the biggest questions companies face when they communicate their sustainability efforts is "How much information should we release?" No company is perfect, nor has any leader done all that can be done within a company, so it's only fair that some are a little hesitant to be fully transparent about their social, environmental, and financial performance.

So how transparent should you be? Will the value it brings to shareholders and customers be outweighed by the risk that competitors could learn from the processes and procedures that lead to your success? Could you accidently be opening yourself to potential liability down the road?

These are all good questions because it takes guts and it takes leadership to be transparent. It's not for the faint of heart. I know that most managers would rather not disclose any information on an area in which they aren't doing well. But this is where transparency can uncover the hidden opportunities and risks that can help a company make the changes it might need or want.

For example, when SBC started working with a large service-based client on its first CSR report, one of the things we came across was that although more than half of the employees were women, there was a noticeable income disparity between men and women. Now most of this was overseas, where culturally this might be more acceptable, but by being forced to seek information regarding this issue from a reporting stance, the client had to think about how to respond. It pushed this issue up to the management level, as opposed to something traditionally handled by HR, and the company began to address the issue head-on.

A different example about transparency was with one of our government clients. The agency was afraid to disclose any employee information, due to risk concerns. They were averse to disclosing HR information because they had had one sexual harassment complaint a few years back (which turned out to be false and was dismissed), and they still felt as though it was a black mark against the organization.

We were able to show them that any issues they had were below the average number for a government organization their size and well below those in the private sector. This helped the organization realize that their management and the policies that they had put in place were in fact doing the job. This helped alleviate their concerns about disclosing this information externally, and turned an issue that they were afraid to talk about on its head.

Who Will Be the Roadblocks to Transparency?

As you can imagine, human resources and legal are the typical roadblocks to transparency. It is in their nature to be cautious regarding external disclosure (especially the first time) because that is what they've been trained to do, so it will be more than just management that will need convincing.

HR might not be sure why you are asking these questions because they might never have had to disclose this internal information before. Legal, of course, is worried about future liabilities from disclosing internal information, so it too wants to hold all information close to the vest. Therefore, whenever your company discusses transparency or takes on a new reporting scheme, you'll want to involve representatives from HR and legal in the initial meetings so that they understand what is being disclosed and why, and be sure to communicate that this level of transparency has management's blessing.

I believe that the best way to approach this is to first get all the information on the table and then decide what information can be stated publically versus what should be kept private for internal use only. This will help avoid running into obstacles from HR and legal throughout the process. Also, be sure to remind everyone that it's always up to your company to determine what information it discloses.

My Personal Lesson with Transparency

I haven't been immune to the concerns about transparency either. In fact, although I was willing to disclose more than what my competitors and peers were doing, socially and environmentally, it wasn't until after the financial crash of 2008 that I truly understood what it meant to be fully transparent.

Like many companies, as we headed into 2009 we were facing a harsh financial reality. Many of our clients were telling us that they loved us, and that we had done exceptional work, but due to budget cuts on their end, we were not likely to have any work with them for the next year or two.

All of this put tremendous pressure on our company's bottom line. Like most CEOs, I was stressing about how I was going to meet payroll while also trying to decide how much of the financials I should share with my employees. So I said, "The heck with it. If we won't be 100% transparent, who will?" So on March 1, 2009, I opened up my books to every employee in my company.

I had never considered doing this before. In fact, although I had read case studies of other organizations doing this, I had never known anyone who had personal experience with this level of transparency. But with revenues declining and my not being able to sleep many nights, I felt that everyone would benefit from understanding the true economic reality. I figured that I had little to lose and much to gain.

We started with an honest and frank discussion about the state of the budget and forecasted revenues, and we talked about what that could mean for everyone. The employees, of course, had been feeling anxious too, but now trust was created and this provided them with the opportunity to speak frankly, share their fears, and, more important, engage and feel empowered to help come up with a solution. "It made it so that there were no surprises," Senior Consultant Ruth Lee said. "It showed trust through all tiers of the company and fostered a stronger team feeling that we're all in this together."

We immediately started brainstorming ways to save money, get new clients, and improve our process efficiency. "By presenting the situation transparently, we could all ask ourselves what we could do," said Lee. What was amazing was that this new level of transparency led to increased morale, a better financial understanding of the company by my employees, and a feeling that we were all in control of the situation.

So instead of me just saying no to new equipment purchases or ideas, together we would decide to hold off on that purchase for the next few months. In fact, in many cases it was my employees themselves who mentioned shifting some expenses into the future and canceling others. This financial transparency continues to this day in how we make shared decisions. In fact, more often than not, nowadays, it is my employees who are saying no to things to which I typically would have said yes.

What I learned was that if I trusted my employees and showed them respect, they would engage. None of this was easy, but instituting our open-book policy was a leap of faith that resulted in one of the achievements that I'm most proud of with my firm.

Additional Lessons from My Transparency

Five years into this experiment, I've realized a few things now that this level of transparency has become "normal." The first is that after you show this level of transparency, you cannot pull back or people will start to wonder why and become anxious again. Second, we became transparent during a crisis, but after conditions improved, sharing financials just seemed like business as usual. So in order to keep people engaged, I needed to make the open-book policy more relevant to the issues of the day and again make it personal for them, as opposed to just becoming information shared from management.

Transparency will be tough at first, but if you want to have the most engaged workforce and stakeholders of the twenty-first century, transparency is key.

Tailor Transparency to Your Company

Although expanding our level of transparency and dialogue from social and environmental to include full financial transparency was important for my company, the issues and their importance will vary by company. For your company, the transparency might involve disclosing female/male ratios to CDP investors, providing information on gender pay gap differences to the GRI, broadcasting your environmental goals and progress to stakeholders, or whatever is important to your company and stakeholders at the time. Know that whatever the topic of conversation might be, there is real business value in being transparent, whether it's mitigating potential PR disasters, getting good ideas and constructive criticism, forging and strengthening relationships, or turning skeptics into proponents of your organization.

Lessons Learned

The following are key takeaways from the "Communicating Sustainability Internally" chapter:

- Continuous communication is key.

- The goal is for everyone in the company to speak to sustainability with one voice. People should know the vision and what sustainability means to your company so that every effort or action can be communicated as building on that vision.

- Share the good and the bad. This will show authenticity and minimize charges of "greenwashing."

- Find alignment in your communications between departments: marketing, PR, sales, HR, supply chain, CSR, philanthropy, community affairs, public affairs, and investor relations. Look for opportunities to mutually reinforce and leverage each department's communications.

- The medium of communication might be just as important as the message. Younger stakeholders and employees will prefer visual, electronic, and social media, whereas older stakeholders might prefer more traditional communication methods.

- There are a various ways to report externally; choose the one that is right for you, that meets the needs and concerns of your stakeholders.

- Transparency is tough. It builds trust, but each company needs to determine the right amount of transparency for itself at that point in time. You don't need to go from where you are to 100% transparent tomorrow; it is a process that takes time.

Individuals Interviewed for This Book

I am grateful for all the wonderful insight and ideas of the following colleagues and friends who so generously gave their time, input, and wisdom to this project:

Aleen Bayard, principal, MarketZing, November 1, 2012

Ben Packard, former vice president of global responsibility, Starbucks Coffee Company, January 7, 2013

Bob Willard, author and speaker, Sustainability Advantage, January 23, 2013

Cecilia Utne, senior consultant in intercultural solutions, Shepell. fgi, January 23, 2013

Christie Manning, visiting assistant professor of environmental studies, Macalester College, February 8, 2013

Claudia Capitini, former sustainability maven, Eco-Products, September 17, 2012

Dave Low, director of sustainability practices, Kidder Matthews, August 16, 2012

Dawn Danby, sustainable design program manager, Autodesk, December 11, 2012

Derek Eisel, former global environment program manager, Expeditors, November 30, 2012

Eli Reich, CEO, Alchemy Goods, August 10, 2012

Gifford Pinchot III, co-founder and president, Bainbridge Graduate Institute, May 11, 2013

Howard Behar, retired president, Starbucks International, November 2, 2012

Jason Boyce, social sustainability manager, Nature's Path, June 1, 2012

JD Norton, global employee engagement, eBay Green, July 2, 2012

John Koriath, core faculty and lead for leadership and personal development courses, Bainbridge Graduate Institute, August 28, 2012

John Zmolek, executive vice president, Verity Credit Union, August 28, 2012

Karen Stevens, former strategy manager, Boeing Employee Credit Union (BECU), August 21, 2012

Kevin Hagen, former director of corporate social responsibility, Recreational Equipment Inc. (REI), January 11/April 11, 2013

Mary Kay Chess, change management lead, Bainbridge Graduate Institute, August 27, 2012

Mike Bellamante, executive director, Climate Counts, January 29, 2013

Molly Ray, former global responsibility manager, Pan Pacific Hotels, August 23, 2012

Patrick Drum, CFA, CFP(R) senior portfolio manager, UBS Wealth Management, December 18, 2012

Ross Freeman, former environment and sustainability manager, Stevens Pass, September 9, 2012

Sarah Martinez, senior sustainability manager, Target, October 5, 2012

Suzanne Savannah Hansen, sustainability director, Macalester College, February 8, 2013

Terra Anderson, change-management practitioner, August 8, 2012

Citations and Endnotes

Chapter 1

1. Daniel Mahler et al., *"Green" Winners* (Chicago: A.T. Kearney, 2009), retrieved from https://www.atkearney.com/documents/10192/6972076a-9cdc-4b20-bc3a-d2a4c43c9c21.

2. Natural Capital Solutions, *Sustainability Pays, Studies That Prove the Business Case for Sustainability* (Boulder: Natural Capital Solutions, May 2012).

3. SRI in the Rockies: the premier industry conference for socially responsible investing in the United States.

4. US SIF Foundation, *2012 Report on Sustainable and Responsible Investing Trends in the United States,* 2012, retrieved from www.ussif.org and www.triplepundit.com/2012/11/total-sri-assets-374-trillion-enough-move-needle/.

5. Milton Friedman, "The Social Responsibility of Business Is to Increase Profits," *The New York Times Magazine* (September 13, 1970).

6. Conference Board, "The Conference Board Leading Economic Index," May 21, 2013, retrieved from www.conference-board.org/press/pressdetail.cfm?pressid=4453.

7. Kyle and Richard Rudden, "Sustainability Index Update," Target Rock Advisors, October 10, 2012, retrieved from www.targetrockadvisors.com/dox/reports/Target%20Rock%20Quarterly%20Sustainability%20Index%20Update%20(Q3-2012).pdf.

8. Anonymous, "2011 World's Most Ethical Companies," Ethisphere, 2011, info available at www.businesswire.com/news/home/20110315006776/en/Ethisphere-Announces-2011-World%E2%80%99s-Ethical-Companies.

9. Gregory Stewart, Scott Bernard, and Ed Fruscella, *Trends in Environmental, Social, and Governance Investing* (New York: BNY Mellon, 2013), retrieved from www.bnymellon.com/foresight/pdf/esg-investing-1012.pdf.

10. Spolanka, "Digital Textbooks and Open Educational Resources," May 3, 2011, retrieved from www.libraries.wright.edu/noshelfrequired/?p=2225.

11. Carbon Disclosure Project Web site: https://www.cdproject.net/en-US/Pages/About-Us.aspx.

12. CDP S&P 500 Report 2011, "Strategic Advantage through Climate Change Action."

13. Sara Stroud, "Shareholders Bring CSR to the Boardroom," Sustainable Industries, May 19, 2011, retrieved from http://sustainableindustries.com/articles/2011/05/shareholders-bring-csr-boardroom.

14. Peter Lacy et al., "A New Era of Sustainability," UN Global Compact & Accenture Report, June 2010.

15. Kelli Johnson, "National Green Buying Research Study," Portland: Green Canary, retrieved from www.greencanary.net/news-item.php?id=685.

16. Environmental Deference Fund Web site: www.edf.org/.

17. Cone Communications, "Consumers Take Responsibility for 'Green' Actions but Aren't Following Through, According to Latest Cone Communications Research," Boston: CONE, April 3, 2013, retrieved from www.conecomm.com/stuff/contentmgr/files/0/a70891b83b6f1056074156e8b4646f42/files/2013_cone_communications_green_gap_trend_tracker_press_release_and_fact_sheet.pdf.

18. One news, "Environment, Social Factors Influence Consumers," June 24, 2013, TVNZ, retrieved from http://tvnz.co.nz/business-news/environment-social-factors-influence-consumers-5474228.

19. Jennifer Schwad, Fortune Green, Huffington Post, May 2013, retrieved from www.huffingtonpost.com/jennifer-schwab/fortune-green-consumers-w_b_3254512.html.

20. Michael Rendell, Report: "Managing Tomorrow's People," London: PricewaterhouseCoopers, 2008.

21. Michael Rendell, "Millennials at Work 2011," PricewaterhouseCoopers, May 2012, retrieved from www.slideshare.net/PWC/pwc-millennials-at-work-2011.

22. Stanford, "MBA Graduates Want to Work for Caring and Ethical Employers," Stanford Business School, January 1, 2004, retrieved from www.gsb.stanford.edu/news/research/hr_mbajobchoice.shtml.

23. L. Rowledge, Igniting the Core: Employee Engagement and Sustainability (Mercer Island, WA: EKOS International, 2010), retrieved from www.ekosi.com/index.php?page=engaging-employees-in-sustainability.

24. Ibid.

25. David B. Montgomery and Catherine Ramus, "Including Corporate Social Responsibility, Environmental Sustainability, and Ethics in Calibrating MBA Job Preferences," Stanford Business School, December 2007, retrieved from https://gsbapps.stanford.edu/researchpapers/library/RP1981.pdf.

26. J. Hittner and G. Pohle, IBM *Attaining Sustainable Growth through Corporate Social Responsibility* (Somers, NY: Institute for Business Value, 2008), retrieved from www.natcapsolutions.org/business-case/IBM2008business-case.pdf.

27. Eddy S. W. Ng, Sean T. Lyons, and Linda Schweitzer, *New Generation, Great Expectations: A Field Study of the Millennial Generation* (Ottawa: Springer Science Business Media, February 16, 2010), retrieved from www.academia.edu/1410939/New_generation_great_expectations_A_field_study_of_the_millennial_generation.

28. E. Mills, "The Greening of Insurance," *Science* 338 (December 14, 2012): 1424, retrieved from http://insurance.lbl.gov/opportunities/ro-12-summary.html.

29. Rosanne Skirble, "NASA: 2012 Was 9th Hottest Year on Record," Voice of America, January 6, 2013, retrieved from www.voanews.com/content/the-year-2012-was-9th-hottest-year-on-record/1585020.html.

30. Bob Willard, January 23, 2013, videoconference interview.

31. International Financial Corporation Web site: www.ifc.org.

32. "A Buddhist Declaration on Climate Change," retrieved from www.ecobuddhism.org/bcp/all_content/buddhist_declaration/.

33. John Thavis, "Pope Urges International Agreement on Climate Change," Catholic News Service, November 28, 2011, retrieved from www.catholicnews.com/data/stories/cns/1104646.htm.

34. Julie Halpert, "Judaism and Climate Change," Yale University, February 2012, retrieved from http://fore.research.yale.edu/climate-change/statements-from-world-religions/judaism/.

35. "Weekly Retail Gasoline and Diesel Prices," U.S. Energy Information Administration, retrieved May 2013 from www.eia.gov/dnav/pet/pet_pri_gnd_dcus_nus_w.htm.

36. Weekly Reports, "Petroleum and Other Liquids," U.S. Energy Information Administration, retrieved May 2013 from www.eia.gov/petroleum/reports.cfm.

37. "European Climate Registry," Wikipedia, retrieved May 2013 from http://en.wikipedia.org/wiki/European_Climate_Exchange.

38. Joseph Mangino, "Fact Sheet—Proposed Rule: Prevention of Significant Deterioration and Title V Greenhouse Gas Tailoring Rule ACTION,"

U.S. Environmental Protection Agency, retrieved May 2013 from www.epa.gov/NSR/fs20090930action.html.

39. Phil Plait, "2011: The 9th Hottest Year on Record," *Discover Magazine Blog*, January 20, 2012, retrieved from http://blogs.discovermagazine.com/badastronomy/2012/01/20/2011-the-9th-hottest-year-on-record/.

40. "Registration, Evaluation, Authorisation and Restriction of Chemicals," Wikipedia, retrieved May 2013 from http://en.wikipedia.org/wiki/Registration,_Evaluation,_Authorisation_and_Restriction_of_Chemicals.

41. Mitchell Katz, "FTC Issues Revised 'Green Guides,'" Federal Trade Commission, October 1, 2012, retrieved from www.ftc.gov/opa/2012/10/greenguides.shtm.

42. C. Laszlo and N. Zhexembayeva, *Embedded Sustainability, The Next Big Competitive Advantage* (Stanford, CA: Greenleaf Publishing Limited, 2011), 79.

43. Ibid.

44. Interface, Environmental, retrieved May 2013 from https://www.interfaceflor.com/default.aspx?section=3&sub=4.

45. Jason D. Schloetzer, Matteo Tonello, and Melissa Aguilar, "CEO Succession Practices: 2012 Edition," The Conference Board, April 2012, retrieved from www.conference-board.org/publications/publicationdetail.cfm?publicationid=2168.

46. Bureau of Labor and Statistics, "Employee Tenure," news release, September 18, 2012, retrieved from www.bls.gov/news.release/pdf/tenure.pdf.

Chapter 2

1. World Commission on Environment and Development (WCED), *Our Common Future* (Oxford: Oxford University Press, 1987), 43.

2. Eli Reich, August 21, 2012, personal interview.

3. Dawn Danby, December 11, 2012, personal interview.

Chapter 3

1. Hunter Lovins, "The High Rate of Return on Giving," Sustainable Industries, September 18, 2012, retrieved from www.sustainableindustries.com/articles/2012/09/high-rate-return-giving.

2. C. Laszlo and N. Zhexembayeva, *Embedded Sustainability, The Next Big Competitive Advantage* (Stanford, CA: Greenleaf Publishing Limited, 2011), 85.

3. Ross Freeman, September 9, 2012, personal interview.

4. Peter Lacy, Tim Cooper, Rob Hayward, and Lisa Neuberger, *A New Era of Sustainability*, Accenture, 2010, retrieved from www.accenture.com/SiteCollectionDocuments/PDF/Accenture_A_New_Era_of_Sustainability_CEO_Study.pdf.

Chapter 4

1. The Global Reporting Initiative, 2013, retrieved from www.globalreporting.org.

2. The Climate Registry, 2013, retrieved from www.theclimateregistry.org/.

3. Carbon Disclosure Project, 2013, retrieved from www.cdproject.net.

4. Janet Ranganathan et al., *The Greenhouse Gas Protocol*, World Resources Institute and World Business Council for Sustainable Development, March 2004, retrieved from www.ghgprotocol.org/files/ghgp/public/ghg-protocol-revised.pdf.

5. "Pareto Principle," Wikipedia, retrieved May 2013 from http://en.wikipedia.org/wiki/Pareto_principle.

6. Ben Packard, January 07, 2013, personal interview.

7. Walmart Sustainability Assessment, retrieved May 2013 from www.bpaww.com/Bpaww_com/HTML/iCompli/Downloads/2012/CSR/Walmart_Sustainability_Assessment.pdf.

8. Philips, Philips Supplier Sustainability EICC Tool, revision 2013, retrieved from www.philips.com/shared/assets/company_profile/downloads/Philips-Supply-Sustainability-Audit-tool.pdf.

9. Arizona State Sustainability Supplier Questionnaire, 2013, retrieved from www.asu.edu/purchasing/forms/sustainability_IA.pdf.

10. Robert Pojasek, *10 Key Questions That Focus Suppliers on Sustainability*, Green Biz, October 6, 2009, retrieved from www.greenbiz.com/blog/2009/10/06/10-key-questions-focus-suppliers-sustainability.

11. Claudia Capitini, September 7, 2012, personal interview.

12. Ibid.

13. "Life Cycle Assessment," Wikipedia, retrieved May 2013 from http://en.wikipedia.org/wiki/Life-cycle_assessment.

14. "About the Consortium," The Sustainability Consortium, 2013, retrieved from www.sustainabilityconsortium.org/why-we-formed/.

15. "Higg Index," Sustainable Apparel Coalition, 2013, retrieved from www. apparelcoalition.org/higgindex/.

16. World Resource Institute, 2013, retrieved from www.wri.org/.

17. Cecilia Utne, January 23, 2013, personal interview.

18. Patrick Drum, December 18, 2012, personal interview.

Chapter 5

1. Daniel Pink, *Drive* (New York: River Head Books, 2009).

2. Ben Packard, January 7, 2013, personal interview.

3. J. Collins, *Good to Great* (New York: Harper Business, 2001).

4. Based on Chris Laszlo and Nadya Zhexembayeva's *Embedded Sustainability, the Next Big Competitive Advantage* (Stanford, CA: Greenleaf Publishing Limited, 2011), 16.

5. L. Rowledge, *Igniting the Core: Employee Engagement and Sustainability* (Mercer Island, WA: EKOS International, 2010), retrieved from www. ekosi.com/index.php?page=engaging-employees-in-sustainability.

6. C. Laslo and N. Zhexembayeva, *Embedded Sustainability*, 164.

7. Rowledge, *Igniting the Core.*

8. The Natural Step Canada, 2013, retrieved from www.naturalstep.org/.

9. Kim W. Chan, *Blue Ocean Strategy* (Boston: Harvard Business Publishing Corporation, 2005), 12.

10. Terra Anderson, August 8, 2012, phone interview.

11. "Can We Learn from Formula 1 Pit Crews to Improve Patient Care in Emergency Departments?" Deloitte Touche Tohmatsu, 2011, retrieved from www.deloitte.com/assets/Dcom-Australia/Local%20Assets/ Documents/Industries/LSHC/Deloitte_Emergency_Department_ Journey_in_the_new_World.pdf.

12. "5 Whys," Wikipedia, retrieved May 2013 from http://en.wikipedia.org/ wiki/5_Whys.

13. John Koriath, August 28, 2012, personal interview.

14. Packard, personal interview.

15. Kevin Hagen, January 11, 2013, personal interview.

Chapter 6

1. Dawn Danby, December 11, 2012, personal interview.

2. Mary Kay Chess, August 27, 2012, personal interview.

3. Sustainability at Harvard, "Green Loan Fund," retrieved May 2013 from http://green.harvard.edu/loan-fund.

4. L. Rowledge, *Igniting the Core: Employee Engagement and Sustainability* (Mercer Island, WA: EKOS International, 2010), retrieved from www.ekosi.com/index.php?page=engaging-employees-in-sustainability.

5. Dori Meinert, "Make Telecommuting Pay Off," June 1, 2011, retrieved from www.shrm.org/Publications/hrmagazine/EditorialContent/2011/0611/Pages/0611meinert.aspx.

6. Rob Reuteman, "Companies Embrace Telecommuting as a Retention Tool," CNBC, September 30, 2011, retrieved from www.cnbc.com/id/44612830/Companies_Embrace_Telecommuting_as_a_Retention_Tool.

7. Dave Low, August 16, 2011, phone interview.

8. Ross Freeman, September 9, 2012, personal interview.

9. Kevin Hagen, April 11, 2013, personal interview.

Chapter 7

1. Kevin Hagen, April 16, 2013, personal interview.

2. John Koriath, August 28, 2012, personal interview.

3. Mary Kay Chess, August 27, 2012, personal interview.

4. Ibid.

5. Benjamin Zander, *The Art of Possibility* (New York: Penguin Books, 2002).

6. Ibid.

7. Chess, personal interview.

8. Kevin Hagen, January 11, 2013, personal interview.

9. Ibid.

10. Cecilia Utne, January 23, 2013, personal interview.

11. Ibid.

12. Claudia Capitini, September 17, 2012, personal interview.

13. *Toward Engagement 2.0: Creating a More Sustainable Company through Employee Engagement* (Washington, D.C.: National Environmental Education Foundation, January 2011), retrieved from www.neefusa.org/pdf/Toward_Engagement_2.pdf.

14. Chess, personal interview.

15. Terra Anderson, August 8, 2012, phone interview.

16. Stephen Covey, *The 7 Habits of Highly Effective People: Powerful Lessons in Personal Change* (New York:. Simon & Shuster, Inc., 1989).

17. Dawn Danby, December 11, 2012, personal interview.

18. Anderson, phone interview.

Chapter 8

1. Daniel Pink, *Drive* (New York: Riverhead Books, 2009).

2. Nikki Blacksmith and Jim Harter, "Majority of American Workers Not Engaged in Their Jobs," Gallup, October 28, 2011, retrieved from www.gallup.com/poll/150383/Majority-American-Workers-Not-Engaged-Jobs.aspx.

3. S. Agrawal et al., "The Relationship between Engagement at Work and Organizational Outcomes," Washington, D.C., Gallup, 2009, retrieved from www.natcapsolutions.org/business-case/The%20RelationshipBetw eenEngagementAtWork&OrganizationalOutcomes_2009.pdf.

4. K. Dam, "The Truth Will Out: The Power of Employees," CSRHub, May 2012, retrieved from www.csrhub.com/blog/2012/05/the-truth-will-out-the-power-of-employees.html.

5. Melcrum, *The Bottom Line Benefits from Engaged Workforce, Study Confirms* (London, United Kingdom: Internal Communications Hub, 2006), retrieved from www.internalcommshub.com/open/news/isrsurvey.shtml.

6. John J. Heldrich, Cliff Zukin, and Mark Szeltner, "Net Impact Talent Report: What Workers Want in 2012," San Francisco, Net Impact, May 2012.

7. National Environmental Education Foundation, "The Business Case for Environmental and Sustainability Employee Education," Washington, D.C., 2010, retrieved from www.neefusa.org/BusinessEnv/white_paper_feb2010.pdf.

8. Laura Taxel, "Green Mountain Coffee Roasters: Towards a New Business Model," Worldinquiry, 2004, retrieved from Case Western Reserve, http://worldinquiry.case.edu/feature_gmcr.cfm.

9. Dawn Danby, December 11, 2012, personal interview.

10. L. Rowledge, *Igniting the Core: Employee Engagement and Sustainability* (Mercer Island, WA: EKOS International, 2010), retrieved from www.ekosi.com/index.php?page=engaging-employees-in-sustainability.

11. Ibid.

12. Associates' Personal Sustainability Projects, Walmart, retrieved May 2013 from www.walmartstores.com/sites/sustainabilityreport/2009/s_ao_psp.html.

13. R. Bemporad, "Employee Engagement: Five Companies That Get It," *Triple Pundit,* February 2012, retrieved from www.triplepundit.com/2012/02/employee-engagement-five-companies/.

14. Associates' Personal Sustainability Projects.

15. Tauschia Copeland, May 3, 2013, personal interview.

16. Kendra Cherry, "Learning Styles Based on Jung's Theory of Personality," Education Psychology, retrieved May 2013 from http://psychology.about.com/od/educationalpsychology/ss/jung-styles_2.htm.

17. Eli Reich, August 21, 2012, personal interview.

18. J. Hittner and G. Pohle, *Attaining Sustainable Growth through Corporate Social Responsibility* (Somers, NY: IBM Institute for Business Value, 2008), retrieved from www.natcapsolutions.org/business-case/IBM2008business-case.pdf.

19. Terra Anderson, August 8, 2012, phone interview.

20. Gifford Pinchot III, May 24, 2013, personal interview.

21. Rowledge, *Igniting the Core.*

22. Pinchot, personal interview.

23. Ibid.

24. Ibid.

Chapter 9

1. Ben Packard, January 7, 2013, personal interview.

2. Bob Willard, January 23, 2013, video conference interview.

3. L. Rowledge, *Igniting the Core: Employee Engagement and Sustainability* (Mercer Island, WA: EKOS International, 2010), retrieved from www.ekosi.com/index.php?page=engaging-employees-in-sustainability.

4. Jeffrey K. Liker, *The Toyota Way* (Madison, WI: CWL Publishing Enterprises, 2004).

5. Ibid.

6. "Lean Manufacturing and the Environment," U.S. Environmental Protection Agency, retrieved May 2013 from www.epa.gov/lean/environment/.

7. "PDCA," Wikipedia, retrieved May 2013 from http://en.wikipedia.org/wiki/PDCA.

8. Rowledge, *Igniting the Core.*

9. David A. Lubin and Daniel C. Esty, "Lessons for Leaders from Previous Game-Changing Megatrends," *Harvard Business Review,* May 2010.

10. Akhila Vijayaraghavan, "Puma Puts Financial Value on Environmental Impact," Triple Pundit, April 19, 2011, retrieved from www.triplepundit. com/2011/05/putting-value-environmental-impact/.

11. "PUMA's Environmental Profit and Loss Account for the Year Ended 31 December 2010," PUMA, 2012, retrieved from http://about.puma. com/wp-content/themes/aboutPUMA_theme/financial-report/pdf/ EPL080212final.pdf.

12. Kieran Timberlake website, http://kierantimberlake.com/home/index. html.

13. Rowledge, *Igniting the Core.*

14. "7 Amazing Examples of Biomimicry," Mother Nature Network, www. mnn.com/earth-matters/wilderness-resources/photos/7-amazing-examples-of-biomimicry/sharkskin-swimsuit.

15. Molly Ray, August 23, 2012, personal interview.

16. Terra Anderson, August 8, 2012, phone interview.

17. Christopher Pinney, "Increasing Impact, Enhancing Value," Report, Arlington, Council on Foundations, 2012.

18. "Resilient Supply Chain," Green Mountain, retrieved May 2013 from www.gmcr.com/Sustainability/SupplyChain.aspx.

19. Ibid.

20. John Koriath, August 28, 2012, personal interview.

21. Dave Low, August 16, 2012, phone interview.

Chapter 10

1. Chris Strashok, "Mountain Equipment Co-op: A Co-operative Business Model," Community Research Connections, May 13, 2011, retrieved from http://crcresearch.org/community-research-connections/crc-case-studies/mountain-equipment-co-op-co-operative-business-model.

2. Ben Packard, January 7, 2013, personal interview.

3. David A. Lubin and Daniel C. Esty, "Lessons for Leaders from Previous Game-Changing Megatrends," *Harvard Business Review,* May 2010.

4. R. Bemporad, "Employee Engagement: Five Companies That Get It," *Triple Pundit,* February 2012, retrieved from www.triplepundit. com/2012/02/employee-engagement-five-companies/.

5. Andrea Moffat and Andrew Newton, *The 21st Century Corporation: The Ceres Roadmap for Sustainability* (San Francisco: Ceres, 2010).

6. Robin Ferracone, "The Role of Environmental Sustainability in Executive Compensation," Farient Advisors, April 26, 2011, retrieved from www.farient.com/blog/blog_current/the-role-of-environmental-sustainability-in-executive-compensation/.

7. Moffat and Newton, *The 21st Century Corporation.*

8. Thomas Singer, "Linking Executive Compensation to Sustainability Performance," The Conference Board, May 2012, retrieved from http://comunicarseweb.com.ar/download.php?tipo=acrobat&view =1&dato=1339073125_Linking_Executive_Compensation_to_ Sustainability_Performance.pdf.

9. Ferracone, "The Role of Environmental Sustainability."

10. Liz Maw, "Sustainability-Engaged Employees More Satisfied, Study Shows," The Living Principles, July 5, 2012, retrieved from www.livingprinciples. org/sustainability-engaged-employees-more-satisfied-study-shows/.

11. M. Dewhurst, M. Guthridge, and E. Mohr, "Motivating People: Getting Beyond Money," McKinsey, New York City, 2009, retrieved from www. mckinseyquarterly.com/Motivating_people_Getting_beyond_ money_2460/.

12. Daniel H. Pink, *Drive* (New York: Riverhead Books, 2009), 145.

13. Christie Manning, February 8, 2013, personal interview.

14. Claudia Capitini, September 7, 2012, personal interview.

15. "Study Shows Employees Learn Best from Video Games," UC Denver, 2010, retrieved from www.ucdenver.edu/about/newsroom/newsreleases/ Pages/Videogamesmakebetteremployees.aspx.

16. Laurence Goasduff, "Gartner Says by 2015, More Than 50 Percent of Organizations That Manage Innovation Processes Will Gamify Those Processes," Gartner, New York City, April 12, 2011, retrieved from www. gartner.com/newsroom/id/1629214.

17. "Tech Trends 2012: Elevate IT for Digital Business," Deloitte, 2012.

18. Paula Owen, Ph.D., "Can Gaming Teach Us to Live More Sustainable Lives?" The Guardian, London, March 11, 2013, retrieved from www.guardian.co.uk/sustainable-business/gaming-gamification-save-the-planet.

19. Mario Herger, "Sustainability Quiz—How SAP Teaches Employees about Sustainability Initiatives," Enterprise Gamification, April 12, 2012, retrieved from http://enterprise-gamification.com/index.php/en/ sustainability/84-sustainability-quiz.

20. Derek Eisel, December 4, 2012, personal interview.

Chapter 11

1. Claudia Capitini, September 17, 2012, personal interview.

2. John Koriath, August 28, 2012, personal interview.

3. Dawn Danby, December 11, 2012, personal interview.

4. Capitini, personal interview.

5. L. Rowledge, *Igniting the Core: Employee Engagement and Sustainability* (Mercer Island, WA: EKOS International, 2010), retrieved from www. ekosi.com/index.php?page=engaging-employees-in-sustainability.

6. Deborah Fleischer, "Green Teams," Mill Valley, Green Impact, 2009, retrieved from www.greenbiz.com/sites/default/files/GreenBizReports-GreenTeams-final.pdf.

7. Molly Ray, August 23, 2012, personal interview.

Index

C

calendar, reinforcing message with, 246-247

California
Global Warming Solution Act, 29
Transparency in Supply Chain Act, 20

Capitini, Claudia, 87, 156, 240, 265

Carbon Disclosure Leadership Index (CDLI), 14

Carbon Disclosure Project, 14

carbon taxes, 29

career development opportunities, 182-183

Cascade Designs, 164

CCAs (Climate Change Agreements) program, 29

CDLI (Carbon Disclosure Leadership Index), 14

CDP (Carbon Disclosure Project), 14

Cedar Grove Composting, 37

CEOs, focus on sustainability, 15

change management, 141
assessing company culture, 155-156
change management methods, 156-157
"initial nice," 156
uncertainty, dealing with, 158
breaking down silos, 162-164
business case: freight efficiency, 155
challenges, 142
change management star, 145-146
coordinating across departments, 162-164
emotional impact of change, 142-144
engaging the skeptics, 165-166
finding common ground, 166
group discussion versus one-on-ones, 166-167
outside consultants, 167
worksheet, 167-175

Hagen-Wilhelm Change Matrix, 6, 146-154
methods, 156-157
phased approach, 144-145
questions to ask, 161-162
stages of change, 143
understanding employees, 158-161

Chess, Mary Kay, 143, 157, 266

Cisco Systems, 137

Clarke, 130

Clarke, Lyell, 130

Clif Bar, 231

Climate Change Agreements (CCAs) program, 29

Climate Counts, 266

Climate Exchange (ECX), 28

climate legislation, 28-29

climate risk in SEC filings, 30

collective behavior style, 159-160

Collins, Jim, 194

communication
to employees, 47-52
external reporting, 256-258
internal communications, 245
aligning communication efforts, 250-253
continuous communication, 245-247
putting sustainability into relatable terms, 248-249
sharing best practices, 251
sharing both good and bad, 247-249
social feedback loops, 238-239
social media, 254-256
storytelling, 249
transparency, 258-262
using calendar to reinforce your message, 246-247
to stakeholders, 67-70

company boundary, determining, 76-80

G

gamification
  engaging alphas via games, 240-242
  examples, 242
  explained, 239-240
  innovation and entertainment, 240
  matching games with culture,
    242-244
Gap analysis, 91-96
Genesis Covenant (Episcopal
  Church), 25
GHG (greenhouse gas) emissions
  GHG (greenhouse gas) protocol, 79
  impact on company value, 13
  sources, 81
giving. *See* philanthropy
Global Warming Solution Act, 29
goals, 45-46, 103
  absolute versus intensity goals,
    117-118
  corporate goals, 108-110
  departmental goals, 108-110
  individual goals, 108-110
  integrating, 107-108
  KPIs (key performance indicators),
    119-122
  North Star goals, 103-107
  order-of-magnitude goals, 114-115
  responsibility and accountability,
    125-126
  setting, 110-119
Good to Great (Collins), 194
Gore, Al, 106
"green," FTC (Federal Trade
  Commission) ruling on, 32
Green Mountain Coffee Roasters,
  182, 220
Green Sports Alliance, 25
green teams, 222-224
Greenbiz, "10 Key Questions That
  Focus on Supplier Sustainability," 87

greenhouse gas (GHG) emissions
  greenhouse gas (GHG) protocol, 79
  impact on company value, 13
  sources, 81
grievance mechanism, 70-71
group discussion versus one-on-ones,
  166-167
group-oriented behavior style, 159-160

H

Hagen, Kevin, 126, 138, 141, 266
Hagen-Wilhelm Change Matrix,
  6, 146-154
Hansen, Suzanne Savannah, 266
Harvard's Green Loan Fund, 134
Higg Index, 89-90
Hong Kong and Shanghai Banking
  Corporation (HSBC), 203
HSBC (Hong Kong and Shanghai
  Banking Corporation), 203

I

IBM
  On Demand Community
    (ODC), 255
  Environmental Management System
    (EMS), 208
IFC (International Financial
  Corporation), 23-24
Igniting the Core (Rowledge and
  Figge), 107
IIRC (International Integrated
  Reporting Council), 34
impact giving, 221
improved data over time, 99-100
inclusiveness of baselines, 77
  80-20 rule, 81-83
  beginning with end in mind, 78-82
  products, 88-89
  supply chain, 83-88

Q-R

quarterly focus, 13-14

Ray, Molly, 213, 258, 266

REACH (Registration, Evaluation, Authorisation, and Restriction of Chemicals), 31

Real Time Environmental Impact Tool (RTEI), 209

recognition, 237-238

Recreational Equipment Inc. (REI), 126, 266

recruiting, 18

Registration, Evaluation, Authorisation, and Restriction of Chemicals (REACH), 31

regulation
    accounting standards, 33-34
    climate legislation, 28-29
    climate risk in SEC filings, 30
    Dodd-Frank Wall Street Reform and Consumer Protection Act of 2010, 33
    energy prices, 26
    external reporting, 35
    FTC ruling on "green," 32
    ISO standards, 34-35
    overview, 26
    toxins, 31
    U.S. mayors' climate commitment, 29-30
    water, 31

REI (Recreational Equipment Inc.), 126, 266

Reich, Eli, 48, 194, 265

Reilly Industries, 221

reinsurance companies, 21-22

relatable terms, putting sustainability into, 248-249

relevance, 80

reporting
    external reporting, 35, 256-258
    sustainability reporting, 208-209

resolutions by shareholders, 14-15

resources, dedicating to sustainability, 134-135

responding to supplier questionnaires, 85-86

responsibility, assigning, 125-126

results, communicating to stakeholders, 67-70

Return on Sustainability (Wilhelm), 9

rewards and recognition, 237-238

Rowledge, Lorinda, 107

RTEI (Real Time Environmental Impact Tool), 209

S

SAC (Sustainable Apparel Coalition) Higg Index, 89-90

SASB (Sustainability Accounting Standards Board), 34

scorecards, 68

Scott, Lee, 116

SEC filings, climate risk in, 30

senior executives, 229-230

setting goals, 110-119

shared ownership, 195-196

shareholder resolutions, 14-15

Shepell.fgi, 265

silos, breaking down, 162-164

skeptics, engaging, 165-166
    finding common ground, 166
    group discussion versus one-on-ones, 166-167
    outside consultants, 167
    worksheet, 167-175

SMS (Sustainability Management Systems), 208

social feedback loops, 238-239

social media, 254-256

social personality type, 191

solitary personality type, 191

Speck, Esther, 227

sponsors, 197-198